T0354477

MODERN-DAY PRAYERS
FOR
A
MODERN-DAY WORLD

MODERN-DAY PRAYERS FOR A MODERN-DAY WORLD

PRAISES FOREVER AND GLORY CHANT

Evette Forde

iUniverse

Modern-day Prayers for a Modern-day World
Praises Forever and Glory Chant

Copyright © 2016 Evette Forde.

Canada 1118676 and United States of America# TXu001-952-356
Library of congress #2015901306

iUniverse books may be ordered through booksellers or by contacting:

iUniverse
1663 Liberty Drive
Bloomington, IN 47403
www.iuniverse.com
1-800-Authors (1-800-288-4677)

Because of the dynamic nature of the Internet, any web addresses or links contained in
this book may have changed since publication and may no longer be valid. The views
expressed in this work are solely those of the author and do not necessarily reflect the
views of the publisher, and the publisher hereby disclaims any responsibility for them.

Any people depicted in stock imagery provided by Thinkstock are models,
and such images are being used for illustrative purposes only.
Certain stock imagery © Thinkstock.

ISBN: 978-1-5320-0826-9 (sc)
ISBN: 978-1-5320-0827-6 (e)

Library of Congress Control Number: 2016916709

Print information available on the last page.

iUniverse rev. date: 11/23/2016

CONTENTS

POEMS

Note: All scripture quoted, was chosen from the English Standard Version of the Bible unless otherwise noted.

Some of the prayers in this book are for meditation.

Example: Prayer 11 titled (God's Bountiful) paragraph six. If you quietly chant the words written in paragraph six, you hear the voice of the LORD speaking to your heart, showing you creative ways to improve your life. (Sacrosanct pâtre)

ABOUT THE BOOK

Modern-Day Prayers for a Modern-Day World: Praises Forever and Glory Chant is a collection of contemporary lyrical, abstract prayers and poems. The work was written passionately in a realistic way to encourage readers.

It will enrich your life and motivate you to study the New Testament and the book of Psalms. While tackling issues relating to humanism and sociology in the twenty-first century—

The prayers and poems are inspirational, soul-searching, and humorous. Originally written to awaken and encourage the audience. Some of the topics are controversial.

Focusing on the social, family, nature, and politics, this book can open your mind to a variety of emotions. Furthermore, it features a real life-changing testimonial.

DEDICATION

To my loving children, mother, father, grandmother, and friends,
My hope is that one day we can all walk the earth in
peace and love with an abundance of joy, wisdom,
knowledge, understanding, and respect for one another
so we all can live, enjoy, and appreciate this marvelous
world. May God of the Universe, in his infinite
wisdom, protect and guide you always and forever.
God is capable. One day, all will realize he is the one and only
God of the Universe, Adonai, and the way to eternal existence.

Love dwells in all living things.

TESTIMONIAL

I had an allergic reaction to peanuts and went into anaphylactic shock. They rushed me to the hospital. The doctor put me on medication that made me drowsy. The same night, around two thirty in the morning, I woke to the loud sound of my fire alarm system. When I opened my eyes, smoke and fire were coming under my front door and making its way up the walls of my living room. My apartment was filling with smoke.

As I lay in bed, dazed yet concerned for my life, I looked up at the ceiling. I quietly said to God, "God, are you going to leave me here to die in this fire?" I felt the power of the LORDS grace embracing me. Six angels appeared around my bed to comfort me. I felt a sense of peace and safety. The LORDS assurance and strength came over me. I remembered there was sand in a bucket in the bathroom that I had collected from the lakeshore.

I got out of bed and went directly to the bathroom. I turned on the bathroom tap and filled the bucket with water. I started pouring the water and wet sand on the fire. The fire was becoming uncontrollable. A still powerful voice came to me and said, "Take the wet sand in the bucket, and throw it on the fire."

The fire started to subside, so I took water from the bathroom tap and continued pouring it on the fire. The fire was climbing the wall, reaching the ceiling. I started throwing water and wet sand up toward the roof. When the fire was under control, I found my cell phone and called the fire department.

When the firefighters arrived, one of them said to me, "Come and work for us." I am a witness. The LORD comes when you call. Trust and believe in him. He will be there to see you through all things, even unto death.

PRAYERS

1
GUIDE US

Oh Dear LORD, guide and protect us through these difficult times. Bring our minds and souls back to you. Let us feel your presence while keeping us safe in your precious love and confidence. Safeguard our hearts; bring us joy, happiness, and contentment. We trusted you in the days of old. Your steady hands guided us and kept us safe.

You have guided us with your never-ending love, patience, understanding, and wisdom. Today we have become compliant and were led astray by deceptions. Keep us safe and steady and forever knowing that you were there with us at the beginning of time and you are with us in the present. And you will be with us until the end of our age.

O Mighty Father, your love is sufficient to keep us safe. Guide others who lost themselves and in disarray. Only you know the hearts of men. We need your valuable guidance today. Guide us, O Father. You are the Alpha and Omega. You are the shining light that keeps us steady and safe. Heavenly Father, who's still on the throne, guides us all, keeping us steadfast and protected in your blessed bosom.

Return your precious love that once filled our hearts for you. Guide us through these trying times. Forgive us for turning our backs on you, O Heavenly Father, for you are the Alpha and Omega. You are the shining light that keeps us steady and safe. Keep us confident in your love, joy, and happiness once more. O LORD and Dear Father, guide and protect us, and remove fear and confusion from our hearts and minds.

O Mighty Father, your love is sufficient to keep us safe.

Guide others who lost themselves and in disarray. Only you know the hearts of men. Comfort us in times of difficulties. You are the great Comforter. In the days of old, you guided us with your loving patience, understanding, and wisdom. Forgive us for our transgressions against you.

Your steady hand has guided us through the centuries, Mighty LORD. Hear our pleas, forgive us, and continue guiding us today. Close the doors to our hearts and minds to continuing fear.

Keep us safe and steady, always knowing that you were there with us from the beginning of time, you are with us in the present, and you will be with us at the end.

Guide and keep us steadfast in your blessed bosom. Guide us through these difficult times. Stay with us. Restore our souls with your blessed assurance and quiet confidence.

Selah.

2
THANKFULNESS

O Mighty Savior, thank you for your grace. You promised to be with me through all my endeavors. At times, I feel you are not there for me. Thank you for your everlasting love and provision. When darkness falls, and men's inherent selfishness tries to suffocate and confuse me, you send your spirit of rationality and consistency to take away the fears and confusion.

O Heavenly Father, thankfulness is in my heart and soul for you. Thank you for sending your angels to watch over me and keep me in perfect peace. Thank you. You have restored my confidence. God is great. His love and protection are sufficient for a lifetime. Be with me at the time of danger and uncertainty. Thank you, Heavenly Father, for being a good provider.

I am forever thankful to you and put my trust in you. Some men's hearts are filled with evil and are ungrateful and wicked. I want to give you thanks, O LORD. Even though evil men lay traps for me, be with me in all things, while I use the wisdom and understanding you give me to fight against them. In all things, I give you thanks. O Great Father, thank you for your love.

You extended your love to the birds in the air, beasts of the fields, and fishes in the ocean and continued your love to me. Thank you for giving me the courage to live without fear and doubt. When the spirit of discontent tries to enter my space, you send your active mind.

And never-ending presence to give me the confidence and courage to pursue, resist, and persevere. LORD, you have the power to remove any negative obstacle that stands in my way. Thank you, O Father of hope, when my efforts crumble, and my endeavors become fruitless, you alone understand. Thankfulness is implanted in my heart, always and forever.

With every breath of air that enters my body, I express gratitude to you. Forever more thank you for life. Lord, I thank you for the big and small blessings. Your loving, tender mercy holds me through all things. Thank you for giving me the courage to withstand the devil's tricks.

As the old traditional song goes,
Satan is a sly old fox.
I will catch him, and put him in a box.
Lock the box and throw away the key for the whole world to see.
(*Author unknown*)

O LORD, men, have forgotten to thank you. Satan's cunningness has penetrated their minds. Therefore, the angels in heaven continually bless you and give you praise. My heart will forever be filled with thankfulness and glory to you, Abba Father.

Selah.

3

SIXTY YEARS OLD

The sun has risen. It's another day. It's fine. It's a good day. "This is the day that the LORD has made; let us rejoice and be glad in it" (*Psalm 118:24 ESV*). My life's journey brought me to be six years old.

(*Say your age.*) Everlasting one, your love, kindness, and tender mercy is the strength that possesses me.

The love I possess for you, heavenly Father, O LORD, has kept me through these years. In many ways, your faithfulness to me has shown me love and kindness and has protected me from life's dangers. You have given me opportunities to enjoy the handiwork of your creations. When I was in dangerous situations, you sent your angels to camp around me.

They protected me and showed me love and understanding. Your patience, loving-kindness, and unconditional love have guided me through motherhood. Your loving strength held me in times of darkness and kept me together through all things.

If not for your mercy and loving-kindness, O LORD, I could not have received the knowledge, wisdom, and the bountiful good blessings you showered upon me.

If I didn't put my complete trust in you, I would lose, in disarray, and live in confusion. You placed love in my heart and soul—for me, primarily; then love for others. You taught me to give to myself first and to show mercy, compassion, understanding and patience to others afterward. The wisdom, knowledge, and fortitude you gave me made me react in an instant to others who treated me unfairly.

They came to unleash their manipulative, forceful strength on me, but your everlasting love protected me. You, O LORD, sent your Mighty wisdom and understanding to show me how to deal with them. You, LORD, through the power of your Holy Spirit working through me, dealt with them, for your name's sake. For this, O LORD, I give you all the glory.

When certain unpleasant, mindless situations perpetrated by others, arise from the evils of this world, made me angry and helpless. I had no fear! Not even fear could conquer me; you rescued me, lifting up my soul from the anger. My kindness to others was taken and replaced with misery and misused. Your patience gives me wisdom, understanding, knowledge, and unconditional love—the kind of love I give to my children.

Because of your light and loving spirit, the sunshine stayed in my heart, mind, and soul. Keep on loving me; O Heavenly Father. Your love is sufficient to hold me at this moment and always. I will continue to trust and expect miracles in the precious name of Jesus Christ, the LORD God of hosts, now and at the end of my days. Amen.

Selah.

4
LOVE

God's love is a precious gift sent from above. God and his angels send Love. Love is everlasting and forever. The Mighty LORD commanded us to love one another. He is the root and offspring of King David. Love is the source of all things. Love formed creation. God is the life of love. Love is an entitlement from Jesus Christ that was commanded by God and given to his children.

Love is infinite. Love begins patience, wisdom, understanding, and knowledge. The infinite Mighty LORD first commandment says to love one another. The ultimate goal is to love oneself first and then others. Love matures by the truth. The truth evolves by love for self and others.

This primary and principal goal will bring about unequivocal love and understanding for life and others and will take you to a higher existence. Love is continuous and everlasting. Love is the only begotten son of God. Love is the beginning and the end. The Mighty LORD smiles down upon love.

He is in love with love. The All Mighty Father has stockpiled an abundance of this great love for his children. Love thy neighbors through understanding, wisdom, understanding conformity, and respect so you can connect with the Kingdom of God. Love, with compassion and adaptation, came from God.

Enjoy yourself, and obey the Heavenly Father's rules, written in his commandments. If men had real love for themselves, they would love and respect their fellow men. Love is giving and receiving. Love was embedded in your heart and soul before you created. Love removes fear and doubt; love the LORD night and day.

Love is forgiveness and unconditional. LORD, you love your children unconditionally. We are all wandering around in this heartless, loveless wilderness called earth. The LORDS angels can purge the land from this loveless, endless misery. Love is giving and receiving. Love is pure, flowing from the heart and soul.

Love removes fear and doubt. Love the LORD night and day. Learn to forgive yourself unconditional through love. LORD, you loved your children unconditionally. We are wandering in this passionless wilderness called earth. The LORDS angels can purge the land from this endless misery.

So let's get in tune with ourselves and reconstruct love in our hearts, minds, and souls. This beautiful inner element called love previously existed in our hearts.

Selah.

5

MERCY AND FORGIVENESS

Father, I humbly seek your mercy and forgiveness. LORD, I know your loving mercy can wipe away my past wrongdoings and my transgressions. In the morning, show me new directions with ways to redeem myself from my wrongdoings, giving me wings to fly. Wipe away the tears of my unfortunate victims; grant me mercy and forgiveness. Renew my spirit.

Teach me to love, make my heart tender toward others. Forgive me for the cruelty I imposed on others. Forgiving Father of the universe, you're the one who sees into the hearts of men. Extend your mercy and forgive me. Heavenly Father, you are the judge, the Alpha, and the Omega.

El Shaddai, you are the morning star, the holy one, the pure. You are the worthy one, the sweet nectar of life. You are my LORD and Savior, the beginning and end. Flow patience into me like a steady, unbroken stream. My love for you is never-ending and continuous.

Your love flows through me like a never-ending river. Heavenly Father, convey life through me with streams of constant, unknown vibes that reach my soul and flow into my heart, causing it to flutter like a feather. Have mercy on me; teach me forgiveness, while renewing my hope in you. Your compassion, understanding, and daily forgiveness give me confidence and long life.

Eternal, Immortal, Invisible King, who dries the tears, you are the one who eases life's pain. You are the LORD softly whispering to my heart, "its okay. Continue. Keep on pushing until you come to the end of your life's journey. I am your light at the end of the dark tunnel." Have mercy on me; shield me from the world's insanity.

LORD, mercy, and forgiveness are in your tabernacle. The angels sing. Stretch forth your loving mercy and forgiveness, blotting out all of my sins, renew my life, and giving me wings to fly like an eagle so that I may soar above my iniquities.

Selah

6

THE LIGHT AND THE LORD

Your temperament and features are like a lion mixed with a lamb and that of eternal, beautiful, glowing souls of angels. These words, "Let there be light," (*Genesis 1:3*) which you said, O Dear LORD, are displayed and revealed through the spectacular aurora borealis, the forming of the view of the world.

The light of the LORD, soothing, calmly overflowing and glowing with positive intriguing energy, the forces of love (repeat these words), I can do all things through the Mighty Father, your kingdoms filled with gold and silver. The realm in which you reside is magnificent, and your temple surrounded with peace and courage.

By infinite luminous white and yellow, soft, gleaming lights—lights so bright it blinds the natural eye and will hide your soul forever. Your dark silhouette is absorbed and penetrates these brilliant yellow flames. Your face adorned with bright, white-golden glowing light. Men and women cannot fathom the depths of your existence.

Powers of Jesus Christ, who strength me" (*Philippians 4:13*) (*repeat*).

Your magnificent body adorned with constant sweet power and mercy, all embedded in your light—this unknown light yet to be absorbed by men and women. LORD, you sit on the throne of life surrounded by your eternal flame. Heavenly Father you are the maker and keeper of this great light.

So much beauty and splendor; endless, unfolding, everlasting light; warming, embracing the light.

Light filled with power and glory—only the worthy can understand, endure, and enter. You are King of Kings, LORD of LORDS. Who possesses no fear? Your skillfulness, impressive splendor, and splendid glory and great, magnificent light that have filled the earth for centuries.

The light is a gift to humankind, this illuminating light. LORD, only a few humans, can understand and absorb this light that offers them a chance to redeem themselves.

You're the never-ending light of this world and the worlds to come. This glorious light magnified. Natural humans or beasts cannot fathom the light you generate.

My being enjoys the strength of your light. You showed me your light before my conception. How glorifying and energizing in the mind of a child. You are the precious light of creation, the sweet nectar of life. Pulsating from the sacred heart of Jesus Christ, God the Father, at the beginning, where the spoken words.

"Let there be light" (*Genesis 1:3*). These words said by the Blessed Father, without a doubt, or fear, spoken with surety and confidence, never pondering. The darkness in the heavens unfolded. The light manifested itself with authority, might, and trust, entirely orchestrated by the Holy Father, the great, mighty, awesome God, surrounded by his illuminating light, viewing this world.

Selah.

7

THE UNGODLY

The wicked shall see their day, minute by minute, hour by hour, day by day. Purge yourselves of your transgressions. The wicked shall not see the face of God, whether in their youth or glory days or old. Consistently redeem yourselves for the sake of the unborn babies and be forgiven.

The adults will be held accountable for the sins of their children. The ungodly shall vanish from the earth and never reenter the earth's realm or see the light of the LORD make amends and intersection for their sins. Redeem yourselves while the time is right. The ungodly, shall thirst for water and long for the word of God and the grace of his light.

Their souls shall live in darkness. The ungodly will not have peace in their hearts and will forever be in need. Redeem yourselves. The intolerable wander around in the darkness, trapped in a world filled with hopelessness, sorrow, and joylessness. The ungodly will not see the light of the LORD.

They forever live in confusion and drama, seeking the souls of the upright who walk in the light of Jesus Christ, who redeems you from your sins. The ungodly and their children shall not inherit the earth and will be led away by false gods. The unreasonable shall walk in the land of the living and not see the glory of the LORD.

Oh, how good it is to see the children of God, happily living in the land of plenty, to worship the one and true living God of salvation.

Redeem yourselves, and your minds will be set free. The ungodly shall deny the LORDS ever-devoted Spirit. They will forever be misguided, worrisome, and without faith, hope, understanding, and wisdom.

The wicked shall stumble and fall, per his enemy's wishes. Redeem yourself. The ungodly shall not know the rainbow; their minds shall be lower to the ground and will not be lifted up above their enemies. Redeem yourselves. The wicked shall see the flaming objects descending in the night skies and will be afraid. And they will say, "It's the end of the world."

Heavenly Father said, "Unto him *(God the Father)* be glory in the church by Christ Jesus throughout all ages, world without end. Amen" *(Ephesians 3:21)*. Man will destroy himself but, the world will stay. Believe and redeem yourselves. The ungodly shall burden with problems not relating to their existence. Redeem yourselves. The wicked shall long for wisdom, peace, understanding, and the love of God and not receive it.

The Ungodly shall deceive others, use, abuse, and discriminate against others for gains. Redeem yourselves. The ungodly shall be like the dark clouds that block out the sun. Redeem yourselves. The wicked shall stumble and fall between the children of God. Redeem yourselves. The ungodly shall walk among lions and tigers and will be swallowed up by life's negative drama.

Redeem yourselves. The unsociable will long for peace of mind in the land of the living and will not conquer the children of God. *(Blasphemous)* Redeem yourselves. These words of wisdom to the ungodly—seek you first the kingdom of the LORD and his mercy. Cleanse yourselves of your transgressions and the kingdom of God will open up before you.

Ask his forgiveness. He will show you the way. The Mighty LORD is in control of all things. He sees inside the hearts of the wicked and the Ungodly. To the outrageous, when you come to the end of your lives and need the LORDS mercy and forgiveness, it will be too late. The word of God has spoken—the lawgiver and judge, God the Father.

Selah.

8

THE DIVINE PLAN

The Heavenly Father designed a divine plan for humankind. His plans consisted of living in love and harmony with each other and caring for his creations. He came to endure the pain and suffering for the remission of man's transgressions and shortcomings. Today, as in yesteryear, men and women are alone. They do not fit into God's divine plan and are separated from the will of God, struggling day by day in confusion.

They fight and devour their brothers daily for their possessions and nothing at all and without cause—their stupid ideology and so-called possessions, lying, cheating, envy, jealousy, greed, dysfunction, dissatisfaction, and corruption and sinful ways. Everything has turned upside down. The mineral of the earth has poisoned the souls of humankind, blinded by their desires, enslaving the minds of their brothers to satisfy greed.

These men and women of greed and corruption only perpetuate fear in the spirit of God's children by failing and misusing them. Their subconscious minds are filled with trickery, designing traps of confusion and discouragement. Abba, Father, good and kind, gentle God of the universe, who is within all things and slow to anger but can and will dispense anger in a split second—help us to succeed in all our endeavors. Protect our minds from those whose hearts filled with bad intentions for your children and the kingdom.

Protect our minds, bodies, and ideas from those who are hungry and thirsty for fame and power. LORD, like in the days of old, men and women have technically advanced and are still continuing in their evil ways, increasing horror and terror. Half of the world is hungry and distracted. It appears as though they want us all to be hungry and feel afraid. They have us worried and are installing climate fear and terrorism fear while taking away our rights and freedom.

There is even confusion about the way we grow, dispense, and eat food. We might think these new voices for change and progression are dynamic acts for the better, when it's actually for the worse. LORD, they have convinced us to send our children, friends, husbands, boyfriends, girlfriends, mothers, fathers, and well-wishers off to these strange lands to fight; to bring civilization and the love of a good God to these parts of the world. They were hoping the LORDS precious light would shine on these areas of the world.

Their sacrifices and efforts met with ungratefulness and destruction. They were taken advantage of, killed, inflamed by godless, talentless individuals; dirty. People who are ignorant, mindless, destructive uncreative and fortified this world with confusion. You, LORD, are still our love, guide, and mentor. Bring us together as one people. Let us make circles our lives. Protect us from the wild forces that are bent on destroying us. Help us to respect our communities and stand up, for your name's sake.

Give us ideas and energy to act on these thoughts. Administer your organizational spirit within us, so we can come together as one and stop the bickering among ourselves. Ever loving and faithful Father, sword and shield of righteousness, send real leaders with integrity and honor our way, to shine the light on our efforts and to make a peaceful and divine world for our children. Making us a success, lift and hold up new leaders who would fight for your glory and honor.

Send a real leader who will lead us to victory among this destruction. Strengthen our governments with new powerful men and women with leadership and power beyond the realm of the natural eyes. Return Mighty men and women of God, our Jehovah, securing their lost souls. That once fought for our freedoms gave us victory by resurrecting brave people. Help us bring success to our lands and the LORD and Savior Jesus Christ.

The All Mighty God, commission men with strength and power who will fight to restore your name and honor. Dispense fear and love again to these countries that would not accept the name of God, Jesus Christ, and the true glory of our LORD and Savior Jesus Christ. Lead us to victory and your peaceful kingdom. Send us new soldiers who can help us make our ideas, dreams, and ideology into reality once more.

Remove fear and doubt from our minds, replacing with courage, wisdom, and knowledge. Protect our idea, so we first may become worthy among you, LORD, and then among men and women. Show us how to rebuild and be good custodians of your creation. Dear LORD, we are experiencing negative things at the hands of others.

Only you can curtail and protect our minds so that we don't think you have given up on us and are not important to us. LORD, make us not be afraid to speak our minds freely, without the other party taking it critically and seriously. Give us victory in these times of struggle and uncertainty while we obey your will for us. Keep us steady in your divine plan for the children of God and men and women. Your will is imperative for the glory of your kingdom.

The All Mighty Father is the one who will deliver this world.

Selah.

9
PATIENCE

Give me patience, so I know you are the one who provides for the birds and the beasts in the fields and you will adequately provide for me. LORD, give me the patience to know you will provide for me abundantly and richly. Give me patience to know you will give me victory over my enemies. Give me patience to know you are the strength I seek. Jehovah you are the one who can deliver me from my despair.

O LORD, you said, "May you prosper personally as your soul prospers." Beloved, I pray that in all things thou mayest prosper and be in health, even as thy soul prospereth." (*John 3:2 ASV*) LORD, you can say the word, and in a quick second, your word will come to life and deliver me from my despair. When my guards were down, the enemy attacked me, making me weak and confused. Give me guts to know you will give me victory over those who steal my thoughts and ideas. Give me the patience to deal effectively with those who wish me evil.

They indulge in my time to monitor my every thought and deeds as they try to use my positive energy, while their wishes are for evil against me. Let them not prosper over me. Send your divine inspiration to keep me focused and steady. O Mighty LORD, the clouds in the air listen to your commands. They are still and know that you are the LORD, who does Mighty things for those who love and obey him.

Give me the patience to understand that the battle is not against the flesh but instead is a spiritual warfare. Mighty LORD, help me as I prosper in personal wealth to continue to be humble before you. Give me patience to love and enjoy the simple things in life, understanding my needs and those of others. Let my enemies stumble and fall, give me leverage over my enemies. Give me patience. Heavenly Father, show me patience through your loving-kindness, understanding, and mercy.

So I can win over my enemies and put them under my feet. Give victory over life's "crab in the barrel" syndrome. Give me the patience to know that I am not in this fight alone, but you are my keeper. You will give me favors over those who used and abused me and took me for granted. Often when I was weak, helpless, and destitute, Satan's children misused and abused me. God stood with me in the trenches. Ever-loving God, the merciful Father, give me the patience to forgive them.

But let me not fall prey to them again. Give me patience. "Seek, and you shall find; knock, and it will be opened to you" (*Matthew 7:7*). The LORD may not be there when you call, but he is a right-on-time God when you need him; he's right on times when you truly need him. Be still and know he is the all Mighty God. He is slowly but surely arranging your blessings. The LORD is good at all times. He is the most Influential Father of the Universe.

Selah.

10

MY LORD, MY PROVIDER

My LORD, my provider, you have been providing for me from my youth. You have been my mother and father. My brother and sister, Let not my enemies conquer over me. LORD, I am poor and needy. Mighty Father, you provide for the birds in air and fishes in the ocean. The LORD gives without reproach.

He is not cursed with envy or jealousy and will make a way out of no way for me. My LORD, my provider, I put my trust in you whether things are good. You are my everlasting friend to the end, my God, My provider; you are the author and finisher of my faith. Heavenly Father you have been with me thru my ups and down.

I am forever giving you the praise in all things. I pray expecting miracles O, LORD, my savior, and provider.

My LORD, my provider, shows me your purpose for my life. Makes me into the person you intended me to be.

When others were pretending to care to seek my soul and destroy my soul, they extend superficial love filled with envy and jealousy.

Their love can't compare to your love, O, Mighty One I am in need. Do not forsake me I pray, putting all of my confident in you O LORD of Wisdom and Understanding. You are there to hold me together when my mother and father forsake me. My LORD my provider you are there to holding me together through all things. My friends betray me causing pain and suffering.

You delivered me from the hurt and disappointments; remove all obstacles in my way. That hinders me from succeeding in my endeavors; my breath belongs to you. Your Omni Present will continue to provide. For me every day in all ways, provide for me bountifully; bring me into a huge place of abundance making me know prosperity like I never knew before.

Selah

11

GOD'S BOUNTIFUL

The Highest God, your name is embedded on the tip of my tongue. And continually lift my head above my enemies, at no time allowing my feet to stumble. Mighty God, your love and tender mercies are as bountiful as the wheat in the fields and never-ending. Exceeding joy, plenty, and abundance come from within your kingdom.

Highest Father, who always catches me when I fall, I owe my life to you. Blot out all my past transgressions. O Mighty One, I am forever in your debt. Forgive me my debts as I forgive my debtors. Help me seriously to forgive my debtors. Give me the wisdom to become productive and experience bounty, according to your will.

You fill the fields with plants and animals to nourish our bodies, and flowers are pleasing to our eyes and minds. Mighty God, you're a well-to-do God and not a meager God, but a generous God. You're the God of the Universe, made from an affluent existence and not a meager one, commanding lavishly.

Speaking words of abundance and perfectly covering the earth with water, vast and plentiful as no one can do. Varieties of fishes were called into existence to roam the depths of the blue sea. Plants and flowers carefully painted in a variety of colors, abundantly engulfing the surface of Earth. Everything you created set up in abundance.

What joy to know Mighty is your name, O LORD! Bountiful God, using one voice with one intention, you commanded the light into existence with an abundance that flows and surrounds the universe. Before this world formed you were present, silent Father, our sculptor, and Potter, Creator of all things in abundance, without shame or excuses.

You bountifully and consistently provided for the children of men and women and the beasts of the field, the ones you created and adore. I richly appreciate your efforts and the bountiful of your abundance, thanks to you. "Ask, and it shall be given unto you. Seek, and you shall find. Knock and it shall be open" (*Matthew 7:7*). (Chant)

You will receive God's bounty, sacrosanct patre. Generous God, sacrosanct pâtre, ample God, sacrosanct pâtre, bountiful God, sacrosanct pâtre, plentiful God, impregnable, benevolent God, invincible, most Mighty God, unassailable, the Universe belongs to you, bountiful God; the world belongs to you, bountiful God.

Selah.

12

NEW FRONTIERS

Son of God, who ascended from the grave into the heavens—they fail to understand you are bronze with a glowing yellow light that men and women cannot touch. Humankind has yet to wash away their faults and to cleanse their souls, denouncing evil, racism, transgressions, and darkness.

The LORD is omnipresent in humankind. Humankind does not heed to his still small voice that existed in them from the time of their conception. He is presently dissatisfied with men's and women's evil deeds and is losing patience. His commandments will reestablish in the new frontiers. Vileness is present on earth, so vile that the LORDS feet refuse to touch the ground again.

You alone, LORD, are the true Savior of this world and worlds beyond, magnificent one, all Mighty God. We are venturing out into space, seeking new frontiers, looking for unknown adventures, brand new colonization, and new places to control, yet we have not mastered the Ten Commandments! Praise the LORD; our minds filled with darkness, hatred, greed, jealousy, racism, inequality, and peccadilloes—you name it!

Help us, O LORD, to replace these unnatural emotions that exist in our souls with the light of the LORD Jehovah God, the everlasting light of this world. The kind of light only you can provide; LORD, your precious light overcomes darkness, hatred, greed, jealousy, racism, inequality, and peccadilloes. LORD, this world—men and women, children, plants, animals, water, air, earth—beneath our feet is suffering from pollution and darkness.

It is in desperate need of your warm, blessed light of love that cleanses the land and the minds and souls of men. The light of peace and love you once gave the world has dissolved and replaced with mayhem and chaos. Your children persecuted for the color of their skin. Love your brother as you love yourselves.

Jehovah it is just a matter of time before the fallen angels who are engaged in a life filled with disobedience to God—racism, raping, exploiting children, senseless killing, fighting in the streets—will return to their barbaric and uncivilized ways to take advantage of the children God. No one can help us, God. Our world leaders are all out to lunch.

Their concern is misleading and powers manipulating, they only fill their pockets with the earth's swag, dear LORD, Prince among Princes, and King of the Earth. Hear our prayers for new leaders—men and women who would stand up for you. Modern-day men and women have gone mad and are drunk with the spirit of the ecumenical world.

LORD, give wisdom, understanding, courage, and strength to new leaders who will govern us according to your will—leaders who will put you first in all things. The LORD of hosts lives on high and is slow to judge and quick to love unconditionally. Give real wisdom, courage, and understanding to men and women so that they can make a better world for our children—the world without racism, filled with peace, love, freedom of speech, and respect for one another.

As they make plans to venture out into these new outer-realm frontiers and to create a brand-new world, let us hope that these unknown worlds will be devoid of transgressions, corruption, confusion, discrimination, and darkness. Mighty LORD, your unused kingdom must be devoid of this darkness. Transplant the hateful part of men's and women's hearts. Sin has corrupted the inner lining of minds. Replace with your love and peace, Prince of Peace and Joy, who sits on high.

Ruling from your kingdom, keep shining your light on your beloved servants. LORD, whose nature is of lamb and lion, you give wisdom and knowledge to those who first seek you. LORD, the captain, and redeemer of our ship, captain of our lives. The LORD is searching our hearts. He is the lawgiver and bestows mercy on us. He is purging the land of evil for his eternal kingdom, selecting and separating the courageous willing and pure from among us.

He is always surrounding us with his eternal light, burning out corruption and confusion from the minds of men and women. Nothing is impossible for him. O Mighty God, your glowing fire can renew the spirit, bodies, and souls. The real intentions for your new frontiers are not known to man. They don't believe you are the Savior, King of Kings.

Selah.

13

KING OF KINGS, LORD OF LORDS

Light of nations, he is the King of Kings, LORD of LORDS. Humankind and humanity have ignited the spirit of hate and destruction by ignoring your LORD and worshiping strange gods. The LORD is making his presence known. He is the first and last King of Kings, LORDS of LORDS. He is our Redeemer in times of trouble our salvation and strength.

Our omniscient light of the nations is the King of Kings and LORD of LORDS. Christ is LORD. Be careful which God you are serving. Make the world a better place for the children. Every knee shall bend and call upon the name of the LORD Jehovah. The time will come when God sends his angels to purify the earth.

As the light of the nations, he is the King of Kings and LORD of LORDS. Christ is LORD, the Mighty God. The Father is on a high. He is sitting in his kingdom on the golden throne, surrounded by the gleaming of his powerful, blinding light eternal, a glowing powerful, radiant heart of light. He is waiting patiently for humankind to come to their senses.

They turn the Garden of Eden into a place of vileness. LORD, The Light of the nations. King of Kings and LORD of LORDS, (*Revelation 19:16 NASB*) Christ is LORD; he is LORD of the Universe. The light of all the nations, he is the King of Kings and LORD of LORDS. Jesus. Christ is LORD. The time is upon us to renew our faith, hope, devotion, and strength in the LORD, putting aside fear and doubts.

Protect your mind and soul with the armor of God the father to fight the spiritual battle that is at hand. He delivered the children of Israel. Our Father, who is in heaven, helps us to purge the earth and renew your sovereignty. King of Kings, LORD of LORDS, (*Revelation 19:16 NASB*) you alone can save us. Put an eternal end to these confusions and destruction.

Every progress and greed humankind endures bent on destroying God's creation. They filled with hatred, greed, hopelessness, and worshiping death. Life is cheap to them. While they denounce our LORD and Savior Jesus Christ, help us to use wisdom to corral the LORDS enemies. Give us victory and triumph.

LORD of hosts; cleanse the earth of all iniquity, delivering your children from the original sin. Who is on the LORDS side in these times of doubt and uncertainty? The LORD God is the one to turn to for all things, more so especially today when the evildoers are always fighting against the name of the LORD.

Omnipresent, omniscient—the universe belongs to God. Jesus Christ is LORD, King of Kings, and LORD of LORDS. (*Revelation 19:16 NASB*)

Selah

14

DELIVERANCE FROM POVERTY

Wealth befits you, my supreme Father, LORD of the living flesh. You alone know my heart's desires and honor my request. Grant me my heart's desires. I will continually praise your name in all the earth. I will forever lift up your name on high to the world. Deliver me from poverty and ignorance. Bring deliverance to my meaningless situation.

The Great Deliver, you know the hearts of my enemies. With envy and jealousy, their wishes are to see me go under in the pit on anguish. You knew my poverty. My tears have touched and soaked your robe. I am the first and not the last. I beseech you on high. Send now prosperity, rescuing my soul from this yearning spirit of wanting. LORD, your courage, and confidence are fountains of living waters.

Create in me a special gift to offer you and your angels in heaven so that I can pass these gifts on to others. The angels can release me from this poverty and into prosperity. LORD, you are my deliverer. Let my head be lifted up high above my enemies. "The stone, the builder, rejected has become the chief cornerstone." (*Psalm 118:22*). LORD, look within my heart. I am the top and not the bottom.

You dry my tears when I weep. Send heavenly opportunities, opening doors that were once closed to me here on earth. Hasten your deliverance from this misery. Block all poison arrows that may come my way to deceive and misguide me and take me in another place, distorting my blessings of prosperity. When I was down in spirit, you lifted my head and my mind, giving me strength and creativeness to keep on the move.

Bring great blessings to the daughters of Abraham (*or sons of Abraham*) that none can take away. As my soul prospers in all things, so do my blessings increase, the blessings you promised in your words. Even as my soul prospers, shed your light on my current situation. Bring me to a place where I can find financial security and serenity. Deliver me from this poverty. Make my family proud of me.

Let me be a blessing to myself, my family, and others. All of my soul belongs to you. Heavenly Father, keeper of the universe, Abba Father, you delivered Daniel from the lion's den. Nothing is too difficult for your intervention. Deliverance came to the children of Israel as they stood in doubt at the seashore. My faith in you is more than a mustard seed. In times of uncertainty and doubt, send your angels' strength to dispute doubt.

Look down on me; make me worthy of receiving wealth. O one, whose heart filled with mercy and compassion for your beloved servant, (*reader: say your name here*), hasten to deliver me out of this uncertainty and lack. Give me victory over poverty.

Selah.

15

COMFORT IN TIME OF TROUBLE

The great Comforter, the Advocate, comfort me in time of trouble. Make an intercession on my behalf. Reassuring God, Comforter in time of trouble, I shall want for nothing. My needs met according to your blessings. Shield me from my enemies and their suspicious minds, trickery, and hurt.

You are the granting Father. In this time of sorrow, hide my bewilderment in your pergola in time of trouble. When my father and mother forsake me, you, LORD, stand with me in time of trouble. When my friends disappoint me, you stand with me and comfort me. When my opponents jab my soul with their forks and knives and try to eat my soul, you come to me in time of trouble.

When others bring drought, doubt, and fear at my feet and surround me with disbelief and their belief system, you come to me, giving new hope, renewal, joy, happiness, and faithfulness. You shield me in time of trouble. When my dreams, hopes, and desires for success are trampled on by others and the spirit of defeat, hopelessness, and despair rises inside of me to pull me under, you stand with me.

Comforting me in time of trouble, raising me up in strength and glory, giving me victories—you are the constant light that shines on me, giving confidence, and courage. You hide my mind and soul and close my heart and soul from those whose purposes were to bring me unhappiness, dissatisfaction, and discontent with my life.

You are always comforting me in time of trouble, blotting the unclean spirits with the blazing fire of those whose intentions for me are evil.

You blot them out like a raging fire and nourish my soul with confidence and the everlasting victory of success.

You raise me up in strength and glory, giving me victories over all things in time of trouble.

Your reassuring spirit is always close in my mind, waiting for me to say "Abba Father" You listened to my cries in the period of crisis and comforted me. You alone, LORD, are my redeemer and counselor and an advocate with the Father, Son, and Holy Ghost. Jesus Christ, on behalf of the followers of Father God, plead my case to the LORD.

The LORD of truth and light is steadfastly sitting on the right hand of God the Father; he brings comfort in time of trouble.

Selah.

16

IN TIMES OF UNCERTAINTY

In times of uncertainty, sadness doesn't last for long. Your very presence is with us in these times. All he was asking us is to love one another and trust him. There are waves of discord, bias, and double standards when it comes to religious tolerance and accepting and respecting each other's established norms. LORD this is happening not only in our country but around the world.

Mighty LORD of all, you are aware of these circumstances. The Christian and the Jewish nations are being pushed aside, slaughtered, and persecuted by factions within society and the media. Believers in the faith conned into closing their eyes and minds to the violence, which becomes them. LORD, you warned us that this day was imminent, and now it is upon us.

LORD, we are living in times of uncertainty. LORD, in spite of these things, stay with us in mind, body, and soul, keeping us strong in our faith in Jesus Christ. In times of uncertainty, all you ask of us is to love one another. In the times of doubt, you are present.

All he is asking of us is to love and trust him. Lord, in times of danger, you are present. All he was asking us is to love and trust. In times of fear, bad health, and death, you are present. All he wants is for us to love each other. LORD, I know you are not dead. Your present, loving spirit is with us in these circumstances.

The light that we once knew seems to be vanishing from our hearts and minds. However, a tiny ray of your precious light is still shining through these painful circumstances.

All you desire for us is to trust. All the LORD was asking us is to love and trust.

All you desire for us is to believe. All God is asking us is to love. All you desire from us is not to doubt. All he was begging us was to love and trust. In this time of need, you are present.

All he was asking us is to love and trust. In times of danger, you are present. All he asks us is to love.

LORD, due to the random violence perpetrated against Christians and Jews, we are calling upon all the Christians and Jews to make peace in their minds with their God. Every time, day and night, in their going out and coming in, as they prepare themselves for the battle of their lives, in times of confusion, you are present. All you ask of us is to love.

All you desire from us is to trust. All you ask of us is to love. All you desire from us is to believe; all you ask of us is to love. When injustice strikes and the spirit of uncertainty arise, all you desire from us is not to doubt. In times of danger, you are present; all you ask of us is to love. All you ask of us is to love.

In times of uncertainty, the battle belongs to you in all its glory and splendor. In times of uncertainty, the spirit of self-hatred and guilt has consumed the minds of some of our leaders. The others are ruling with past vengeance and lots of deceptions. The heads of state seem to be confused and are in disarray. Our young people are being fooled day and night by people whose goals are to mislead them.

Evette Forde

They have entrusted their lives and well-being to deception. All you desire from us is to trust in you. All God was asking us is to love. All you desire for us is to believe. All he was telling you is to love and trust. All you desire for us is not to doubt. All he is asking us is to love and trust. At the time of need, you are present. All he would like you to do is to love. In the times of danger, you are present. All he is asking us is to love.

In times of uncertainty, you are instant. In times of fear and uncertainty, all you ask of us is to love one another. In the times of danger, you are present. All you ask of us is to love. All you desire for us is to believe. All you ask of us is to love each other. All you desire for us is not to doubt. All you ask of us is to love one another. At the times of need, you are present. All you ask of us is to love.

You are present in the times of uncertainty. LORD, our children, are helplessly being persecuted and slaughtered through no fault of their own. In times of uncertainty, poverty and ignorance are rampant in the African American communities, while their appointed leaders are sliding around from the main issues and these realities. They are only concerned about the flag, carding, and "black lives matter; all life matters."

All you desire for us is to trust. All you ask of us is to love. All you desire for us is to believe. All you ask of us is to love. All you desire from us is not to doubt. All you ask of us is to love. At the time of need, you are present. All you ask of us is to love. In the times of danger, you are present. All you ask of us is to love.

The present-day mainstream media is doing a number on the way they portray African Americans. They either are having a problem with the law, or they are being gunned down on the streets, or they just do not exist up front or in the background of their programming. LORD, all you desire for us is to believe; all you ask of us is to love.

Selah.

17

THE NIGHT THE SON WAS BORN

The night the Son of God was conceived in the heavens, the glorious lights of the Holy Spirit were present. The night the Son of God was born, wise men from the East and all living creatures, big and small, knew of his birth. The angels in the heavens sang songs of great inspiration and joy. The skies above illuminated.

The night the Son of God was born, hallelujah, hallelujah,
The night the Son of God was born, hallelujah, hallelujah.

The night the Son of God was born, praise the LORD,
The night the Son of God was born, Redeemer of Life.
The night the Son of God was born, birth to the world.
The night the Son of God was born, Begotten Son.

He brought the light of wisdom and knowledge into the world, undoing the darkness. Setting men free from their transgression and indulgence, he is the buckler and shield to all those who trust him. Evil men and demons hide their faces from their iniquity. Others purified their souls. He was a gift sent from the heavenly Father.

The night the Son of God was born, hallelujah, hallelujah.
The night the Son of God was born, hallelujah, hallelujah.

The night the Son of God was born, Prince of Peace.
The night the Son of God was born, Omni-deity.
The night the son of God was born, sins forgiven.
The night the son of God was born, he conquered death.

The night the Son of God was born in the image of the Heavenly Father, God transcended light to his children. That was the night the world found joy and peace. The night, humankind was set free. Sin had no place in the world. Redemption came to the world.

The light from the brightest stars followed his birth.
The night the Son of God was born, hallelujah, hallelujah.

The night the Son of God was born, hallelujah, hallelujah
The night the Son of God was born, praise the LORD.
The night the Son of God was born, redeemer of life.
The night the Son of God was born, birth to the world.

Three wise men followed the bright star. The gifted men brought three gifts—gold, frankincense, and myrrh. Jesus Christ is the bread of life. He is living hope for the dead. His birth brought men to their knees, the consecrated heart of Jesus Christ, beloved Son of God.

The night the Son of God was born, hallelujah, hallelujah,
The night the Son of God was born, hallelujah, hallelujah.

The night the Son of God was born, Begotten Son.
The night the Son of God was born, Prince of Peace.
The night the Son of God was born Omni-deity.
The night the Son of God was born, sins forgiven.

The night the Son of God was born. The night the Son of God was born. The night the Son of God was born. The night the Son of God was born. The night the Son of God was born. The night the Son of God was born. The night the Son of God was born. The night the Son of God was born.

The night the Son of God was born, hallelujah, hallelujah,
The night the Son of God was born, hallelujah, hallelujah.

The night the Son of God was born, hallelujah, hallelujah.
The night the Son of God was born, praise the LORD.
The night the Son of God was born, Redeemer of life.
The night the Son of God was born, birth to the world.

These wise men came to the manger to pay homage to the King of kings, LORD of LORDS. With the birth of the King of light, the heavens ignited. There was a presence of peace adorning the manger and baby Jesus Christ. Men and women are given the gift of an Everlasting Father and the opportunity through his blood to live forever and ever.

The night the Son of God was born, hallelujah, hallelujah,
The night the Son of God was born, hallelujah, hallelujah.

The night the Son of God was born, Begotten Son.
The night the Son of God was born, Prince of Peace.
The night the Son of God was born, Omni-deity.
The night the Son of God was born, sins forgiven.

The night the Son of God was born, the angels rejoiced in the stars that were shining brightly. Wise men came from the East. They brought presents of gold, myrrh, and frankincense. King of Kings was born with powers to deliver humankind. God's good will sent a Messiah to bring the light of peace and joy into the darker lower level of this world.

The night the Son of God was born, hallelujah, hallelujah.
The night the Son of God was born, hallelujah, hallelujah,

The night the Son of God was born, praise the LORD.
The night the Son of God was born, Redeemer of life.
The night the Son of God was born, Birth to the world.

Blessed hope; animals lay in the manger and looked on in silence, peace, tranquility, and love as they welcomed his birth. Let us adore him. Jesus Christ, the power of God, who presides over this universe. He sits on the right hand of God the Father, vowing never stepping his foot on this planet again.

The night the Son of God was born, hallelujah, hallelujah,
The night the Son of God was born, hallelujah, hallelujah.

The night the Son of God was born, Begotten Son.
The night the son of God was born, Prince of Peace.
The night the Son of God was born, Omni-deity.
The night the son of God was born, sins forgiven.

The night the Son of God was born. The night the Son of God was born.
The night the Son of God was born. The night the Son of God was born.
The night the Son of God was born. The night the Son of God was born.
The night the Son of God was born. The night the Son of God was born.

The night the Son of God was born, hallelujah, hallelujah,
The night the Son of God was born, hallelujah, hallelujah.

The holy book of the tabernacle opened, and the truth about right and wrong revealed. The human race was given the book of knowledge and understanding, which opened them up to the truth about living and loving in the Garden of Eden. They were given a choice to serve good or serve evil.

The night the Son of God was born.
The night the Son of God was born.
The night the Son of God was born.
The night the Son of God was born.

Selah.

18

TRUSTING THE LORD

Abandoned and tired, I reach for you. Your strength is perfect. In you, I put my trust. Deliver me, O LORD. So my face can shine again with your love, tender mercies, and joy. I sing praises to you every day while I wait patiently. Lord, my trust is in you and waits for your deliverance. O LORD, morning has arrived. O LORD, you are on my mind.

The weather is cold and drab. My circumstance is grim. The heat in the apartment is not working properly. LORD, you alone, knows my circumstances. At all times, I place my trust in you and wait for your deliverance. You, O LORD, know my heart and soul. Protect me from life's misery. I have given all.

Understand wisdom and patience to other, so that they too can experience your love. You alone, LORD, know my heart. The love you give me permits me to endure. Guide my going out and coming in. I trust in the LORD. You're the quiet voice that instructs me to be vigilant and at the same time tells me when to fight.

You have given me songs to sing and joy in my heart. You have given me a smile on my face and patience and confidence in my heart's Holy One. I place my trust in you. I know you will supply the desires of my heart. I patiently wait for your deliverance. Trusting in the LORD without doubting demonstrates to the LORD that you are worthy of his blessings.

I believe you for victory over my failures, keeping me steady. Bring prosperity to all endeavors. God, let me not be ashamed. If I was in the way, then take me out of the way of my success; blow out the oppression of deceitful friends. Send angels to assist me. LORD, don't forsake me in these difficult times.

In you, I put my trust. You alone know the desires of my heart. Your love for me, O LORD, is bright and as assuring as the morning star. Only you know my needs and will provide for me in this time of lack and uncertainty. You, O Trusted Father, can provide for me above the needs of my enemies.

Blessed Father, choose for me my inheritance. Make me know plenty. Let not my past mistakes hinder me from your blessings. I put my trust and hope in you and wait for your speedy deliverance. Open up your sacred heart and pour out blessings that no one I know can attain. My cup will be filled and run over.

Open doors of opportunities and dispense prosperity. My undying abundance of faith is in you. Provide for me new opportunities, trusting in the LORD. Set me up in a large place out of the reach of my enemies. Turn their sneers and rude ways into prosperity for me. In you, I put my trust in you.

Here on earth, where materialism, education, money, position, and wealth, measures your existence, not kindness and love. Turn my love and efforts into substantial opportunities for prosperity. Calm the flames of the evil intentions that come from my enemies. So, that those who have been deceiving me by taking my love, energy, understanding, and patience and eventually leaving alone.

While they were taking me for granted and called me mad, the handiwork did not lead them to anything, but unhappiness. See the evil intentions in their hearts, and protect me from these intentions.

I can't accomplish these things without you. Every effort I made to improve my life has obstructed by men of greed and jealousy.

They have mistaken my kindness for weakness and set the net of a sneer before me. In you, I put my trust. While I'm trusting in the LORD, let not my enemies win over me. Guard my mind, soul, inspirations, and efforts in your pavilion. While trusting in the LORD for my deliverance, let me keep on loving you for the rest of my days and beyond.

My cup filled and ran over in this life and the next. Let me not wander far away from you. With all blessings and things, drought or plenty, forever faithful, you are my rock. LORD, my deliverer. In you, I put my trust. I believe in you, O LORD, All Mighty Father, in you alone, I put my trust, forever leaning on your everlasting strength.

In all things, God always causes us to triumph in Jesus Christ. He wants us to enjoy the silver and gold. However, never put your trust in these things.

You're my redeemer. In you, I put my trust. In the time of need, I called, and you delivered me. I call upon you, O Mighty one, my fortress and hiding place.

The wicked know, and time to time they try to attack me intending for me to stumble and fall. Keep my enemy under your feet, O LORD, and forever living in confusion. Mighty God, I put my trust in you, the LORD of LORDS

Selah.

19

VICTORY OVER MY ENEMIES

They pretended they were my lovers and friends. Only you alone knew their intentions. Give me the strength to fight this emotional battle, giving me victory over all things. Give me victory over poverty, sickness, jealousy, and evil eyes. LORD, hear my prayer remove fear and depression from my heart. Give me victory so sweet that my enemies wonder in amazement. To you, LORD, O God, I pray. Send success before I return to your kingdom.

Let them see that you are for me; therefore, no one can be against me or win over me. Rush to deliver me. Hastily break the chain of ignorance, material external poverty, and poverty of my mind. Let your heavenly lights shine upon me without end. Let my enemies fear you, O LORD. You, who guard the gates of heaven, send lightning and thunder on those who will obstruct me.

Give me victory over my enemies, you whom I love and obey. Let not my blessing is hindered. Male or female, let not any human or beast put their agendas before me. In this world and the one to come, you alone have the power to elevate and provide in abundance while defeating my enemies. My soul has faith within me as I wait on you, O LORD, who is quick to deliver me from my enemies,

Let not my hope in you become worthless. Deliver me from the fangs of the serpents. Like a child, I wait for you. When the ones who are faithless, hopeless, lost and confused intervene and trip me up, come between and shield me, on my behalf and for your name's sake. O LORD, my deliverer, delivers me! O Dear LORD, who sits on the throne of life, sends disaster on those who are jealous of me and wish my demise.

My soul is a wounded lamb. My pain and silence have reached the ears of the LORD, who resides in the Heavens. With every breath, I wait for you, never doubting. I lay in the darkness of poverty, trying to reach the light and your glory, O Holy One, which raises the sun in the morning and shines the moon at night. I believe you will lend an ear to my suffering and deliver me.

Through my endeavors, you stayed with me. Reassuring me through the sufferings and pain, you reached from the heavens and delivered me. My heart is blessed and rejoicing in your name. Only you know my heart. Let not the words, deeds, situations and actions of men or women hinder me from your glory and love in this life and the next. Grant me victory over my enemies.

Selah

20

FAITHFUL FATHER

My soul is drunk with glee, for you have provided for me; you give me songs to sing. You renewed my hope in you; if my heart had fainted, I would lose and unfulfilled. Faithful Father, you are a good provider and a loving Father. You're a jealous God. I am mesmerized by your love; you have taken the riches from beneath the ground and delivered them unto me.

You have given me the minds and souls of men. You will take the wealth of the wicked and give it to me, faithful Father. By grace and everlasting courage, you said – 'Truly, I say to you, whoever says to this mountain, 'Be taken up and thrown into the sea,' and does not doubt in his heart, but believes that what he says will come to pass, it will be done for him". (*Mark 11:23.*)

Devoted Father, now and forever, curses out, the unclean spirit of betrayal who uses people and destroys marriages. All the while, you thought I was in your life to become and remain your servant. I am the servant of the LORD God. Neither man nor women can manipulate or control me for their self-seeking purpose. I guess I showed them. I sure did show you. (*Giving God all the Glory*),

Yellow-bellied bastard, you came from a tribe from hell and thought you could mess with me and what the LORD has joined. Constant Father, Dedicated Father, now and forever, they learned very quickly that they could not mess with me. The All Mighty Father protects my actions. The revenging God shall satisfy my desire for your destruction.

The Ravens shall bring me news of your fate. The angels of darkness shall devour your soul. Let no man deliver you from the trap you set for me. The Mighty God holds the sword of retribution over your life. The Mighty God of Moses, Jacob, and Isaac shall give me victory over your adulterous ways; you are my enemy.

Steadfast Father, faithful Father, now and forever,

O Mighty God, who made heaven and earth, my enemy tried to take the virtues you gave me and use it to destroy me. Show them no mercy. Don't forgive them for their shortcomings. Teach me patience and wisdom so that I can live in this world that's filled with darkness. Shine your everlasting light my way. Stay with me in all struggles.

Remarkable Father, Faithful Father, now and forever,

Anoint me with your boldness and fearlessness to succeed. (*Having no fear*) Blind the enemies that may come m y way to steal my dreams and joy. Let me live in the moment to face my enemies. Go ahead of me and conquer my enemies, giving me victory over their sad thoughts. Keep away fear and discouragement; shield me from envy and jealousy.

Heavenly Father your love is sufficient.

Selah.

21

COURAGE

Give me courage, O LORD, to accept the things I cannot change and to know you are with me in all my undertakings. Give me the courage to understand the things that cannot be known and the power to discern and disassociate from evil. Give me the courage to decipher and withstand confusion and trickery when it raises its ugly head.

Give me the courage to remember to seek you, all Mighty LORD, in all things. When I am weak and facing despair, you are my strength, my deliverer, and my everlasting Father. In you, I place my trust. Give me courage, O LORD, to accept the things I cannot change and know that you are in my corner. Give me the courage to understand the things I cannot learn and the power to disassociate from evil.

Give me the courage to decipher and withstand confusion and trickery when it raises its dirty head. When I am sad and cannot cope with the evilness of this world. You closed my mind, shutting it down, putting it in protected mode. Giving me peace, joy, and understanding, wiping away the tears and confusion placed in my mind.

Give me time to create; let no one take advantage of me. Give me the courage when all odds are against me. Save my life and have it be wealthy and righteous. Give me courage, O LORD, to accept the things I cannot change and know that you are in my corner.

Give me the courage to understand the things I cannot determine and the power to disassociate from evil. Give me the courage to decipher and withstand confusion and trickery when it raises its dirty head. LORD, when I am losing faith in you and myself, you enter into my life with dynamic forces to build me up.

You, O LORD, comforted me and held my heart in the palm of your hands. Thank you for accepting me with all my faults and misgivings. You are the God of old. You were there in the beginning, and you will be there at the end. You rescued the children of Israel out of bondage and enlightened them. You are capable of doing the same for me. O LORD, gracious LORD of Hope,

Give me courage, O LORD, to accept the things I cannot change and know that you are in my corner. Give me the courage to understand the things I cannot apprehend and the powers to disassociate from evil. Give me the courage to decipher and withstand confusion and trickery when it raises its dirty head.

Virtuous Father, the cold wind of failure and discontent is trying to enter my heart and soul to unbalance me. Don't let the world take away the joy and contentment you have placed in my heart from birth. Give me the courage and power to organize my life, putting you first in all things. You are the God, the great God of Hosts. My world is without end, forever and ever, amen.

Selah.

22

LOVE

Love is the first commandment. The word of God, though, the Mighty Father, Jesus Christ, requires us to love one another. Love without demands. Love brings freedom of mind. Love without controlling and conditions. We can do all things through Jesus Christ, who loves us.

Love without an agenda, love without oppression. Pure love untainted. Love without the mind games. His son was sent to show us love, the only begotten Son, Jesus Christ. Love yourself. If you love yourself, you will respect others. Love the LORD first, and you will love yourself eternally. Time to enjoy yourself before its too late; death comes like a thief in the night.

He has love, eternal love, love, never-ending love. If we apply God's the love in our lives, the confusion in your mind disappears. Peace, hope, faith, and assurance appear in our lives. The LORD will restore your soul by the spirit of confidence, order, and organization. The LORD loves. Love is the basis of formulas for living. Learn to love one another in spirit and truth.

The Kingdom of God waits. Anger disappears when you leave the windows of your mind open to the LORDS love, and his light shines through your soul. Love and peace restored. Hatred and bitterness cease. Love brings life and creation and serenity over the power of your mind. Love brings understanding and joy in the LORD and yourself.

Mighty Father, you are the one who first loved us and commanded us to love and inspire ourselves and others. You have brought us out of so many disasters and have given us favors. First of all, you showed us love through the sacrifice of the Lamb, Jesus Christ. The depth of your love is eternal, true, and everlasting.

You have been with through the dark nights and days of war and confusion and have sent your angels to help and comfort us in times of trouble. Your love has guided and protected us in childhood. Your sacred heart filled with patience and love was there for us through the good and bad times. Your love was before us and safeguarded victories in all our wars, trials, and tribulations. LORD, grant us your love once more.

Your love for us delivered us from our enemies. Teaching us wrong from right, disciplining and keeping our minds safe in your love, your undying love for us has shown us the way to live. Love without conditions. We will forever be indebted to you, O Mighty LORD, the Savior of this world.

Selah.

23

WAR AND POVERTY

The threat of war and disasters,
The risk of poverty and death,
The powers of the world are out of control.

However, God is in control. Men have misused the children of God. Speaking with fork tongues they made promises in the past which are un-kept, only blinding the eyes and minds of their subjects with nonsense.

The LORD will always keep his promises to his children. None of this world's confusion and biased events shall destroy the minds of his children. Let not your heart be troubled by rumors of war, death, and confusion.

The LORD has the power over life and death and poverty. He is the one who keeps us from falling. All Mighty God, help us make the right decisions, so we don't fall victim to poverty and despair. Forgiving God, help us take a bite out of the poverty of the mind, body, and soul, dear LORD God of wealth and prosperity.

You were on the cross, taking the lashes and bleeding for your children. Come on, sons of God. Make a stand; rise and get your prize. The time is the present. The time is now, O LORD, for you to rise. The children of God Jesus Christ are at war at this moment against poverty, despair, lack, and bloodshed and over taxation. He gives strength, so we don't lose our faith and hope in him.

He is the beginning and the end—Christ, the power of God. Only he has the authority to bring you out of this dilemma of World War III and the poverty that will arise from these actions. Now is the time for you to beg for God's mercy and acquire fortitude (*true grit*). Victory and everlasting life will be yours.

The powers of God will give you discipline, organizational comprehension, fortitude, wisdom, understanding, and true grit. When you cannot find your way, he makes ways out of no ways. Hold on to his precious garment, and keep on trucking.

Poverty is sometimes a state of mind that will bring you to a place of pure hell and misery. Mighty God and his special forces are always with you if you only trust in him and believe.

Selah.

24

DON'T LOSE YOUR FAITH

Fight for your faith, your belief in God. Beware: your faith tested every day. Fight for your faith, your faith in God. He is the way. Guard your heart; guard your faith; don't lose your faith. Defend your faith in your religion. Don't let others discourage you from praying. Don't lose your belief on account of someone else.

Don't let others lead you astray and lose your prize of everlasting life. Everyone knows at the end of the day, the ones who don't lose their souls are the people who are the winners. The world may test your faith. Lucifer may test your faith. He tested Job. Guard your heart and your faith. Stand up for your faith. Guard your faith; guard your life; stand up for your life.

Know yourself, and fight for your belief. When unbelievers challenged your faith, call upon the LORD, and he will deliver you. Don't be weak in your understanding of the LORD God Jesus Christ. Guard your heart and your faith. Stand up for your faith. Guard your faith; guard your life; stand up for your life.

Be aware of the enemies of your faith. They are knocking on your doors. They are trying to open the gates to your heart, only to destroy your body and soul. God is stationed at the gates of your heart, trying every possible way to deceive, weaken, and break your spirit. Guard your heart and your faith; stand up for your faith.

Guard your faith; guard your life; stand up for your life. Do not allow the devil deception to trick you with his fear campaigns and evil tactics. Sickness and death may test your faith. Relationships may test your faith. People will test your faith. Situations may test your faith; you may not have a job. You might be hungry.

You may face with questioning God and being disappointed with Christianity and end up losing your faith in God. Guard your heart and your faith. Stand up for your faith. Guard your faith; guard your life; stand up for your life. Mighty God, help us to safeguard our hearts, faith, and our lives from the spirit of deception. Guard our hearts and faith; help us stand up for our faith in you.

Guard your faith; guard your life; stand up for your life. Protect your heart; defend your faith. Protect your faith; guard your life.

Selah.

25

PET

The Patron Saint of Animals sent by God look down on all our animals, especially our dogs and cats, and be with them in every way. Give us patience, wisdom, and knowledge in all things to take care of them. Calm our nerves and shower us with virtue to reassure our dogs and cats that we will be there for them at all times and in all things.

Help us to treat them well, for they are willing to please us. The animals take instructions from us sent by God, with the purpose of showing us love and contentment. We need to talk care of them and keep them safe and comfortable. Heavenly Father instructs us to be kind to the animals. He transmits unconditional love for them. God's love radiates through their eyes.

The dog and cats are happy when we take good care of them. Look at us in adoration, willing to be trained and obeying our commands. They are brilliant creatures. The companionship, comfort, and joy they bring are everlasting. The animals are with us in the rain and snow, good times and bad. LORD, you commanded us to love and take care of the animals

They are always there to greet us; they are constantly there for us, showing us they love us and are content—a beautiful feeling from creatures sent by God. Sometimes I look at them and wonder what they are thinking. Who are they, or what were they before they became pets? God bless them for coming into our lives. Blessed Father, thank you,

The LORD speaks to the heart of the animals. LORD, you alone
have a connection to all their souls. Wisdom and understanding
come from your kingdoms. That's why you commanded us to love
and take care of the animals. Knowledge and understanding come
from your kingdoms. Thy wisdom transferred will be done, O
Gracious Father, Creator of All Living things.

Even all the animals in the manger looked on in amazement and
adoration of you at the time of your birth. Thank you for allowing us
the opportunity to live and understand the minds of our pet. Dogs
and cats and all the rest of the animals, Precious LORD, continue
giving us the grace to care for our pets.

Selah.

26

WHEN DARKNESS COMES

When darkness comes into your world, call upon the LORD. When you've lost your faith and feel discouraged, the spirit of despair appears, and you want someone or something. Always know that there is God. His ears are open, and his hands are forever reaching out to you. His heart, ears, and mind are open, waiting for you to call, Abba Father.

O Loving Father, who filled with eternal light, your flames are forever shining for us Eternal Father, who takes away all of our fears and doubt, save us when darkness comes. Take away our blindness; remove the veil of ignorance from our eyes and minds, so we can see the truth—the truth in your love for us when society says we are losers. We are winners in your love.

If we surrender our hearts to you, your love makes us a winner in Jesus Christ, our LORD, and Savior. Your love is sufficient to bring us out of the darkness and into your precious light. Darkness cannot exist in the light. You, LORD, are the light in the darkness. At all times look toward the light—our Father, who is in heaven.

When darkness comes, the LORD saves us from the lies and destruction we face. He protects us from our enemies when night comes. He calls us to glory and virtue. Our days filled with fear and concern for our safety and the safety of our families. Protect our minds and our dreams with steel, saving us from this darkness.

Blessed Savior, you have the power to move mountains and to sit with us in the valleys and protect our minds, and those of our children from misinformation and propaganda served up by those whose intentions are evil. Take away that fear that comes with control. Strengthen us and replace in us the heart of a lion.

Protect our minds and our dreams with steel, saving us from this darkness. Destroy bad habits and replace them with good, heartfelt success. Keep us warm in your love, keep us safe and assured, and take us out of this darkness. Mighty one, give us the wisdom and power to fight against our enemies when they come against us to mess with our minds and souls.

LORD, give us the knowledge, wisdom, and strength and shield us from this darkness. Send the Mighty One who anointed Saint Michael the Archangel to destroy. Raise your sword of protection, and shield us with your strength and divine ammunition. Please, LORD, do for us as you did for King David.

Selah.

27

THE LORD SHALL PRESERVE YOU AND YOURS FROM DANGER

Put all your trust in the LORD and Savior, Jesus Christ. He will guide you and yours from danger. Life is not always about acquiring physical possessions in your strength here on earth. Instead, it is about the state of your mind and soul at the time of your departure and reentry into the Heavenly Realm.

When you choose to put the Kingdom of God first, the window of heaven will open up for you, and you can have all the earthly possessions. Furthermore, if you chose to acquire physical properties in your strength, you would have to trample and hurt your neighbor and constantly struggle to find your daily bread. The LORD shall preserve you and yours from this danger.

What have you done not to be selfish today? Have you lent a helping hand without expecting anything in return? Did you love your brother and give of yourself to others? Did you smile when you looked in the mirror? Were you grateful for all the good things the LORD has done for you? The LORD shall preserve you and yours from danger.

Everything you do in this life must be done to glorify God and must be pleasing to him. His heart filled with love, patience, and mercy for his children and his creation. You would never truly stumble and fall if you put your faith and trust in his loving care. He is the God of compassion, the God of the covenant. The LORD shall preserve you and yours from danger.

He will send spiritual forces to rescue you. Your time on earth is limited; you cannot deny these truths. Live daily for the LORD. Quietly live in your mind, body, and soul for the LORD. Ask him for wisdom and understanding to figure out life and to survive in society. He would keep you through all things. The LORD shall preserve you and yours from danger.

Life may become challenging, tough, and damn difficult, and you may feel as though you have hit a roadblock. Your mind is stagnant in darkness, despair, and lack. These are times when you may have to make difficult decisions. Look up; he is there waiting for you to call on him. He is the light at the end of the tunnel.

The LORD shall preserve you and yours from danger. "Love the LORD your God with all your heart, with all your soul, with your entire mind." (*Matthew 22:37*). Love and enjoy the LORD, your God, and the strength he bestowed upon you to acquire pleasurable things. Do not put your emphasis and power on adoring his creation more than you love him.

Selah.

28

TURNING AWAY FROM GOD

Some people turn away from God the Father and his Mighty strength. Life is full of disappointments, despair, efforts, trials, and failures. Men would take advantage of you and use and abuse you. Don't let their actions turn you away from God and the power of prayer. Prayer brings hopefulness and renews your faith in yourself and God.

The power of prayer is everlasting; the power of prayer is unbelievably real. Some people believe that praying to God alone is not sufficient, so they lose their hope and faith in God. They turn away from God, seeking other strange anomalous gods. They put their trust in strange rituals, indulging in contrary, mediocre practice, and sacrifices.

They still perform all kinds of strange, outdated customs that the LORD died to redeem them. Their schemes are only to confuse the minds and souls of the new and old followers of Christ. Jesus Christ was the last sacrifice. He is LORD of the universe, the most all-powerful overall. He oversees men's and women's minds because they have turned away from God.

They should be calling upon his name (*God the Father*) for forgiveness before they decide to turn from him—Abba Father, we call upon you in the name of Jesus Christ. Turning away from God to another place in your mind is not the answer. Turn to him in all things. That's the answer. Turn to him when trouble comes; don't put your hope and faith in strange mediums, for he is a jealous God.

All Mighty God is on your side. He will not let you down. Don't believe in strange Gods. The Mighty Father is jealous and angry about your betrayal. Cleanse yourself and repent. Ask God for his forgiveness. You denied him by turning away from him. Let your heart rejoice and be glad, for the heavenly Father is a forgiving, kind, and loving Father God.

Today we face confusion and betrayal of citizens against their governments and religions. We need to pull together and fight the good fight for God and the betterment of humankind. He would look beyond your betrayal and deliver your hearts to his alignment. His door is open to the lost sheep. Jesus Christ— is the one, true, living, forgiving God.

Fight the good fight. Fight for our LORD and Savior. Jesus Christ doesn't mind the circumstances or the way things appear to be. His eternal presence is in every situation we face. Let not your heart be troubled, and do not faint, in all cases look toward the light. He is the Light of the world, the light of your circumstances. Turn your heart back to the LORD.

Calm yourself and humble yourself, and return to the God. His arms are open wide, welcoming your soul back into his heavenly realm. His gentle voice will connect with your heart. The sacred heart of Jesus Christ will give you strength to fight the good fight, instead of handing out food, water, and blankets to the persecutors of Jesus Christ, his followers, and his teachings.

You should be giving these necessities to the persecutors of God, Jesus Christ, along with the honorable Holy Bible.

Selah.

29

A PRAY FOR SINGLE MOTHERS

O LORD, my heart is broken and is in disarray by the way that adults and the feminine movements have put aside the important issues facing our teenage women today. Precious LORD of mercy, our young women are made to believe that having children out of wedlock is normal and without consequences.

They are having our future generation of children without the presence of the babies' fathers and are indulging in having several or more than one father for their babies. Often they struggle to raise these children on their own, without financial, emotional, or physical support from these men.

Beautiful Father, have mercy on them and kindly shine your glorious light of wisdom on these single mothers. LORD, you were an excellent, blessed example of a right provider for them to follow. You made provisions for the children of men before you created them and loved them generously enough to keep on providing for them through the ages.

LORD, you created the earth inhabitable for the children of men. By calling the light into existence, the earth filled with an abundance of animals, fishes, plants, air, water, and minerals. These things were created in abundance and are never ending. LORD, this earthly establishment, and its fallen angels came up with a plan to deceive.

These perplexed mothers and fathers to commit this transgression against your kingdom. They are selling themselves short by cohabitating with men who cannot protect and provide adequately for their children. The mothers seem to have put the cart before the horse by not obtaining the right education before they venture out to have their children.

The Mighty LORD loved you and gave you the power to produce children. You are responsible for giving birth to and taking care of these kids. Then you walk away from them, leaving all the responsibilities of childrearing to the mothers and grandmothers. Have mercy on your souls.

Mighty God, hold them responsible for providing for these children. Give these mothers wisdom and strength to raise their children alone. In the glory of you, give them the favor in your Kingdom. Loving Father and powerful one, God who resides in the realm of heaven, look down on these children.

LORD, send your angels to guide and protect them from the spirit of abandonment and destruction. The LORD God ordered fathers to take care of their children and to respect the women who gave birth to their children. His eyes are on the sparrows, and he watches you day and night in disappointment.

He is recording your words, thoughts, and deeds. The LORD commanded you to look after your own. The son of God went to the cross he shed his blood for you and your offspring's. His actions were the example for you to follow. He generously catered to you before you entered the world and kept on providing.

It's a mortal sin to leave a woman in despair after childbirth and not be a good father to your children. The world filled with predators whose job is to seek out the frail and weak and take advantage of their vulnerability and helplessness, exploiting situations. Your children need both parents. LORD, the children, cannot take care of themselves.

They need both parents to have a cordial understanding, with the aim of protecting these kids and providing for them with a proper home filled with love. Fathers, when the spirit of frustration and desertion enters your minds and souls, the first thing you think about your abuses.

Evil confuses the mothers and their children when you should be rebuking these unclean spirits in the name of Jesus Christ, our LORD, and Savior. These spirits will flee your minds and souls. And will make you stronger and wiser. Take care of and love your children and respect their mothers.

Making life difficult for your babies' mother is not the best option and is not the right choice for you and your kids. In the beginning, there was Adam and Eve. You are doing yourself a disservice by having all these unwanted children. "Jesus said, "Suffer little children, and forbid them not, to come unto me: for of such is the Kingdom of Heaven." (*Matthew 19:14KJB*).

He will meet all your needs in the name of Jesus Christ. The heavenly Father frowns upon unwed mothers and the men who are responsible for making it so. Kids should be blessed and protected through the sanctity of marriage with good, loving parents and a decent home. Your children, women, and future depend on your actions and decisions.

In the name of God the Father

Selah.

30

THY KINGDOM COME

Thy kingdom comes into the new world the God of wisdom he who is still to come. The Mighty God, keeper of the earth and every living thing therein give us the wisdom to deal with the social problems we are facing today. The reformation of the last tribes situated in the Middle East. They do not possess the spirit of joy, freedom to choose, wisdom, understanding, cooperation, and gratitude.

A culture that's filled with savagery, bloodshed, and mayhem and one whose daily rituals involve confrontations, killing, and contemplating bloodshed have entered our sphere.

Thy kingdom comes, O Holy One, for they lack the intelligence to understand life, its goodness, and the pros and cons, as they deal with issues about life and freedom. Beautiful Father, other men have taken from us and are trying to destroy us. We are willing to march to hell for your heavenly cause. These people have taken themselves and their ideology too seriously while hindering others from enjoying and practicing their belief system and ideology.

The Thy Kingdom come, Mighty God, hasten to bring this horror to an end. Thy Kingdom come, glorious and spectacular, forgives us for our transgressions against you and your heavenly Kingdom. Your truth will shine on. Bring excellence to the hearts and minds of our leaders. Rebuild and encourage men with new strength and new ideas, and give them courage and wisdom to lead us in the right direction.

The first inject love and honor for you, reestablishing in their hearts courage and virtue to save their kingdoms. Thy kingdom comes, remove from the hearts of men the spirit of compromise, uncertainty, confusion, and doubt. And replace that with men of courage and truth to bring us a new beginning. O LORD, who lives on high logged into the silent hills of the universe. Where the wind blows, and the grass is green and lush; where there are unconditional love and understanding; where men can build, grow food, and create.

Renew our pride in you once more. LORD, fortify us to be vigilant and steadfast in our going out and coming in. There are rumors of nuclear war and sexual uprising. They are talking about peace, but in their hearts, their intentions are for war. Thy Kingdoms come, where hate, fear, confusion, violence, hunger, inequality, and racism cannot reside. Where happiness, joy, and humor live once more, set up your new kingdom here on earth,

Mighty God, we have come a long way in understanding our past mistakes and have made amends to correct our ways. Walk with us, O, powerful spirit of truth and righteousness, and help us to fight this final battle, where your children will be truly set free, and your name will be exalted. You're the great warrior who consecrated King David the shepherd boy and led him into battle, giving him victory over his enemy.

Give us victory in this, our final battle over deception and evil. Let us not be confused with the grace, charm, and charisma of the new uprising of the false prophet and false prophecy, enticing us to believe their teachings are the norm and should be accepted. These modern-day false Nebiim are the unknown future, the beginning, and the end. Turn them back in all their ways. They are the unknown future, the beginning, and the end. Turn our enemies back in all their ways.

Reestablish for your children a new earth, where your compassionate, loving ways can set our minds free from those who would have us conform to their evil, misguided ideology and culture. Thy Kingdoms come, when all men call you Abba Father, Jesus Christ, LORD, and Savior. Every knee shall bend to honor the King of Kings, LORD of LORDS to all men, God of the universe.

Jesus Christ is the Son of God and God the Father is above all things and religions, Christians, Jews, Pentecostal, Muslims, atheist, whoever. He will preside over the synagogues, temples, mosques, chapels, darkness, voodoo, the underworld, under rocks, and in the sea. LORD, every living thing in the air and on the land shall bow before him, saying, "Holy, Holy, Holy LORD God, the Mighty, who was and who is and who is to come. (*Revelation 4:8 ASV*)

"Holy, Holy, Holy, Lord God of Power and might heaven and earth are full of your glory Hosanna in the highest."(*Sanctus*)

LORD, you are our King of Kings, LORD of LORDS, the one, and only Father; you are the Alpha and Omega, the Prince of Peace. The beasts of war that live in the hearts of men shall cease to exist, cleansing them from mental despair and self-hatred. LORD, your new Kingdom will be established here on earth. The elites are setting up large ways to cripple our economies, leaving the middle and poor classes of people with nothing.

They expect us to fight each other and plunge into despair. O, One LORD, sitting in the valley of decision, turns them back; distort them and their plans to destroy your Kingdom. LORD, you are the designer of all things. Your sacrifice on the cross and blood did not shed in vain. Holy Virgin Mother, girdle the hearts and loins of your beloved children as they prepare for war, Thy Kingdom comes, O Mighty LORD of the Universe.

Selah.

31

LOSING MY FAITH IN GOD

Doubt has entered into my heart. O LORD, my faith in you is failing. LORD, you are the beginning and the end. Don't allow me to lose my faith in you. Have mercy on me, and straighten my faith in you. I have permitted myself to be led astray by life's circumstances and situations. Help me to be still and know you alone are God, all by yourself, and you can restore my soul.

I am weak and vulnerable. O LORD, I am at my lowest emotional point in life. My heart got broken from trusting, and soul got. I allowed myself to be fooled by men, causing me to resort to drugs, alcohol, cheating, deception, and other vices. My life has turned in the worst direction, resulting in despair. Lift my soul so I can soar like an eagle once more.

I have lost my faith in God. Send your Mighty hand and save me. LORD—he who enters the hearts of men, he whose teaching and spirit were logged into our minds and souls before we were made men—enter me once more. Enter my life, restoring your love again. Renew my faith in you; remove all obstacles that are hindering me from you.

Your love is guaranteed. I seek forgiveness for my sins. Sacred Heart of Jesus Christ, have mercy on me. Strengthen my faith in you. Restore me, O Mighty one. You knew me from birth and beyond. Have mercy on me and strengthen my faith in you once more. Forgive me for my betrayal; excuse me for turning away from you. God of all grace, renew my faith in you.

The mountains crumble under my feet, O LORD. I am losing my faith in God. My soul filled with darkness and confusion. The thought of suicide and the spirit of nothingness have penetrated my mind and heart. Send me an angel—someone to help me. I need my mind lifted over these problems. Plant my feet on the solid ground, renew my heart and soul.

Blind my eyes, heart, and soul from this negative situation of losing my faith in you. LORD, do not allow me to lose my faith in you. Redeem my soul from these mental and physical thoughts of suicide.

Selah.

32

TRAVELING

My wonderful Father of light let your love look down on me from heaven. Prepare my mind, body, and soul as I am about to make this journey. Go before me, ordering favors and blessings as I go on my way. Keep me steady. Go before me, paving the way for me to have safety and a pleasurable trip. Send your angels to guide and protect me as I go on my way.

Stay beside me; take care of me, keeping me safe until the end of my journey. Give me a gentle, polite spirit with those I encounter and favor with authority and people in high places. If discord, danger, and misunderstanding should come my way, protect me. Go before me, making the way clear and peaceful, if danger should arise. Go before me, and let me be a help to those I come into contact.

Send your angels to guide and protect me as I go on my way. Standing beside me, take care of me, keeping me secure, always until the end of my journey. Dear LORD, if disaster and confusion should occur, dispatches your Mighty angels. Keep me guarded at my departure, arrival, and at my destination. Go before me, detouring danger, letting my heart be at peace with your confidence.

Go before me, providing me with everything as I focus on business or pleasure trips. Send your angels to stand beside me, guide me, and protect me as I go on my way. Jehovah, take care of me and keep me safe, always until the end of my life's journey. Soften the hearts of persons I come into contact with if I have lost directions. Let me not be put to shame; let no man's terror enter my heart or my soul.

Go before me; bring no harm to my physical body in airborne diseases. Go before me; bring no harm to me in the air and on the ground. Send your angels to guide and protect me as I go on my way. Stand beside me, taking care of me, keeping me safe, always until the end of my journey. My life is in your hands, O Kind and Loving Father. Keep me protected in your bosom, surrounded by your love and joy.

Go before me, if by car or plane or train or bus—whatever means of transportation. Go before me. If death comes upon me while I travel, I give the LORD my soul to keep. Send your angels to guide and protect me as I go on my way. Jehovah, God, stand beside me, take care of me, keep me safe, always and forever, even at the end of my life's journey.

Selah.

33

INCREASING YOUR FAITH

Dear Kind and Loving Father, the times are testing the faith of men, and confusion seems to rule. The environment is instilling fear and doubt, causing people to become weak in their faith. Protect our hearts and souls, increasing our confidence in you. Some whose faith has diminished are trying to discredit and discourage our faith in you.

They are planning to infiltrate our souls with doubt their intentions are to weaken our faith in you. Fill us up with everlasting faith so that no man can penetrate our hearts. Guard our minds, bodies, and souls against those who would con our minds for diluting my faith in you. Fortify me with your omnipresence and strengthen me so that my confidence in you can withstand temptation.

Hold on to our frustrations. The fool says in their hearts, "There is no God," (*Psalm 14:1(NASB)* thus losing faith. Others are disenchanted with you, bringing along the spirit of uncertainty and doubt. I increased my faith in you, for others are fighting against me because of my faith in you. Heavenly Father, blot them out for our sake. Strengthen our faith in our homes, jobs, and all our endeavors; increase the faith in our hearts and souls.

Keep us close to you that others cannot penetrate our minds to destroy our experience and our luck in you. Nothing comes between my trust and relationship with you. LORD, increasing my faith in you, he who parted the Red Sea and worked miracles among men.

Let the wicked intentions of those who want me to stumble and fall by the wayside put to shame.

Let them not win over me to decrease my faith in you. Baptize me with the Holy Ghost, turning them back, letting all disaster befall them, slowing them down and confusing them, making them weak. Grant your humble servants' fruitful desires of victory in everything. Bless my accomplishment; let it be pleasing to you.

O Begotten Son of God, increase my faith in you, let no man steals my faith in you. Carve your love in our hearts, granting favors of victory over all favors. In you, I trust All Mighty God of my strength.

Selah.

34

IN THE VALLEY

My soul is in the valley of decision. I am wondering which way to go. Asleep in the Valley, my heart is grounded in the LORD, who has the power to lead me out of the valley into the light. I am tired, shaded, and despondent in the valley; take me out of this barren existence of my mind. In the valley of no return, get my mind out of this dark, fruitless sphere and into the ever flowing lights.

God alone can set me up on high. As I lift my mind, up to the LORD, fearing no evil without a doubt. As I raise my thoughts and soul, up to the LORD, fearing no evil without a doubt. The valley where all dead bones and broken dreams lie, I straight my soul connecting with the LORD, pleading doesn't allow my dreams dies. Your rod, staff, and loving-kindness will comfort me.

Goodness and mercy shall follow me. In the valley where men's minds go to die, lift me up out of the valley of despair. Resurrect my soul. For you commanded it, generous Father, who stayed with me in the valley and redeemed my transgressions, covering me with these beautiful, gifts of love once more. You are the great Comforter; comfort my soul with hope, steadying my way.

Your light shines into the valley, penetrating my heart and bringing me into the realm of your sacred presence, dear heart of Jesus, precious light of the world. The vultures, serpents, and critters all would like to have a piece of me; even the sky looks cloudy and gray. The Mighty Father who knew me before my conception and took me out of my mother's womb.

The God of the heavens, who sits on his throne, is willing and able to reach down in the valley and deliver me out into his powerful, excellent light.

Selah.

35

PRAY FOR SUCCESS

O Mighty God, only you know about my desires to be successful, rich, and famous. Your tender love and kindness will give me a good favor from others. I depend on you for everything. My mother and father did understand they forsake me, but you, LORD, will not forsake me.

My friends are all jealous and would like to take my place. I have extended myself to others and have gotten nothing in return. Hasten to my rescue. Hide my desires from my enemies. Lift me up in a large place that my enemies cannot attain. Protect my soul and my efforts so my enemies cannot discourage and destroy them.

Speak to me in a soft voice, giving me courage and wisdom as I go from day to day. When those who believe they are better and more accomplished than I am fighting to maintain their make-believe status by trying to put down my accomplishments, they do not understand and have never actually tried to attain something major, nor have they perfected an actual discipline.

Let the powers of all the saints who reside in the heavens of Crystal City find satisfaction with my efforts and approve and bless my efforts. Let not my efforts are in vain; glorify and dispense your heavenly pleasures of success upon your servant. Success will come to me as swiftly as the bite of a cobra and as lasting.

Making others' accomplishments and concrete acquisitions look like chump change. They boast and cheat, taking from others, making others suffer so they can acquire more status and wealth in the material world. LORD, help me to succeed. Renew my spirit; help me to succeed in this life and the life to come, without hurting or trampling others.

O, LORD, my Maker, you alone knows my past accomplishments and will bequeath me my heart's desires

Selah.

36

SAFETY FROM ENEMIES

O LORD, keep me safe and secure from my enemies. If men had their way, they would eat my soul. They are pretending to be my friends but would destroy me, daily distorting my words. Their hearts and minds filled with envy and jealousy of me; secure me from enemies. O, God of the righteous who saves me from the spoiled and Mighty. Provide safety from my enemies.

Protect me from those who smile in my face but criticize and talk about me behind my back. Keep on shining your everlasting light on my soul and sending safety from my enemies. I employ your strength to safeguard me and your wisdom to maintain me, giving protection from my enemies. Keep me on the straight and narrow path, administering safety from enemies.

Never allow me to stumble and fall, grant me safety from my enemies. Give me good favor among other things and bountiful blessings, showering me with protection from my enemies. Shine your light forever my way; let not my adversaries' jealousy penetrate my soul and my well-being. Send your wind and the tides to reassure me; wash away the envious eyes of my enemies while I keep my mind and spirit on you O LORD, increase my safety from my enemies.

Let me not be fooled, take life for granted, or let others sway my mind. When my enemies try to trick me into leaving my station, only to devour and consume me, send your sword of protection to slay my enemies unto death. Let not the pestilence that flies day and night, destroying the earth's realm, have authority over my soul.

Let your love continually surround me, enabling protection from my enemies.

Let my enemies not come within feet of my mind or person. Release your angels in heaven, to surround me with their holy vengeance, which bends the sword of death against me as they melt in the pit of fire. Secure me for your Kingdom; I will be forever loving, more faithful to you. Administer safety to me from my enemies so that I may glorify you in your Kingdom.

Selah.

37

OFFERING THANKS

Captain of salvation, you were with me in times of confusion, danger, and uncertainty. You were with me when others did not understand your plans for me. These are prayers offering thanks to you, All Mighty God, Father of life. You stood beside me in times of trouble.

These are prayers offering thanks to the All Mighty God.

You guided me in my adolescent years, putting hope, joy, laughter, and happiness in my heart. My childhood filled with fear, abuse, hurt, and confusion. When I became pregnant in my teen years, you lifted me and set me on high. These are prayers offering thanks to the All Mighty God.

When my mother and father abandoned me, and there was no one, you were my parents. When there was no baby's father, you were my baby's father and my keeper. I am forever indebted to you. You held me up in every way. These are prayers offering thanks to the All Mighty God.

You love me and have given me beautiful children and grandchildren. You led me through the wildness in perfect wisdom, knowledge, and understanding. I lift you on high. When I became sick, your hands held me gently, close to you. These are prayers offering thanks to the All Mighty God.

You give me patience, real understanding, and wisdom and showed mercy. When I did not love myself, you sent your tender loving care and magical efforts, glowing from above with tender mercy. Your hands opened wide, and your lily-white garment protected me and taught me to love myself.

Your precious blood hides my spirit from my enemies. When the world came at me with raging forces, you were the one who stopped the forces of defeat. I give thanks to you in the morning, evening, and late in the midnight hours. I called on you late at night, when the fires of hell tried to destroy me, and you sent your angels to protect me.

In the middle of the night when the spirit of harm sought to engulf my mind Heavenly Father, giving me strength and patience. I called upon you, and you sent your angels to save me. These are prayers offering up thanks to the all Mighty God. You lifted my soul and guided me through it all. You stood by me in my decisions, good or bad.

I cannot thank you enough. You promised to be with me in the days of old and at the time of my death and beyond. These prayers are offering up thanks to you, the all Mighty God.

Selah.

38

PRAY FOR OUR COUNTRY, THE STARS AND STRIPES

Let us pray for our country, the Stars and Stripes. The battle is at our front door. We are concerned; guard our soldiers, giving them an abundance of courage in time of the fight. Bring them victory over evil. O LORD, baptize our country's leaders with your Holy Spirit as you baptized King David in the days of old so that they can rebuild our nation, triumph over evil, put things in perspective, and take care of the needs of our citizens.

Resurrect men of strong convictions, courage, and virtue so that they can make sagacious decisions about our future safety and economic well-being. LORD, you are our very present help in time of trouble. We trust in Jesus Christ, our LORD, and Savior. Help us to look beyond the betrayals and mediocrity of the chosen leaders and the provocations by others. Their intentions are to destroy our ideals and exceptionally Great country. "In God, We Trust" "(*U.S. Twenty Dollar Bill*) must be our battle cry.

Further, let us know unequivocally that these are the times when believing Christians ought to become more serious about their faith and ideology, rededicating their lives to the Holy Spirit through Jesus Christ, our LORD, and Savior. LORD, with all the talk about terror, war, hate, and change of political and religious direction, show compassion and mercy to your children. Keep them safe and confident in your love and sacrifices. Give them courage and stamina to live and uphold our constitutional laws.

And fight for the betterment and advancement of our county. Mighty one, LORD of the universe, you've blessed our country in the past. Bring us together as one to live with confidence and courage, at no time shying away from saying your name in all the earth. Tighten our faith, making us stronger to fight this battle in your precious name, never allowing us to stumble and fall. Blot out and confuse our enemies to the fact that this race does not belong to the swift, cunning, and ignorant.

But to those who endure, fighting and taking no prisoners. Help us to break the will of our enemies.

Give our leaders victory over all present obstacles facing them today. If we must take up arms to defend your name and our ideology, then blessed Virgin Mother, be with us in the trenches and depths of despair. LORD, anoint us once more with your Mighty blood. Lead us on to a glorious victory.

Forgive us for our debts as we forgive others; show us brand-new ways to bring ourselves out of these debts, sending a new spirit of creativeness to create employment and bring prosperity to our nation, like you did years ago. Let us be still and know that you are the LORD and victory in all things. Give our citizens insight, comportment, and endurance to know that you are there at all times and in all things. Even with the betrayals by our politicians, pollution, confusion, and danger, give us patience with our country's leaders.

Help them to lead us in ways that do not compromise our belief system, having the convictions to bring us jointly as one nation, one people. Together we stand; divided we fall. God bless our country. LORD, forgive the United States of America for the never-ending atrocities perpetrated against people of color and for present-day transgressions, especially for the inhumane and economic genocide that done to the decedents of Alkebulano (*Africa*).

They must compensate and respected for past atrocities committed against them. They were given a raw deal and are in dire need economic stability. LORD, bring together members of the Caucasian and decedents of Alkebulano (*Africa*) races living in America and around the world. You, command us to take care of the fragile and needy in Jesus Christ and protect our neighbors in Jesus Christ, our LORD, and Savior. We protect the weak against the strong, obeying your commandments and principles, only to be called America's world police.

Why don't you stay out of other countries' affairs—those arrogant Americans? Our arrogance came from trusting in God. When tyrants, vicious dictators, and suppressors grip God's children, destruction and disaster strike parts of this world. You commissioned Mighty men of courage to take the light of justice to these hit regions of the world. The afflicted accepted our generosity and turned against us. Christ, they thought we wanted them to conform to our ideology.

God, bless our nation for freeing the minds of the oppressed ones. The clock is ticking. These kind gestures, once attainable for those blinded by their ignorance, are no longer available. God, instill solidarity in our nation's citizens. Build up new armies with men and women of great conviction to the LORD. Bless our past heroes who sacrificed their lives for freedom and equality.

Bless them as they sleep in your precious name. Resurrect their spirits to fight the final battle between good and evil. The Stars and Stripes—"In God We Trust" (*U.S. Twenty Dollar Bill*)

Selah.

39

CALL ON HIM

Night and morning, the Mighty Father watches over us. He promises he will never leave us alone. His love is sufficient to hold us. All you have to do is trust in him. All we have to do is call on him.

His loving-kindness is forever. He is all wisdom and understanding. He is the beginning and the end. What you do is believe in him. All you have to do is call on him.

He is the bright shining morning star. He is a just God and our Savior. He is the bright morning star. All you have to do is call upon him and converse with him; he is the LORD—the retired psychologist.

His plans were for you to live in peace. His grace is sufficient and everlasting. He was with Moses when he crossed the sea. What you have to do is ask for his forgiveness. All you have to do is call on him.

He was in the fire with Shadrach, Meshach, and Abednego. He closed the lion's mouth and put love in their hearts for Daniel. He turned water into wine, and it's still flowing. All you have to do is trust and obey. All you have to do is call on him.

Call on him,
All you have to do is call.
Call on him.
All you have to do is call on him.

Selah.

40

HIS LOVING-KINDNESS

From the beginning of time, his light has shined—never failing, never at any time ending. He sent its booming thunder and lightning, reminding you of his covenant. He sent his sunlight willingly to brighten up your soul. He sent his angels to assist you and gravity to hold you up and keep you standing each day. Open your ears and eyes to his loving-kindness.

He endured pain and suffering to demonstrate his love for you. He sent the rain to wash away your tears and sun to dry your eyes. He holds you in the palm of his hands, his loving-kindness. His loving kindness sent his Son, who bled on the cross for you. Open your ears and eyes to his loving-kindness. Defending Father and refuge in the days of our trouble ease all human afflictions.

So that man doesn't have to suffer himself greatly for the sins of the world. He gave his mercies to keep you confident, and the skies and the oceans to ease your mind. Open your ears and eyes to his loving-kindness. Love the LORD with all your heart and his Mighty hands will deliver you, freeing your mind from fear and worries. The LORDS, his heart is as big as the moon and is as bright as the sun.

And gentle eyes look down on you with compassion and mercy. He commanded the earth to yield food, never ending. Open your ears and eyes to his loving kindness. He made the mountains protect you from the storms. His adoring kindness will prevail forever. He is the Mighty One who rules the universe.

His loving kindness waits submissively patiently for you to repent, saying Abba Father. You are in the trees, sun and moon, the babies, the love, your love, is in the animals on the ground, the birds in the air. Open my ears and eyes to see your loving-kindness. All things work for good to those who love God.

His loving-kindness keeps us from falling, day to day, Faithful Father.

Selah.

41

THE WAR IS AT HAND

The war is at hand. My Father who lives beyond the heavenly realm protects us at all times. Bring peace to the minds of your children. Guide them through this life's spiritual warfare and racial unrest. The war between men and women has started; they have become lovers of themselves.

The children of God are concerned; protect us from the killing and mayhem. The war is upon us. Supreme Being the Shepherd of our souls is with us in the valley of decision, when plowshares turned into swords. The war is at hand. The children of Israel, Christians, and all other religions are under attack.

The sons of men are wrestling daily with their thoughts about rumors of war. Ideology, philosophy, radicalism, racial unrest, and sexual identity, and spiritual warfare is confused with who they are in Jesus Christ. Safeguard us from the hate and propaganda; redeem us from these deceptions.

The war is at hand. Send your angels to administer immaculate wisdom, understanding, and strength. Real leadership, the war is at hand. Prepare your concealed quarters to hide the minds of your children from these deceptions. LORD, you are our hiding place, our shield and high tower. God All Mighty keeps us safe as we go on our way.

Guard our minds, strengthen our hearts, and give us the stamina to endure these modern-day trials. Give us the victory again. Let us not be fooled by thinking others are better than we are and have guilt. Strengthen our faith in you; make us true believers in God once more. In God, we trust.

We are confident in you until the rivers run dry and the moon drops from the sky. The war is at hand; make haste deliver us from this evil. Do for us as you did in days of old; do for us like you did for King David. Give us the victory in Jesus Christ, our LORD and Savior. The war is at hand.

The war of all wars is being waged to steal the joy of the LORDS children and those living in Christ Jesus, our LORD, and Savior.

Selah

42

SACRED HEART OF JESUS

(*Le coeur sacré de Jésus*) Sacred Heart of Jesus, the everlasting Father who made heaven and earth, your blood was shed for our sins. LORD, when looking into your loving eyes, we see your soul. Your sacred heart speaks to us of love—love forever shining through; love that brings extensive understanding.

All the world needs love; all these blessings come from the heart and soul of Jesus Christ—kind Jesus Christ, the sacred heart of Jesus, Maker of mine, peaceful glory, gentle humility, your heart beating, wrap around, sealed with love for your children. (*Le coeur sacré de Jésus*)

The sacred heart of Jesus,

Who held me in the womb? (*Le coeur sacré de Jésus*) The Sacred Heart of Jesus' love that blinds hate, love ends hurt and pain. LORD, in time, hate (*Le coeur sacré de Jésus*) the sacred heart of Jésus that bleeds with sadness and suffering beckoning us to love each other. (*Le coeur sacré de Jésus*) The sacred heart of Jesus, so gentle and genuine, brings me to you in love.

He is the Savior of all. Waiting with arms stretched wide, divine compassion, and strength embedded in his eyes. The (*Le coeur sacré de Jésus*) Sacred Heart of Jesus, as soothing as a lamb, your blood was not shed in vain.

(Jesu mitis et humilis corde) — *(Jesus meek and humble heart.)* Prays for all the saints who surround you in the Heavenly Kingdom that illuminated with the perfect light, order, organization, love, respect, abundance, creativeness, and immaculate peace

In a place where the minds and souls of saints are forever whispering your name, Jesus Christ, King of Kings, LORD of LORDS. Imperial Majesty, how marvelously complete are your creations. The Heavens and earth filled with your glory.

Jesu mitis et humilis corde — (Jesus meek and humble heart.) The gentle Lamb of God's last sacrifice, the sacrifice made for the remission of mankind's transgressions. God of Salvation, your kingdom is being dismantled in the name of promiscuity, complete selfishness, and madness.

These acts are perpetrated by the fallen angels of the earth to bring about the destruction of your children. They are forced to go along with the evil program intended to cleanse the land with your glory. They are compelled to go along or be hunted down by the spirits of imperfection and banished from enjoying their freedom and earthly prosperity.

Jesu mitis ET humilis corde, — (Jesus meek and humble heart.) who rolled away the stone and rose from the grave, rose up to meet the great Father in Heaven. The heavenly kingdom opened up, welcoming him back home into its realm to sit by your Father's side, teaching us not to fear death, promising to be with us through life and death.

Gentle Lamb, *(Le coeur sacré de Jésus)* the sacred heart of Jesus, the apple of the Heavenly Father's eyes, all nations must acknowledge that you are the one and only true God of all with supernatural powers to save humankind and this world.

Le coeur sacré de Jésus, ¬ (*The Sacred Heart of Jesus*)
Jesu mitis ET humilis corde, — (*Jesus meek and humble heart*), that's filled with compassionate and embedded with love so high! It's hard to understand his infinite, wisdom and immeasurable silent greatness.
(*Corazón Sagrado de Jesús; Amor Tan Grande Que es difícil de entender*)
Sacred Heart of Jesus; — *love so great it's hard to fathom (Sagrado Corazón de Xesús; - Amor tan grande que é difícil de entender)*

Sacred Heart of Jesus; — *love so great it's hard to fathom (Sacred Heart Íosa; - Grá mór mar sin tá sé deacair a fathom)*

Selah.

43

DESTROYING EACH OTHER

God made men, but they are daily destroying each other, not showing love. They are destroying each other, not stopping to think that love is the answer; love is the key. They blinded by ignorance and confusion, lack of understanding, and self-control.

Guarding your heart and soul does not allow evil to enter. Guard your heart so that fear cannot come.

LORD, what about the children? What about their souls? God sent his son, Jesus Christ, to demonstrate his love for humankind. Love, Love beyond understanding, and love beyond hate. Humanity has come a long way and given intelligence over animals. (*Or so they think.*)

Guarding your heart and soul does not allow evil to enter. Guard your heart so that fear cannot reside.

Sad to know in this century, day, and age of technology and man's super-intelligence, we still are having problems loving each other. Why can't we respect each other as humankind, instead of destroying each other? The LORD is thinning out the herd, calling and seeking the hearts of men.

Guarding your heart and soul does not allow evil to enter. Guard your heart so that fear cannot come.

He is seeking those who will not stand up and commit themselves to love him and obey his words. Remove fear from your minds and stand up for the righteousness of the kingdom of God. Purge your urges be strong in your mind, never letting anyone bring you down or turn you around.

Guarding your heart and soul does not allow evil to enter. Guard your heart so that fear cannot come.

Envy and jealousy—destroying each other over earthly possessions, religions, sexuality, race relations, abuse, treaty, uneven distribution of the world's wealth, misuse of power, pollution, fishing, raping the land, and defaming each other's character. Harden the hearts of men, so that evil cannot enter; fight the good fight.

Guarding your heart and soul does not allow evil to enter, Guard your heart so that fear cannot come.

The wealthy and well-known people, bragging and boasting about their superficial fame it is the powers of the heavenly fathers. That granted them the opportunities to become famous and rich for the whole world to see. The media is supposed to open the minds of people. Don't be confused and cause division.

The Lord said to love one another, and do not use your powers to deceive humankind.

Selah.

44

COME BACK TO THE LORD

Look to the hills from where your help comes; your help comes from the LORD. He is LORD God on high. He sits at the altar, waiting for you to return to him. Modern-day churches mock God and try to imitate him can't be imitated. Come back to the LORD. Walking away in disarray, they came to the conclusion that there is no God. They walk by sight and not by faith.

They walked away and lost their faith in God and their religion. Please don't mention the Bible to them, for men would turn up their noses and correct you in jail. Don't be an atheist. Today, you can't even find one Bible in the dresser drawers in hotels anymore. We can't mention the name of the LORD in our schools or sing his name in our anthems. Come back to the LORD, people.

Don't let fear and disappointment ruin your lives.

Come back to the LORD, all Mighty One. He forgives us. The LORD anoints and awakens the hearts of men to a great revival. Send your divine Holy Spirit to reside in the hearts of men and the churches, to defend us in the name of Jesus Christ, our LORD, and Savior—the name of Jesus Christ, God.

In these times of uncertainty, the followers of Jesus Christ have to come together and return to the LORD to fight the good fight. The LORD is making his presence known. He is preparing to make significant changes in the hearts of humankind. He will resurrect strong men to fight against the subjugation of others and the threat of another religion trying to take the place of Christianity.

O LORD, all these things are happening because men have fallen short of the glory of God. Disobeying the LORD, come back to the LORD. Call upon him. He is patiently waiting for you to call. Don't deny him three times like Peter did. The Mighty LORD is beyond denial. He defeated death by rising from the grave. Christians disenchanted with their religion because of all the corruption they experienced in the churches.

The all Mighty God only wants you to repent for the sins of denying he exists and seeking out strange gods. He is patiently waiting for you to ask his forgiveness and mercy but not to sell out your faith to strange gods. Today the LORD is testing the hearts of humankind; the great test is on. He wants to see if he is going to be sold out once more and hang on a cross again.

The LORD is using the Islamic religion to show Christians that they have strayed far from him and needed to return to him. Mighty God is a jealous God and wants you to repent and come back to him for help. Your past help in victory always came from the LORD, your God.

Selah.

45

BROKEN HEARTS

Surely God can mend broken hearts, just as he can lift your spirit up. He can dry away your tears. Only he can set you free to love again. Put not your trust in men, for they will disappoint you.

Surely God can protect your heart from being hurt. Only he can protect you from deception. Naturally, he can send you the right one. Only the King of kings can deliver glory and victory. Put not your care in men, for they will disown you.

The enemy of life sends death and destruction and knows how to hurt your mind and soul. God is the sole one who can deliver you from the enemy of life. God knows how to send his love and mercy to heal you from the pain. Only,

God alone can deliver you from the pain of a broken heart. Only "Satan is a sly old fox" if you catch him, toss him in a box. Lock the box, and throw the keys for the world to see". (*Author unknown*) Satan understood betrayal long before you came on earth.

Put your trust in the LORD God Jesus Christ at all times and his will. Replace the spirit of betrayal and despair with a new spirit of genuine love. God will guide you in the way you must go. He will send you the right one to see you through.

Trust in him. He has the power to protect you from hurt. We are all vulnerable to having our hearts broken. Only our Father, who is in heaven, our LORD, and Savior, understands.

Selah.

46

PRAY FOR HOPE

Dear Heavenly Father, my heart is weary and in disarray. I am losing my faith in you. I have put my trust in men and things of this world, and they all failed me. My heart and soul strayed away from you.

Because of lust, greed, and unclean desires, return to me you are hope so that I can cleanse my soul from these infirmities. Send your Holy Spirit into my mind like a white dove, O LORD, the spirit of hope.

Renew my hope and faith in you once more, so I can mount up with wings like an eagle. Have an abundance of mercy on my soul, O LORD, Mighty one, whose bloodshed for me. Let my heart and mind feel the spirit of the white dove of hope once more.

I have been walking through this world of darkness, trusting only in the things I could see. O wretched spirit of defiance and hopelessness, I rebuke you in the name of Jesus Christ. Spit out this evil, confused. Unclean spirits from within me.

I am ejecting you from my mind and soul. Heavenly Father, forgive me for discarding the Holy Spirit of hope and the covenant you gave me from my conception and replace it with the spirit of darkness, blinded by life's glitter.

Serving two masters, I forget my soul and the laws you had placed in my heart before I came into this world. The Holy Laws wrote upon the liner of my gentle heart with your blood. I was nothing but particles, atoms floating around in the darkness.

I was scattered and lost in darkness. You joined me together from these tiny pieces of particles, breathing life and love into me. Renew my hope in you, O forceful LORD, Mighty LORD of life.

Selah.

47

FORGIVENESS FROM THE LORD

Forgive me, O LORD, for all the confusion. I cursed the world. You have given me dominion over the animals and sustained me, giving me everything that was good and pleasing. You gave me the desires of my heart. I forgot about you and turned to the things you gave me, worshiping and praising them all day long. My pain is deep; my soul longs for your forgiveness. I am only an unstable human being, living for myself. I harmed my brothers in so many ways, lying and cheating, taking things that were not rightfully mine.

Hide my sins beneath your blood and show mercy, for I unknowingly hate myself as much as a tempest. I had feelings of envy and jealousy toward my brothers over their land and their blessings, so I resorted to spreading confusion, hate, rage, pain, and misery on my fellow brothers. Using the powers you gave me to manipulate my brothers' lives; I caused their lives to fill with sadness and pain. Forgive me, O LORD for strangling the wealth from other nations and using it for my alleviation

You alone have the power to forgive my soul. My heart cries out to you for complete forgiveness. You, O LORD, sit on the high seat of judgment and seek those who are honest, steadfast, and uncompromising. You are a jealous God who commanded us to serve, worship, and love. My transactions are weighing heavily on my mind, like the yoke I placed around the necks of the children of God. I cheated and limited them from their share of the glory and blessings you provided for them.

Mighty Father, your sacred heart bleeds when one of your children goes astray. Have mercy and take away the darkness within my soul, and let me live again. Have mercy on me, O LORD! Forgive me for judging others. Have mercy on me, O LORD! Excuse me for using and abusing others. Have mercy on me, O LORD! Forgive me for turning away from you and worshiping another god. Have mercy on me, and renew my soul and my faith in you.

Forgive me, O LORD, for all the confusion. I cursed the world. You have given me dominion over the animals and sustained me with everything that was good and pleasing. I forgot about you and turned to the things you gave me. My pain is deep; my soul longs for your forgiveness. I am only an unstable human being, living for myself. I harmed my brothers in so many ways—lying and cheating, taking things that were not rightfully mine.

Hide my sins beneath your blood and show mercy, for I unknowingly hate myself as much as a tempest. I felt envy and jealousy toward my brothers over their land and their blessings, so I resorted to spreading confusion, hate, rage, pain, and misery on my fellow brothers. Using the power, you give me to manipulate my brothers' lives, causing their lives filled with suffering and pain. Pardon me, O LORD, for spreading colonialism and worshiping greed.

You alone have the power to forgive my soul. My heart cries out to you for complete forgiveness. You, O LORD, sit on the high seat of judgment and seek those who are honest, steadfast, and uncompromising in their faith. You are a jealous God who commanded us to serve, worship, and love. My transgressions are weighing heavily on my mind, like the yoke I placed around the necks of the children of God. I cheated and limited them from their share of the glory and blessings you have provided them.

Evette Forde

Mighty Father, your sacred heart bleeds when one of your children goes astray. Have mercy and take away the darkness within my soul, and let me live again. Have mercy on me, O LORD! Forgive me for judging others. Have mercy on me, O LORD! Excuse me for using and abusing others. Have mercy on me,

O, LORD and forgive me for turning away from you and worshiping other Gods. Have mercy on me, and renew my soul and my faith in you.

Selah.

48

MERCY AND KINDNESS

Stretch forth your loving hands and shower us with mercy and compassion. The world today is filled with pain and suffering. Cover your children with your mercy and compassion.

Keep us close to you, never allowing temptation and confusion to derail us as we make our journey back home to you. The great, Mighty one, who formed all things, showers us with mercy and kindness every day.

Have mercy, O LORD, have mercy, O LORD. When we face our mortality, show us mercy and compassion. Give us peace, joy, and courage. Your compassion helps us to live one day at a time. Your compassion and kindness are forever faithful.

Let us feel your mercy, LORD, and kindness one minute at a time. (Let us remember your love when the wind blows and touches our skin.) Cleanse our anxieties, depression, worries, and fear with your mercy and kindness.

Your compassion shows us a good life and healthy living; everlasting is the Spirit of God. Where would we be if it was not for your blood, so powerful, that was shed on the cross? The earth quivered when it came into contact with your blood.

Greatest Father forever lives. We would be altogether lost today, residing in a state of total unconsciousness, if it was not for you and your precious blood. LORD, your blood was not shed in vain.

Selah.

49

UNDERSTANDING DEATH

Mortals are we all, but Jesus Christ promises everlasting life. LORD of the universe teaches us to live and deal with our mortality. Let us live one day at a time; help us to understand. We must live before we die; many acts like they came on earth to stay, so they walk around with their faces stuck in a frown—no hello, no joy, no love, no "How are you doing today?"

Lighten up and live because tomorrow promised to anyone. Death, O LORD, is just the beginning and not the end. Hold on to the good things in life and not the worst. Live, share, and love, my dear LORD, in time of death and sadness, send your angels to administer hope and faith to those who are struggling with your love and compassion.

Give them the grace to understand that the process of pain, death, and sadness are also part of living. Teach them so they can understand the process of life and death when they are grieving for their loved ones. Bring understanding to those who are having problems thinking of their mortality; their faith must be strong.

The Mighty LORD took the sting out of death by dying on the cross. Let us not forget death. Have mercy on us while we are living. When we are born, find the powers to rejoice, consider the LORD every day of your life. For in death, there is no repenting. Celebrate life; light a candle for the dead so they can find their way back to the heavenly Father.

You have to Light a candle, say a prayer to the Holy Father and make intercessions for the soul or souls of the dead, Make the intercession with the Heavenly Father on behalf of your loved ones for the remission of their transgressions so they can make the transition to the resurrection. Let us not remember them as dead, but as living in Jesus Christ. Let us not forget your loved deceased in life.

Celebrate the goodness of their lives, knowing that they will not be gone forever but will be with the LORD when they fulfill life's process. Just to be reformed and given second chances, even third chances or as many chances as they desire to celebrate life and love.

Selah.

50

TIME OF SICKNESS

O LORD, my physical body, is failing me. The spirit of fear and concern is upon me. My present health and fear of the unknown are causing me to be mentally distracted. I am concerned about my young children. Heavenly Father, pain is consuming parts of my body, and I am always feeling tired.

The cause might be a chemical imbalance. LORD All Mighty, you healed the sick. I am hopeless and weary. Help me to endure. If it's your will, send your active healing spirit to mend my body. I place my hope and confidence in you. Quietly and patiently, I trust you for healing by conventional or unconventional healing methods.

You alone endured emotional and physical pain upon the cross and suffered, knowing the discomfort of pain. Administer your spiritual grace for me to understand that you experienced and had the ability to endure my pain. If it were not for your loving-kindness and tender mercy, I would not make it through this pain and suffering.

Rebuke the spirit of suffering and pain. Let it befall my enemies. I make intercession on behalf of my body, repenting for the mistreatment and the abuse of my body. Resurrect the built-in medicinal components that instilled in my body before my birth so my body can help heal itself. I place my body in your care to bring about healing.

If my reckless behaviors caused me to mistreat my body, then forgive me, whether done intentionally or unintentionally, consciously or unconsciously.

You, O LORD, are the healing master of the universe who cured leprosy and raised the dead, Mighty God, Father of all things. In time of sickness, O LORD, deliver patience and grace while I consulted with the medical professionals to find a cure. Eliminate all stress, fear, and anxiety from my mind. Transcend your wisdom and knowledge through these professionals to ensure the right diagnostic, providing my speedy recovery. Faithful Father, send your healing powers to me in time of sickness. I will be forever indebted to you, O Holy LORD of my life.

Selah.

51

PROTECT YOUR LOVE ONES

Magnificent heavenly Father, thank you for loving me, keeping me safe and caring about me all through these years. Father, I cleanse myself of all earthly desires. And put aside grief and strives. I am coming before your throne this morning.

Father, first to offer thanks to you and second to ask you this favor, LORD, for the protection of my family—interceding, channeling my heart to your heart, seeking protection for my love ones. (*Say their names*)

Transcending through your Son, Jesus Christ, and all the saints in heaven, sending your spirit of protection to administer taught me on behalf of my family. At your command, O LORD, the Mighty Savior, the angels dispatched.

Day and night, minute by minute, you sit on high in silence, listening to those who call your name. You are the protector of all protectors. Your omnipresence felt minute by minute. The angels obey your commands without hesitation. Commission your angels to aid and assist my family.

Lift me up above my present financial situation so I can be of great help for my family. Let them see your favors flourishing through me, administered in your name, Jesus Christ (*the Pearl of Great Price*) so they can forever live in the spirit of hope, faith, and your blessing.

Help them not to glance at past disappointments but to look to the future with much confidence. O loving Savior, I put my trust in you at all times. Shed the veil that blinds me from your truths and blessings. Open up my mind to believe you.

I ask these favors with confidence, knowing that are there for me, and you care. Protect my loved ones from present and future dangers. Protect them from every human-made deception. Considerable is my faithfulness, God unto you.

You, LORD, call those things that are not as they were—any weapons form against me, and family shall not prosper. They shall be condemned you, for the LORD Jehovah shall protect my family and me (*reader: call names of relatives*) from the terrors of the nights and the poisonous envious arrows that fly by day.

The pestilence that stalks in the darkness if the day or the plague that destroys at midday none will come near me because you love me says the LORD. (*This prayer can be said morning noon or night, minute and hour*)

Selah.

52

HAVING PROBLEMS STUDYING

O LORD God, give me the patience to endure this learning venture I have undertaken. To become a full-time student at [reader: name the college or university] to study [name the course of study]. All Mighty Father, whose ultimate confidence formed the earth, grants me infinite.

Understanding and wisdom to comprehend the material presented to me by my teachers and instructors. Let not the noise of daily life obstruct my studies. For me to be blinded from my goals of becoming a [name the profession or course of study], King of eternal, immortal, invisible strength eliminates.

Heavenly Father, eliminate any distractions that may hinder my concentrate and give my teacher (say the name of instructor) the professionalism, and virtue so gets undivided attention. You, O LORD, know and see the future. My brain has to undertake the task of understanding new materials. It is imperative, for me to achieve this accomplishment today and the continuing terms.

My efforts will not only benefit myself but will also benefit someone else. I am experiencing lots of noise with voices from my limitations and around. My friends and family don't seem to care about my education. Give me, O LORD, the time and space. Open up my mind, eliminating all anxiety, fear, and negative distractions.

Show me how to finance these efforts. O LORD, At all times I put my trust in you. Bring enlightenment and amplification to my brains, distracting my opponents from distracting me and leading me astray from my purpose. Be with me, O LORD, in the classroom, on the bus, at home, at the library, on the computer.

Let not be afraid. Send good study partners to accompany me in time of study to utilize my time wisely. Clear my mind and add knowledge and wisdom to my brain—fortitude. Help me with this challenge I have undertaken; make my mind receptive to wisdom, understanding, and knowledge.

Show me how to accomplish this discipline and eliminate my financial burdens. Save my opinion and make these ventures I have undertaken bring fruitfulness give me the training to overcome obstacles. And control my thoughts to perfection so that the outcome of my efforts will be active.

I will be forever grateful, asking in your name on your promise. Jesus Christ.

Selah.

53

KNOWING THE LORD

Bring yourself to know the LORD. He will change your life; gently ask him into your life. O Precious LORD, forgive me for my transgressions against you, myself, and humankind. Blessed Father, I am giving you permission to enter my life. Make me know you better and be bountiful. Personally Knowing the LORD is the beginning of my wisdom and knowledge.

LORD, I am lost and living in sin's darkness. Send your light of perfection to enter my soul. Show me your love and strength. I did not believe you were real and thought that you were a myth or some fake existence. I was forever living in disarray. Forgive me for doubting, and let me not fall by the wayside. I believe you are nonfictional; reveal your eternal powers.

My heart will rejoice with glee, and I will serve you in strength and truth. LORD, allow me to dedicate my energy to helping you and accomplishing your will my entire life. I beg your forgiveness. Forgive me for not knowing that you are the LORD. Let me know your mercy. I did not believe that you are Jesus Christ, who bore pain on the cross for my sins. I beg your forgiveness.

I want to know that you are the LORD. Teach me how to forgive myself so that I can forgive others. "Ask, and it will be given to you; seek, and you will find; knock, and the door will be opened to you." (*Matthew 7:7*) Uncover my heart into your ever-blessed light so that I can win your love with all my heart and soul. All Mighty God, your strength, and energy have lifted my head.

I put my confidence in you.

Knowing you, LORD is the beginning of wisdom, knowledge, and understanding.

Your love will keep me in perfect peace. He will enlighten your soul.

Knowing you, LORD is the beginning of wisdom, knowledge, and understanding.

"Your kingdom comes, your will be done, on earth as it is in heaven." (*Matthew 6:10*)

Knowing you, LORD is the beginning of wisdom, knowledge, and understanding.

You have the power to change the minds of men and women.

Selah.

54

HELP IN TIME OF TROUBLE

O LORD, in time of trouble, helps me, for men flutter their lips and harbor deception in their hearts. If I should fall, do not give my enemies victory over me.

O LORD, in time of trouble, help me and be by my side at all times, shining your divine light on me. Others tried to blind my way with their tricky, false religion deceptions, hatred, and confusion. (*You, LORD, stood up and blocked their evil ways.*)

O LORD, in time of trouble, helps me. Their minds filled with darkness and despair. They use magic and tricks and deception to attain their goals. Their intentions are not to make my life easier but to make my life harder.

O LORD, in time of trouble, helps me to escape the ignorance and darkness that exists in the minds of men. Let me not fall victim to their deceptions. Precious LORD, make them the recipient of their mischievous, deviant thoughts.

Let their destructive thoughts and unorganized instincts not hinder me and block my way. Turn their cynical ways into a victory for me.

O LORD, in time of trouble, helps me. Send your honorable servants to finish them off for your name's sake. Father, eliminate them from the face of the planet, showing no mercy.

Help me, O LORD, in time of trouble. For your name's sake, my enemies will devour me. They set me on fire, decapitate my head, and take my heart out of my body. (*Send redemption to my soul.*)

O LORD, in time of trouble, helps me. Lift my heart up high so that my adversary cannot reach my soul. They derive plans to draw my soul down to the ground with them. (*Hold my soul in the palms of your hand.*)

Help me, O LORD, in time of trouble. O Majestic Father, LORD of the universe, protect my soul from my enemies. Help me, O LORD, in time of trouble. (*Hasten to be my helper.*)

Selah.

55

DECEPTION

O LORD, let no man deceive us. Guard our intellect. Satan is busy walking the earth, looking for the souls of men to devour and corrupt. LORD is vigilant about defending our spirits that Satan cannot reach them by any means.

Let not Satan deceive and weaken our hearts with his insincerities. Satan is jealous, narcissistic, and corniness. He camouflages and appears to be kind and loving, even gentle. He is a man of many disguises, penetrating the souls of men in disarray.

Let not his elegant and deceptive ways blind us from his truth. He is a liar and a thief, the thief of men's souls. Cast him in the lake of eternal fire. Protect me from his deceptions; protect my mind from his deceptions.

Cover us and protect us with your precious blood, from the top of our heads to the soles of our feet, our right side and left the side, our front, and back. Circle your blood around us; protect our souls from Satan's deceptions.

O Mighty Father, we call upon you to save us from Satan's deceptions. O Great Father, we urge you to protect us from Satan's deceptions. Guard our hearts and souls against Lucifer's tricks; mark the doors of our homes once more with your precious blood.

O Strong Father, we call upon you to save us from Satan's deceptions! O Mighty Father, we urge you to protect us from Satan's deceptions. Even our friends and families are sometimes used as tools.

O great Father, we call upon you to save us from Satan's deceptions! O Mighty Father, we call upon you to protect us from Satan's deceptions. They have even taken your name out of the schools.

O Mighty Father, we call upon you to save us from Satan's deceptions! O great Father, we call upon you to protect us from Satan's deceptions. Along with the threats of World War III, a dark storm cloud is hovering around, filled with confusion, deception, and pain.

In the wink of an eye, the Mighty God of gratification,

H capability is like the fangs of a serpent and strength as a lion's jaw. He shall restore his kingdom on earth. He is capable of powers, and strength as a lion's jaw.

God's fangs will deliver us from Satan's deceptions.

Selah.

56

CONCERN OVER JOB

O my Father, Mighty LORD of the universe, you alone knows the thoughts in my mind; you know my concerns and my needs. My job, O LORD, is on the line extremely! Very much! Give me a favor; my job is on the line. My mind is weary and confused; my wants are more than my needs. I am concerned about my job; my thoughts and confidence are disturbed over these concerns.

Because of this dilemma, I cannot sleep at night. My mind is distracting me from my slumber. Let me not ponder and worry; give me the confidence to know that when one door closes, another one opens. Administer your love and patience, knowing that you are with me at this moment in the situation. You, LORD, knew me from the beginning, and you will be working to steer me in the direction of a new job.

O LORD, erase these moments of uncertainty and bring confidence to my mind and soul. I know that you have a plan for my life. You open up doors of opportunities. If it is that I need to re-educate myself, subsequently, in my mind, make it so. O LORD, if you have another mission for this restless soul, then anoints me from head to feet so I can fulfill your desires.

LORD, I am doubtful if this uncertain period of my life designed for me to grow and serve you. If so, LORD, grant me the power and strength to grow in wisdom and to satisfy you. Let me grow into confidence and gracefulness. A fortune is always at the end of a rainbow. You are the bright light in the tunnel of darkness.

Bring real hope and an excellent opportunity to my existence. Let not your anger for me lead me astray and stop you from guiding me onward to new possibilities. If, O LORD, there is a brand-new experience I must undertake, then guide me. You provide for the birds in the fields and are a blessed Father and a good provider. Help me through this difficult time of unemployment.

You provided for me in my youth and will continue generously to take care of me until I am old. Hold me up in this time of unemployment uncertainty, letting your love and grace guide me on. If it's your will, send bigger and better opportunities. My cup filled and ran over with your love and certainty. LORD, you are my light, strength, and salvation. The universe will open and restore a blessing none can restrain.

Selah.

57

A CHILD'S PRAYER

Dear Mighty Father who rules this universe.

Look upon this little child; helpless am I.

Happy am I for entering into this world.

Help my mother and father to do well and provide for me.

Gentle Jesus; give them the patience to show me love and understanding. Give them health and joy to share their love, undivided attention and unconditional love with me; You conceived me with the rules of life embedded in my soul and your love in my heart.

Gentle Jesus, Maker of mine,

Golden of all hearts, Jesus Christ,

Joy and happiness fill my heart.

Protect me from the darkness of this world while I fulfill my life's journey. Gentle Jesus, Kind Heart of Jesus, keep my heart peaceful and filled with joy and contentment and your laughter. Keep away unwanted spirit, as I lay to sleep.

Send the right angels to watch over me while I am asleep.

Gentle Jesus; send the angels to peaceful camp around me. Thank you for sending me here on earth with love and joy in my heart, fortify me with peaceful sleep, Love mother and love father for ever more.

Gentle Jesus; safeguard my soul from death and danger. Hide my soul in your pavilion. If I death day or night. I give my heart to you. O, Dear LORD, keep my heart in your blessed blossom. Amen.

Selah

58

DEATH OF FATHER

My merciful Father who is in heaven, Father, my soul is grieving because of the death of my father. You called up my dad and took him away from me. You alone know my pain. You called him to your kingdom for other duties and higher wisdom, love, and understanding.

His loving, presence, and listening skills here on earth were impeccable. The LORD had another mission for him. LORD, help me to understand and cope with this sadness of great loss and my thoughts of the unknown world. I know my father's protective, loving spirit will guide and protect me.

Help me to understand your plans for infinite wisdom life and living. I sat and talked with him. Relay my love to him through your high power. Somewhere in your kingdom, he lies. Let him know I miss him, his love, and understanding. One day the white dove will carry me to meet him.

I Light a candle for his soul; say a prayer for his resurrection. I miss him; let him sleep in peace as his soul rests in your gentle bosom. I know at the end of my journey I will see him. My present thoughts about him are real living ones, knowing he still lives inside of me.

LORD, hold me closer to you at this moment. O, Majesty LORD of old, Wipe my tears, console my soul and let the tears that flow from my eyes fall into your gentle bosom. Wipe away my tears with the hem of your lily-white garment. Comfort my soul as I genuflect at your feet. Let the Glory be to you.

Majesty of old, you alone know the pain of death. You took the pain of mortality on the cross. LORD, I interceded on behalf of my father. Accept these intercessions and forgive him for his wrongdoings. Passionately take care of his soul as he lay in judgment.

LORD, you alone know the pain that sin brings. I loved my dad as he dearly loved himself. The love he gave was silent and unconditional. My love for him is perpetuity. Keep my father in your dear arms, and guide his eternal soul toward your precious light.

Jesus Christ the Son of God, LORD, defeated death on the cross. Allow my dad to live again, be with the spirit of my father at this time. For only I know only you LORD, can take his place in my life. I need you; All Mighty LORD. I know you are with me at this time and always. I honored my father.

Selah.

59

DEATH OF MOTHER

Guide me and hold me through these terrible times. I am grieving for my mother. My mom passed away; I can't find the strength, understanding, and energy to go forward. Alternatively, grant wisdom to conceive this ordeal. My mind and soul are in disarray. I am alone in my thoughts and can't understand why.

Help me to understand; help me not to lose my faith and love in you and the light. Be with me at this moment, retaining my confidence in your bosom. Send your angels of understanding to hold me. Your grace and love are sufficient to keep me. Thank you for sending me a mother she tried to provide me, with her patience, love, and understanding.

Show her knowledge in heaven, and dry away her tears of the disappointment of this world. Take her home to your kingdom, adoring her soul with your loving-kindness and mercy. Gently watch over her soul while she sleeps during the day, and keep watch over her soul at night until we come together again in the resurrection.

Once more, your love, LORD, is sufficient to hold me at this time of the unknown. You took the sting out of death. Looking into the life of my mother, she was a giver, not a taker. She thought me to forgive and endurance. My knees are buckling, and my heart smashed. As I genuflect before your feet seeking your mercy and guidance.

The only consolation I have is to hold on to is the glory of your resurrection. Knowing that one day, she will enjoy the resurrected.

Like did in the name of Jesus Christ. Send angels to hold and console my brother, sisters, her grandchildren, and great-grandchildren. Her hard work and dedication to her family recorded in the book of life.

Let her soul rest in peace with you, forgiving her all transgressions committed against you and humankind. Give her new life; one filled with love for self, joy, and happiness. She went to be with her husband. He waits for her in the unknown world as they both look forward to the resurrection. I honored my mother.

Selah.

60

PATRON SAINT OF ANIMALS

Saint Francis of Assisi, patron saint of animals, the Mighty LORD anointed you to intercede on behalf of the animals. We come to you in humility, asking you to give us wisdom and patience to take care of and protect our animals. I see your grace through the eyes of the animals. They too deserve love and attention.

Shining through from their souls, kindness, respect, faithful love, unconditional trusting, and patience, they are our best friends, smart and pleasing. What wonderful companions—they bring joy and happiness to us and always wait patiently for us in anticipation of our coming home.

They wait with joy, appreciation, and wagging tails of joy. They are intelligent. You can see the love and affection coming from the LORD above when you look into their eyes. They protect us from danger and bring joy and contentment to our hearts. Have mercy on them; keep our pets in your grace.

Saint Francis of Assisi, the patron saint of animals, watches over our pets, our companions, our home buddies. Keep them healthy, without reasons for them to become hyperactive and disobedient. Keep us from becoming unproductive, so we can continue to provide and protect them. They are our best friends.

Selah.

61

PROTECTION FROM THE EVENING NEWS

Dear LORD, protect my mind from the evening news, the producers, and anchor persons. (*What a trip!*) They all seem to have the same tone in their voices. I can't tell one from the other as they brainwash and confuse the minds of their viewers. They turn every segment of the news into a fiasco, from the time you wake until morning until the sun dissipates and sometimes it goes on forever. LORD, they are only pimping out their viewers and confusing their minds.

Mighty LORD, they are pumping the blood faster into the vessels that go into the brains of their viewers, just creating anxiety, confusion, and despair. What a cynical, mindless means of controlling human minds—the news stories and the happy segments they conjure up and the ways they produce and convey these messages are merely deploying fear, tension, and drama all in the world.

You cannot sit on the dinner table at your evening meal without your food exploding in your stomach. The anchors, viewers, and eyewitnesses and man-on-the-street interviewer who are a part of these productions appear to be in disarray. The news filled with superstition and hopelessness, triggering depression, fear, and anxiety; disrespecting and promoting racism; characterizing individuals; confusion; and teaching self-hatred.

LORD, look down on them; you alone know the truth. The weatherman's views on the weather are appalling, and you sometimes wonder if you should go outside or stay indoors. When the weatherman says you should walk with a coat or umbrella, if you decide to listen to him and take whichever, you are not only leaving the house with an umbrella or a jacket but with your mind filled with confusion. You do not need either.

However, with fear and anxiety absorbing your minds, why can't they say, "Tomorrow will be sunny," and leave out the chance of rain or cloudy or wind-chill factor? LORD, when this is all over, and your mind is fully overwhelming, they turn the news and weather segments into a talk-show theme, with puppets for news anchors perpetuating nonsense and stories of their personal lives.

Superficial puppets call themselves anchor persons, all Mighty LORD. They are anchoring themselves. Where is the news—the real news, news to uplift the spirit and encourage the mind; friendly news about people doing positive things, helping each other, living together in respect and harmony? With only one second left in the broadcast, they offer you one second of a fuzzy story. (*Humanistic stories; then those fuzzy are taken away in a quick second*.) And back to the lies.

LORD, at the end of the news shows. They show you for one second, an emotional, humanistic story of a dog or a cat rescue. So you can make contact with your soul, feel-good story, and call it happy news segment. (*For examples saving a dog or cat, some raccoon story or something swaying and controlling minds*) That just doesn't make any sense at all, like a heart-wrenching story of a young child dying from cancer. LORD, why are these young kids dying from cancer?

Save our minds and our souls. Set us free from this daily hype. Send your noble spirit to rescue our minds for this morning, evening, and breaking-news hype. Our Holy Father, send us your amazing love and perfect understanding and humanity.

Selah.

62

GOING ON A TRIP

Go before me, O Precious LORD. Pave the way for a safe trip. Give me favor with those in authority and others I meet along the way. If I should lose my way, and fear and uncertainty step in, send your earthly angels to assist me in a safe and helpful way. Send blue skies and the sunshine to warm and put joy and confidence into my soul.

Dispatch joy, happiness, and contentment, you who made heaven and earth. If disasters beyond my control should strike, take my heart to safety in your loving bosom. Lord, let me feel your love and hear your voice beckoning men and women. Make my trip safe; bring success to my efforts, and make provisions for me upon my arrival.

Go before me, securing a safe place for me to spend time, clear my mind, and help me find relaxation. Like the American Express, I can't leave home without you and your assurance. I am taking you with me, O LORD, wherever I go. You are my guiding and shining star. O LORD, how good and pleasant it is when I come to you with my thoughts and trouble.

You are the redeemer of my soul and the pilot of my life. You had drafted a map of my life's journey before I entered this realm. Your love sends me to your doorstep by a comprehensive understanding. So I can live again. You gave me confidence in the past. And will continue in the future.

Keep me safe and protected by your love, blinding my enemies while giving favor to me. If, for some reason, disaster strikes while I am traveling, let me hold on to you with my soul and carry you to the other side of my life. If it is your will that I continue to live, then bring me back safely to my home in perfect peace,

Shield my soul to engage in your magnificent omnipresence, and endow your illuminating light. Mighty Father, you are everlasting. When I go on a trip, be with me, the King of Kings who calmed the waters and parted the Red Sea.

Selah.

63

RACE RELATIONS

Mighty Father, sorry to bother you again, but there is a problem with race relations, in many countries around the world, especially in America and Canada. Heavenly Father, your first commandment said to love and respect one another. You have given humankind domination over the animals and made them with reasoning powers higher than the animals. Theoretically, LORD, you did not create humanity to mentally or physically misuse and one another.

Your love is sufficient to hold us together and to take us to a higher level of consciousness. O LORD, you told us to be good and kind to each other. However, in the minds of some men, loving and accepting others of a different race and culture seems to be a problem. This distracting, dangerous problem is happening more so to those who were born with white skin tone; black lives matters, but all lives matter.

Hatred has engulfed the minds of men and women and has overtaken the core of their souls, blinding and shutting their hearts, minds, and souls to your first commandment—to love one another. When Caucasian males or females are experiencing low self-esteem and falling from society's grace, their hearts are bleeding. They identify themselves with the people of color and seek their mercy, love, understanding, wisdom, and creativeness from the people of color. (*Africa and her descendants*)

Everlasting Spirit of creation has mercy on the souls of these unseen men. Who wants to see people of color confused and in disarray?

For years, they have been tracking and mistreating people of color (*Africa and her descendants*). These invisible men and women filled with deep hatred and greed have devised a plan to start a race riot today. LORD, the racial struggle between white and people of color was to be mended with the integral of a black president.

Mighty LORD, instead of compensating the descendants of slaves for past injustices and exploitation (*example: the cotton fields of Alabama*) and all other acts of slavery in the West Indies. And Africa, these same men have embraced a different culture, giving them respect, employment, bank notes, and special privileges, turning them into middle-class and upper-class citizens. Then they set them loose on the people of color (*Africa and her descendants*).

These Arab and Asian cultures, along with a select set of the Caucasian race are together fighting a secret economic war against people of color (*Africa and her descendants*). The elites assist the Asian and Arab culture to gain economic strength and educational leverage over the people of color (*African descendants*), while the Asians build up themselves, their communities, and nations. LORD.

They have entirely neglected the people of color and their communities in America, Canada, and the continent of Africa. For the people of color (*Africa and her descendants*), all they seem to have for them is to manufacture diseases in Petri dishes and pass these diseases on to people of color (Africa and her descendants) through their food sources, making them sick, miserable, and wanting.

The elites are distracting them with issues that are irrelevant to their present well-being. They are giving them the worst of the worst. Unfortunately, the black leadership from the deceiving black president of America, down to the grassroots ones, is acting dumbfounded about the situation. LORD, deliver people of color

(*Africa and her descendants*) from these evils placed upon them by themselves.

They do not collectively invest in themselves, do not build anything, are hard to train, and gravitate toward niggerisms. They used to be abused and misused by this causation that many of them are still suffering from deep confusion and self-hatred. LORD, this immense inequality, abuse, and misuse are rampant today, just like yesterday, making it impossible for the people of color (*Africa and her descendants)* to become economically stable, Mighty LORD!.

The people of color (*Africa and her descendants*) all promised compensation of forty acres and a mule for their unpleasant experiences they endured during slavery. They did not receive half ass. Today, people of color (Africa and her descendants) are without compensation. Other nationalities subjugated to the same, or less harsh experiences received their payment but not the people of color (*Africa and her descendants)*.

Today's leadership says they are concerned and representing the interests of people of color (*Africa and her descendants)*, especially the snake-oil salesmen of the world. They have embarked on another campaign using the Arab Middle Eastern culture to further instill self-hatred, poverty, and confusion in the minds of people of color. (*Africa and her descendants*),

Sidetracking them, making life economically harder for people of color (*Africa and her descendants*), and separating them from the real issues affecting their lives. The Arab culture and selective members of the Caucasian race are both responsible, for the injustice of disfranchising people of color (*African and her descendants*), making those slaves, and the destabilization Africa.

These are the same cultures today that are in control of the educational, medical, and other leading institutions. The media—television and print—are also playing a prominent role in delivering a pessimistic worldwide persona about people of color (*Africa and her descendants*), identifying everything negative with blackness (negative behavior). If you look at the programming of mainstream television evening news,

You will hardly see people of color (*Africa and her descendants*) doing positive things. It appears as though we do not exist. They portray other cultures in a positive light, as though they alone are capable of and are doing practical things. We do not exist and do not fit into their scheme of things. Holy Father, let not the eyes of people of color (*Africa and her descendants*) be blinded from the truth.

Open their eyes and minds, bring them together collectively, instilling the love of self and discipline. Give them a good favor, and bring them to know this struggle is all about organizing and management of resources and commodities. They are using the science of economic discrimination to keep the people of color (*Africa and her descendants*) down. This mass confusion is the name of the game.

Heavenly Father, have mercy on the people of color, giving them wisdom, understanding, and discipline to build their lives and communities. Shine your everlasting light on their souls. Fill their hearts with deep, passionate love of themselves. Have mercy on them, and do for them as you did for the state of Israel; (*Africa and her descendants*), their prayers, hopes, and disciplines written in the covenants of the LORD.

Open up the souls of people of color (*Africa and her descendants*), so they don't destroy themselves and their communities because of the injustice and double standard they see and feel. Set their minds free from this cancerous, frustrating tyranny that has engulfed their minds. LORD, the present political and economic situation as it pertains to the people of color (*Africa and her descendants*) living in America.

With the new wave of immigrants washing up on our shores, vying for resources, jobs, and economic freedom, it is putting a financial strain on the people of color (*Africa and her descendants)* communities. This lucrative conspiracy against the black communities in America, perpetrated by individuals in higher power, is making the managing of resources worse for people of color. These economic and political conditions are making this situation stagnant.

The outcome looks bleak and uncertain for the people of color (Africa and her descendants) because these new-age immigrants are a bunch of selfish, racially charge individuals who are also against the people of color (*Africa and her descendants*). LORD, the time has come for people of color (*Africa and her descendants*) to respect themselves and build their communities while they are living.

They must put an end to this self-pity nonsense and psychologically and physically kill themselves, police brutality, and radical racial discrimination in the media, and progress forward. It is imperative that the people of color (Africa her descendants) fight hard to leave a stronger legacy for their children. "A man should not be judged by the color of his skin but the content of his heart." (*MLK*) "I have a dream that my four" Martin Luther King's Jr., (*Martin Luther King's Jr. speech August 28, 1962*)

You, LORD, know the content of the hearts of people of color (*Africa and her descendants*). The infinite Father will judge and render justice for his children. Give us the victory. Honestly, help our minds to build a great nation.

Selah.

64

EDUCATING YOUR YOUNG CHILDREN

LORD, help these young pregnant women; assist them to overcome all obstacles. You, O LORD, in your teachings, stated, "Train your children in the way they should go so that when they are older. They will not depart" (*Proverbs 22:6*). LORD, you alone can grant us this favor. When we call upon you, you answer us and bring it to pass with your truth and great unusual nature (*not by our will*).

LORD, you are the author of education, wisdom, and knowledge. Your wisdom and mercy give us the formula for living and open our minds to make real and everlasting plans for educating our young children. Supply us with time, patience, and teaching concepts, before and after we give birth to our children. Send us to take classes in early childhood education, and teach us proper childrearing skills.

LORD, let your wisdom and knowledge pour into our minds and souls. Bless us, creating a burning passion for education in our children that they can enjoy this precious life that you give them. Faithful Father, LORD, implant in the minds of our children peace, patience, tranquility and favorable environment. So they can fully develop their minds.

Protect them, sending only useful information to their brains. Surround them with intelligent mentors, and deter information of ignorance. Safeguard their minds from a world filled with deceptions and unwilling spirits of distractions. LORD, give them the powers of concentration and discipline to answer always when they're called upon.

Bless their mothers, and give them the powers to disarm deception and negative distractions. LORD, while they administer to their babies' knowledge, wisdom, and understanding from within the wombs. LORD, open wide their hearts and minds to your precious voice while educating their young children. Mighty Father, guide the children and their valuable thoughts all the way through to adulthood.

The LORD is the Alpha and the Omega. In your infinite wisdom, guide our children in the way they must go, turning them into successful citizens of this earth forever. Thy eternal wisdom is rooted in great patience and discipline from here to eternity. LORD, send us good, healthy men of conviction to copulate with to reproduce.

Selah.

65

IN TIME OF PREGNANCY

Mighty LORD, this baby I am about to bring into this world has no father. Take hold of this situation and be my baby's father. Send divine help from above, LORD. Keep my mind clean, bright, and loving; keep my body, mind, and soul healthy and affectionate.

Dispatch your peace and joy of life to my baby's mind, and a thirst in his or her soul for wisdom, knowledge, and patience. Assist me to engulf good reading habits and sound materials so that I can enrich my brains and pass it on to my unborn child's brain.

Give talent beyond this sphere to this precious seed planted inside of me. LORD, you called the sun to life—the sun to life; how lovely. To this new life you give me through nature and unconditional love, send patience and understanding from above.

Let the day bring joy and tranquility and at night peace and serenity. Guide this new life into this world. Accompany me. O LORD, while I prepare a place for life to rest. Help me, O LORD, to organize a place where hope, faith, love, and joy reside so my baby can grow up in a loving environment.

Dispatch your angels to surrounding this new life at all times. Lord, I am requesting he or she grow up in a home filled with love, joy, and understanding forever? Bind this birth with your love. Thanks for this opportunity; thank you for this precious life.

Praises to the King of kings, for he gives us life's splendor and glory. In this, my time of my pregnancy, gently cascade wisdom unknown in the brain stems so it can transfer this knowledge on to my unborn child.

Life is good, and the life you bestowed into my womb is moving around inside of me with the vigor of a champion. You poured this life into me like the tree planted by the water of life. Thank you, beloved Father.

Selah.

66

ORGANIZATIONAL SKILLS

You, O LORD, invincible Father, who organized and shaped this universe with methodical and sequential scheduling, you are the Prince of perfection, Mighty LORD, inventor, and organizer of this world. The Saints are all organized and confirmed in your heavenly kingdom. LORD, you expect us to be orderly on your beloved earth. You held the state of Israel with your infinite wisdom and truth and are her keeper. ("Behold, He who keeps Israel will neither slumber nor sleep.") (*Psalm 121:4(NASB)*)

Help the people of color (*Africa and her descendants*) to follow your example by organizing their thoughts, minds, souls, homes, purpose, possessions, and communities with your unforeseen divine wisdom and faithfulness. Mighty LORD, You created and fashioned the Earth in an unrelenting organized perpetual, discipline, rhythmic regular continuously, progressing at unabated life forces. The earth in its consciously organized perpetually, control, rhythmic regularly is steadily improving its inhabitance.

Your example and extensive efforts have helped us to live in a systematized way in the land. Part of your divine plan for humankind was for them to live in an organized, orderly manner. Based on the organizational structure, discipline law and order. Love for self and you, LORD; only send your spirit of methodology to walk among people of color (*Africa and her descendants*). Look into the souls of the children, teaching them the powers of organizing and building communities.

Mighty Father, bring order to the confusion that exists in the minds, and souls of people of color (*Africa and her descendants*). Make them know you rose from death so that they too can rise and organized holding themselves and their nation together. Heavenly Father, extract the confusion and miss trust of self. That exists in the spirit of Africa and her descendants. The world is looking at the situations taking place on the African content.

Other nations are once more taking advantage of people of color (*Africa and her descendants*); they took the Africans for granted and considered us a joke. LORD, all the years of discrimination of a race of people, psychological raping and confusing the African continent has not gotten Satan anywhere. His offspring cannot get past their guilt trip that daily haunts they minds. LORD, it's time for us to look beyond these past injustices and build a better world for all our children.

The entire people of color (*Africa and her descendants*) and their African leaders have not found it fit to produce, build, and organize their country and communities, lifting up their lives to create a better life for their children. Help them to follow your example by organizing their thoughts, minds, and souls and homes, purpose, possessions, and their communities. Help them to follow your example; have them live in an organized, hopeful, futuristic way— the way you planned for men.

LORD, send your spirit of timing to walk among them, to fortify them with complete built-in skills of being organized and love for themselves. Thanking you in advance for assisting people of color, (*Africa and her descendants*) with organizational skills, so that the wolves of this earth cannot enter and lead them astray, gather them and seal them together. If, O LORD, we were not commanded to organize our lives, this world will be in disarray and filled with immense chaos.

We would be living in constant hardship, and everything would be in disarray. O LORD, the Olympic Organizer, you organized the kingdom of Israel. O LORD, our Keeper, help the African continent and her descendants to understand the powers of education, organizing, and taking care of their own. Help them to raise the flag of salvation and systematize their lives.

Selah.

67
STRENGTH IN TIME OF WEAKNESS

"This is the day the LORD has made; let us rejoice and be glad in it." (*Psalm 118:24 (NKJV)*) Let our souls sing of your love and kindness (*Give us strength in weakness*), The Mighty God, who anoints and saves the souls of men and women, strengthen us in the time of weakness. LORD, when people test our faith to start a racial or religious war. (*Give us strength in weakness*).

Men and women of evil have derived a plan to gather my personal information and use it against me and penalize me.

When our souls are sinking, and our oppressor is demanding, (*Give us strength in weakness*), my mother and father are overbearing (*give us strength in weakness*). My job is demanding too much from me.

Sheer frustration and anger are stepping in my way to steal our joy and happiness. (*Give us strengthen in weakness.*) My culture, religious dogma, and everything we built and stand for is under scrutiny. The game of reverse psychology is being played out. (*Give us strength in weakness*)

Remember, King David and Goliath (*Give us strength in weakness*); the children of Israel (*Give us strength in weakness*). LORD, you were there at the parting of the Red Sea and the river's edge (*Give us strength in weakness*), Daniel in the lion's den (*Give us strength in weakness*)—O LORD, you come to us through pure grace and power. Don't let us ponder about whom we are and our life's mission.

Our life's mission is to fight for your name, Jesus Christ, and return to you with our hearts and souls secured and intact. We attempt to save those who are becoming lost in the mayhem and compromising their intellectual, self-control to acquire materialistic gains while they lose their noble souls. (*Give us strength in weakness.*)

Selah.

68

THANK YOU FOR LIFE

Mighty LORD, I thank you for life, O LORD; thank you for life. Thank you for holding my hands and walking with me through these difficulties and disappointments. Holy Father, you were there to dry away my tears; you held my heart in your hands and gave me comfort.

Everlasting Father, when times became rough and tough, you were the shoulders I leaned on. (*Never failing God*) I did not know strength existed within me until you slowly gave power, wisdom, and understanding. Lord, you carried me on your shoulder when I became lost.

I am continually indebted to you. Thank you, thank you, your mercy and strength will see me through to the next level of my life. Your mercy has bravely endured for me forever. When others tried to pull me down, you stood in the gates and hindered them.

You send the sun in the mornings to kiss my face and warm my heart, indulging in your love, and the rain to wash away my tears and teach me to fight and win and to lose and be humble. Your mercy endures forever. Thank you for life and the joy from above.

LORD, I believe you were the last sacrifice. You sacrificed your life for me when you went on the cross so that I don't have to go on the cross—mentally, physically, psychologically—for anyone. Just believe. I can help them a little, but I do not have to sacrifice myself for anyone. Thank you for that wisdom.

Selah.

69

BEDTIME

Heavenly Father, now as I lay my family to sleep, sends your nightly angels to watch over my family while they sleep. "Now I lay me down to sleep, I give the LORD my soul to keep." (*The New England Premier*) Holy Father, guide me and keep me safe through the night.

As I prepare my mind and soul to rest, turn off those unwanted thoughts of anxiety, concern, and the world's silent harmful subliminal noise that enters my mind hindering me from sleeping.

Send your light of protection and your band of perfect angels to watch over me and adequately safeguard my dreams. As lay down to sleep, strengthen me with wisdom; protect my mind and soul from unclean spirits of evil, jealousy, and envy.

Protect my physical body from any dangers. Secure my mind from friends, family, coworkers, and associates, some of whose intentions are evil and filled with envy and jealousy.

If my mind encounters horrible dreams along the way, protect my mind, so these dreams do not entangle or entwine with my soul's peaceful sleep to take my soul away to random, harmful places.

For many reasons, these unpleasant thoughts hinder my mind and soul. Then, when I wake the following morning and look back on those terrible, horrible dreams, my mind is in disarray.

Give me the wisdom and patience to be successful, filling my daily obligations of work and school and taking care of my family. Take me home safely to see my kids, and give me the strength and energy to take care of them.

LORD, adequately protect my family and me against the fiery darts and pestilence that flies by day and night. If trouble comes while I sleep, my confidence is in you, O LORD. If I die before I wake, I give you, O LORD, my soul to take.

Selah.

70

SURGERY

Clean my soul, O LORD; clean my heart and wash away my sins, O LORD. You are the author of life and death and the resurrection. Let not my life be taken away from me on this surgical table; make haste dispatch your angels to surround me and give me the courage to successfully make it through this surgery (*reader: name the surgical procedures*).

LORD, replace my fear and concerns with courageous, graceful, humbling confidence. Comfort me. Let your loving hands guide these doctors as they carry out this delicate surgery (reader: belief in your heart and name procedures, whether minor or major]. If, LORD, for any reasons, this surgery is not necessary or was not meant to be, summon an angle to send new of postponement.

Then send your angels and your mighty white doves ahead of me to enter the hospital and bring news to warn me. Heavenly Father, like a blind man trust in his cane or work dog, I honestly and sincerely imagine and believe that you will hear my prayers; Father, I do not put my confidence in people. I wait and listen to your still gentle voice.

Open the door of heaven, sending a sign from above. Mighty Father, Let me hear your voice and obey, O LORD, who was in the fire with Shadrach, Meshach, Abednego. You, LORD, were in the lion's den with Daniel and with Moses at the vast sea. Mighty LORD, you have the powers to heal the sick and stabilize the minds and hands of these surgeons and doctors.

Yasha, commission Saint Michael to defend me in my time of need, turning these physicians to be servants of the LORD and Savior Jesus Christ. Grant them patience to concentrate and take good care of me. Send peace and reassurance to my soul. I come to you, O LORD, forsaking all worldly noise and my material wants.

My soul has faith in Jesus Christ and his healing powers. As healing comes to my body, make haste assist me through this chapter of my life. God of unforeseen wisdom and virtue, help me through so that my heart can continue to sing praises to you and find joy again in this beautiful life you gave me.

"If I should die before I wake, I give the LORD my soul to keep." (*The New England Premier*) Father, I come to you with a clean heart and resting my confidence in you, God of expected wisdom and the powerful healer.

Selah.

71

COWORKERS

Beloved Heavenly Father, thank you for providing me with this job. My heart is weighing down inside of me because my coworkers are making it hard for me to implement this position (*reader: name the job position*). My coworkers are conspiring against me, making it challenging and overly demanding for me to function in this post.

Mighty LORD, stretch forth your Heavenly hands and protect me from my colleagues. Give me the foresight to maneuver my way through stressful this situation. Make me vigilant in overcoming them and their antics. Provide me with patience and understanding, so I don't become lost in their desire to displace me.

Mighty God, take the lead, to protect my livelihood. I plead my cause to you. (*It's bounded in heaven*)

Bring stupidity to their actions and minds so that they cannot harm me in any way. Send your angels to assist me with strength to successfully continue in this position. (*Reader: name the job position*) Heavenly Father, you alone is God. You are God by yourself and don't need me or anyone else to be God.

LORD, you cannot be harmed nor controlled by humankind.

When I arrive at work, shield me with your strength. Put your whole armor of protection around my entire being. Give me the confidence to carry on in this position without fear and confusion. Always let my coworkers feel the forces of their confusion. Defeat them in their efforts to bring harm by jeopardizing my (*reader: name the job position*).

Let me feel your presence and confidence. Thank you for providing me with this job position, forever carrying your light with me as I go from day to day.

Selah.

72

LAUGHTER

All Mighty LORD, from the beginning, in the present, and in the end, you were and are the joy of my life. LORD, the joy you have given me during my life's journey has touched and inspired many. With joy come laughter, understanding, and contentment of my heart and soul.

Happy am I when I can congregate in my heart and soul with you, LORD of hosts. All Mighty ruler of this universe, you are my joy and strength. LORD, you are love! Laughter and joy are in your tabernacle. The LORD loves laughter and joy; he is the strength of my life. The LORD loves laughter. He has a sense of humor and joy.

He is the force and commitment of my life. Men take themselves too seriously and seem to think there is nothing in their lives that's worth rejoicing over. And when they see that I possess joy and happiness in my life, they seem to think I'm on drugs or I'm crazy. LORD, they believe I am on drugs or something.

What they don't know is that I am high on life and the joy of knowing that you are the LORD of the LORDS, the granting Father of life. You, O LORD Jesus Christ, were a pleasure to the heavenly Father, All Mighty God, after your resurrection. Most of them walk around not saying high to one another. They think you are still dead and don't have a sense of humor.

However, if they only knew you personally, as I do, my LORD, they would indulge in your joy and laughter. LORD, laughter, and joy are in your kingdom. Your joy is my strength. Keep on integrating joy and laughter in my heart and soul. The LORD loves laughter and joy; he is the strength of my life. The LORD loves laughter and joy; he is the strength of my life.

There are wisdom and understanding in laughter. Mighty Father, LORD of the universe, safeguards my soul and keeps your joy in my life forever. You are the joy in my life. My heart loves you in all ways. Your unconditional love and joy are sufficient to hold me. LORD, you were sentenced to death, nailed to a wooden cross on Calvary's hill, died, and laid in a tomb.

After his humiliating death on the cross at Calvary's Hill, Jesus Christ the Mighty Conqueror of mortality, the authenticity that you rose, flatters the heart of the Heavenly Father, with love and joy brings The Glory of God the Father. A pleasure knowing that the stone was removed ascending him to heaven to join his father, God. He took the sting out of dying and death for all.

The LORD loves laughter and joy; he is the strength of my life. Your resurrection gives me joy and happiness.

The LORD loves laughter and joy; he is the strength of my life. O what a glorious day when truth and joy fill the hearts of men. Everything's in his infinite wisdom that the Heavenly Father possessed was given to humankind in joy here on the earth, under the ground, and in the air.

"Make a joyful noise unto the LORD"; (*Psalm 100 (KJV)*)

Rejoice greatly. Rejoice and be glad for the resurrection of Jesus Christ. He is LORD of the universe. You can find real joy (*if you indulge in his love and the transformation of his living soul.*) Live and wash yourselves in his precious blood; he is the cherished lamb who was sacrificed for your transgressions (*he was the last sacrifice*).

The Mighty LORD has a sense of humor. He loves laughter and joy; he is the strength of my life. The LORD loves laughter and joy. He is the force of my life. All Mighty Father, today humankind takes themselves a bit too seriously. Some of them (the faithless) never knew or have forgotten the original meaning and purpose of life.

They lost themselves in the perplexity of life and lost sight of life's real purpose, causing them to manufacture unpleasant and unwanted problems. Be of good cheer; sing and dance in your daily lives, for he lives in spirit and truth, today, tomorrow, and always. Remember the God of old, Pay homage to him

Whose name, is joy, strength, wisdom, understanding, and power lives on in the New Testament. Anoint yourselves in his name and blood as you go on your way. Remember the LORD; lift up his name in your hearts, minds, and souls. Jesus Christ is in father's heavenly kingdom, sitting on his golden throne.'

At the right hand of his Father, All Mighty God. He sits on the right hand of the Father, the All Mighty Father, King of Kings, LORD of LORDS. The LORD loves laughter and joy; he is the strength of my life. The LORD loves laughter and joy; he is the strength of my life. I find joy in knowing you LORD, sacrificed your blood for me on Calvary's cross and your resurrection. It brings me joy and gratefulness existing in my heart day and night. Your resurrection heavily planted in my heart.

Selah.

73

PATIENCE

LORD, grant me patience to understand myself and others. Bless me with your everlasting patience, the forbearance you have shown to men on earth in times of death, uncertainty, anxiety, dementia, fear, divorce and depression.(*all evil*) Teach me patience through all things.

Father of love and understanding, administer to those who seek your face patience, wisdom, grace, and understanding. However, let them not be led astray and taken for granted by others because of their persistence.

Your love and patience, Mighty LORD, architect of fortitude, is sufficient for me to forgive others who have done me wrong. Surround me with your patience. All spiritual forces of the LORD hold me together, instilling patience within me.

Like you nurture and show to a young child.

Forceful Father, most powerful and Mighty, mercifully administer patience to my soul, bountifully and never-ending depths unknown. I will praise your name always in the land of the living and among the dead.

Magnifying and glorifying your permanent presence in all the earth. Precious LORD, take away all uncertainty, anxiety, fear, and depression. Replace them with a calm, flourishing, energetic spirit of confidence. Keep me steady in all things. In all things keep me stable.

My request to you comes from a place filled with darkness, confusion, and despair. Remove the darkness from my life. Come to me, O Loving Father, and replenish my soul with an abundance of patience and confidence.

LORD, let no man or women in their ambitions and mischievous sprites lead me astray to destroy my mind, body, and soul and lose my actual favor and relationship with you Heavenly Father. Fortify my will with patience unmeasured, and running over, so I can resist the devil's temptation.

Selah.

74

CHARITY WORK

LORD, show me the virtue of giving; you are the wonderful originator and a good example of being of service to others. You fed the poor and performed charity work. God the Father, through Jesus Christ,

When my chips were down, and there was no place to turn, you taught me that for my soul to be at ease, I must give and perform charity work to give back to my friends, community, and society.

When my chips were down, you taught me to share some of my time and money with others. I must give and perform charity work in society for my community. The LORD can use all retired professionals in all areas of profession and nations.

In good times and bad, mostly at the right times, LORD, author of giving, you gave your son. Embedded with your prevailing wisdom, you commanded us, through your examples, to follow the principles of giving back and building better communities.

Send these messages to the people living in the disadvantaged communities in America and around the world. For the light of the LORD to shine into their hearts and communities,

They must give to themselves and their communities. Let them know, through your infinite wisdom that they must give back to their communities and society. You will enrich your stay on earth and that of others.

In good times and bad, teach others the real gift of charity work so that they too can bring hope and faith to others. Guide those who are entwined in darkness and pursuing their endeavors,

Keeping them in your heavenly light, and show them your teachings of giving and receiving. They must give and perform charity work, first to themselves and their community.

Help them to be a comfort to others as they slowly make their way back to your purpose and the Mighty Kingdom. LORD, open the eyes of those blinded by the bright lights of greed, confusion, and selfishness.

Cast out the diminishing evil spirit of them and the mentality of the crabs-in-the-barrel syndrome. When we are called to give to others, let not our offerings of good energy and finance took for granted. You alone are God, all by yourself.

Selah.

75

BEING A GOOD FATHER

Heavenly Father, you are the best example of a father. You provided for your children before calling us into existence—forming us from the dust, breathing life into our nostrils, placing the earth beneath our feet and the sky above our heads, and giving us dominion over the earth, animals, trees, food that you commanded.

Heavenly Father, you are the best example as a father. You provided the wind to keep us breathing, and sunshine and rain, the moon, seas, and stars to give us hope for life. Rolling Thunder reminds us of our mortality. Your gentle understanding and unconditional love have kept us for centuries.

Heavenly Father, you are the best example of a father. Thank you for the honor of fatherhood and the opportunities. Teach me through your creative spirit how to be an excellent father. Give me the wisdom and understanding to be a good provider for my children and to walk in your footsteps. Give me the strength and virtue to continue.

Heavenly Father, you are the best example of a father, consistently providing for your children, even though at times we are not worthy because we forget to thank you. Abba Father, forgive us. Beautiful Father, we became blinded by materialism and the constant negative noises. Forever you will extend to us your patience, in spite of our ungratefulness.

Heavenly Father, you are the best example of a father. You prepared and commanded the four elements of the earth to function endlessly.

You provided all the necessities of life to sustain your creation. Mighty one, suffer not the children to come to you. Thank you, God, for being a good Father and provider. You, as our example, help us to be excellent providers for our children.

Selah.

76

DEATH OF A SISTER

LORD, help me through this time. Hold my feet to the ground, for they trembles and wobbles with thoughts of the mortality of my sister. Hold my soul in your hands, and dry my tears. Bring tender healing to my mind.

Heavenly Father, Quietly counsel my mind so I can come to terms with the process of life and death. Son of the highest, in the winking of an eye, my beloved, loving sister has decided return to you.

She went away to meet the Holy Maker of life. She was the only real friend I ever knew. Let her soul follow the light of eternity. LORD, when there was no one for us, we carried each other through the rough times.

Send your light of love to comfort her in death. Give her a calm place in heaven, so her soul can rest in tranquility. Rejuvenate her to a better life in a different time, with kind, loving parents to love and protect her.

LORD, may she find eternal rest as she sleeps in your care in your generous chamber. As she waits for her resurrection through Jesus Christ, may she find new joy and love, erasing and blotting out all her transgressions?

Comfort her children as they deal with this tribulation. LORD, let your angels care for her precious children until they return to join her through your precious blood. Always keep her in their hearts, for she loved them and gave them her all.

She was taken advantage of and treated unfairly in life by others. LORD, you bore her sadness and disappointments on the foot of the cross on Calvary's hill. However, I know and believe you took the sting out of death.

By conquering death at the feet of crucifixion and resurrection (the crucified Jesus Christ); you defeated death. Comfort me so I can be of comfort to my mother; keep me active so that I can be healthy for my mom during this time.

You are the great Comforter. I kneel before the cross I pay homage to you, O Mighty King of Kings. Hold my heart in the palm of your hands.

Selah.

77

DEATH OF A BROTHER

Mighty God, when the devil was trying to discourage and stop me from trying, my big brother stood up for me. He always struggled with his demons of self-hatred, fear, and doubt, lack of encouragement. These confusion and despair perpetrated from a source unknown.

His first betrayed by his mother and father. The first persons he came into contact with and loved. Somehow, he never felt loved and lived a loveless, lonely existence, filled with fear and doubt. Lord, He wasn't given a chance to succeed at anything in life.

He always tried to be a good, protective son but did not receive gratitude or love in return. I light a candle for him and say a prayer for his soul. Heavenly Father, Mighty savor instructs the angels to crown him with peace and glory, for his journey through this small life, is over.

Angel of mercy, grant him forgiveness and a peaceful sleep. Return him to your kingdom and allow him to live once more. Through your resurrection, give him the blessings of love, trust. The things denied him in his time on earth.

Let you soul travel, away from the confusion you experienced in this life. Follow the light my brother to a new life. My god, the father, welcome you into his pavilion. An interaction made on behalf of your soul.

Evette Forde

Only love for you exists in my heart. Thank you for being my brother. God, the Mighty Father, thank you for sending him and made him my brother. He helped liberate my mind. I love him evermore.

Travel, my brother, go to the light, find the love you never receive while here on earth find that love in the hands and heart of Jesus Christ, find peace, joy, and comfort until we meet again in the hereafter, God's servant. He came to liberate. May the Son of the Highest God, take you under his wing.

Selah.

78

PRAY FOR SINGLE MOTHERS

My Spiritual Father and Virgin Mother, who are in heaven, look down on all single mothers, giving them wisdom and understanding to raise healthy, loving children. Send peace and patience at night to ease their frustrations.

Mighty God, you alone know the troubles of single mothers. Send your angels to guide them with insight, wisdom, and knowledge. Shine your light inwardly to see them through; shielding their children from unnecessary anger, pain, disappointments, abandonment, betrayal, and other negative emotions.

King of Kings, LORD of LORDS, an advocate of the poor, counsel for the defense, the lawyers wants one hundred dollars an hour and more to help them attain child and educational funds to support the children. This struggle is killing the mind of the single mother, slowly decreasing her joy and contentment.

Some keep a straight face for the sake of the children; while the fathers are leisurely destroying their children. The children are caught up in the middle of this negative emotional mess. Why, LORD, do men put women and children through these stressful predicaments?

O Mighty Father, help them to see a silver lining behind this cloud. Open the eyes of my husband (or the baby's father) to see the harm that his negative action is having on the children. LORD, have mercy on the women and men, who cast this hurt on women and children.

They bring harm, because of their acts of selfishness and uneducated of adultery. The pain and confusion I see in the eyes of these kids can't be redeemed. Damn the souls of the wild women sleep with men knowing well they are married men. Their actions destroy homes and relationships and cause mothers to raise children on their own. These unpleasant situations of hurt and pain are destroying families.

Home wreckers, their souls should rest in hell, without forgiveness. I curse the day they were born and the women who birthed them. Put them in hell's fire, for they must go there to perish forever for the pain they cause. Show no forgiveness to them, unless they repent of their evil act of home-wrecking and mental abuse women of children.

Selah.

79

PRAY FOR SINGLE FATHERS

Welcome to my world, boys, and sons of David. Show them the strain and pain they have often put women under unnecessary pressure. Open their eyes, making them see the glory and wisdom behind keeping their families together. Single fathers, hear my pray.

The word of God to men is to make this world a better place for everyone, including the children. The firstborn Son of God, born in a manger, was surrounded by animals and straw, with nothing but straw to lay his head.

Fortunately for him, he had a mother and a father by his side. Single Fathers, hear my pray. Help these men to be men and not boys, leaving their mothers and fathers, taking up their responsibilities. Become men, not boys, the chief cornerstone of their families.

Heavenly father, you commanded them to love their babies' mothers so their days would be longer. Turn yourselves into loving and nurturing parent to your children and respect their baby mothers.

Neglecting and abusing your children for your girlfriend is not pleasing to the All Mighty Father. You were given full stewardship over these kids; these are the words of All Mighty Father.

The act of sex was made to enjoy and bear those children. Those kids were gifts from God to be loved, cared for, cherished, and raised in wisdom and truth. O, Yeshua of Nazareth, guide single fathers to put God and their children first in their lives.

Selah.

80

UNDERSTANDING

Heavenly Father, Moses didn't doubt your words. He led the children of Israel to the water's edge to the Promised Land, leading them to safety and freedom. Speak to my heart and soul, destroying this spirit of doubtfulness and uncertainty. Fortify me with understanding. Engulf me once more with the power of positive thinking and a can-do attitude.

Give me understanding and strength, not doubting. Let my soul be filled with a never-ending supply of helpful thoughts, and follow up with specific actions. Give me the power of clear thinking at all times in all things. Let there be light, and the light formed. You did not quiver or doubt. Engulf me once more with the power of favorable thinking; help me to change. My thoughts and my life will follow.

Give me the same courage given to King David when he faced off with Goliath. Gentle Father, filled with confidence and the bright light of positive, eternal energy that flows all around you, making you the author of the power of beneficial thinking, repair my mind and soul from all the negative-thinking people who have camped around me. Engulf me once more with the powers of positive thinking.

Send me your spirit of persistence, foresight, and understanding. Follow me through this stage of my life, turning doubt and fear into courage, and place in me a fearless spirit so that I may conquer my inner fears. Author and Perfecter of Faith, Savior of all men, make my life one of adventure and courage, removing this stagnant cloud of unsuccessful ventures and turning these negative thoughts into successful ones.

Selah.

81

DIET AND DIETING

Let me be healthy, my living one, God the Father. I feel my steps slowing down, and my breathing is becoming difficult. LORD, My doctor, says I need to be on a diet (*because of high cholesterol*). Be with me, O Dear LORD; give me the power to undergo and sustain this demanding task.

Let me live and be healthy, breathing one, God the Father. I feel my steps slowing down, and breathing is becoming difficult. LORD, My doctor, says I need to be on a diet (because of high cholesterol). Choose for me, O Mighty One, the healthy diet program, making this my request possible.

Let me live and be healthy, My Persisting One, God the Father. I feel my steps slowing down, and my breathing is becoming difficult. LORD, My doctor, says I need to be on a diet (*because of high cholesterol*). Give me discipline, strength, and courage to complete this task. Let me be healthy, my Living One, God the Father.

I feel my steps slowing down, and breathing is becoming difficult. My doctor says I need to be on a diet (high cholesterol). Immanuel, choose the right foods for me to nourish my body. Take away the symptoms of depression and anxiety that are hindering me from maintaining this diet. "But I discipline my body and keep it under control, (*Corinthians 9:27 ESV*)
(*https://www.biblegateway.com/passage/?search=1+Corinthians +9:27&version=ES*)

Let me live and be healthy, my active one, God the Father. I feel my steps slowing down, and breathing becoming difficult. My doctor says I need to be on a diet (*high cholesterol*). Holy Deliverer, I am not ready to die.

Father, I need to practice healthy habits and eat healthy foods to maintain a healthy lifestyle while I am alive. Send me a doctor with an excellent diet plan. Save this shell of a human body and my internal organs. Help me adopt great eating habits and disciplines while protecting my body, mind, and soul, Jehovah.

Selah.

82

BAD NEWS ON HEALTH

Heavenly Father, hold my hands as I walk through this life that's filled with ups and downs. My trip to the doctor today has brought me nothing but bad news. As I go on my way, I know I did not come on this earth to stay. Let me continue to live happily and contented. If this is not your will, then make my journey back to your kingdom a painless and pleasurable journey.

Throughout my life's journey, if ever I did not know you personally and did not stop to acknowledge you in my prayers, O Dear LORD, with all of my strength and energy, I solemnly beg for your forgiveness. Take away this spirit of arrogance that has taken hold of me. Replace this spirit with humbleness and love for you. O Spiritual One, your faithfulness is fathomless and stretches out as far as eternity.

You, O LORD, whose faultlessness magnifies itself in the realms of heaven; you, who secretly kept me in spite of my faults, redeem my soul, sending me wisdom and strength to cope with this bad news on health (reader: name the health condition). I place my confidence in your hands, knowing your love is sufficient to see me through this disturbing news. Let this cup of bitterness pass from me.

I am holding on to your everlasting love. Bring me the healing that's necessary. My soul will rejoice, and I will continue to live with confidence, knowing that you heard my prayers and delivered me from this ordeal. I come to you in comfort, peace, and healing, kneeling at your feet. Forgive me for abusing this precious body.

LORD, bring fast healing through the power of Jesus Christ, our LORD, and Savior, in acknowledgment of the Blessed Sacred Heart of Our LORD and Savior.

Selah.

83

UNDERSTANDING SEX

LORD, give me wisdom, courage, and understanding to teach my children the joy, responsibilities, and conscience of engaging in the act of sex. Help me to show them the power of abstinence and control of their bodies and minds, the great High Priest of Wisdom and Understanding. Go forth and multiply the earth; take stock, children of God. It is better not to put the cart before the horse.

Have an education and understanding of life before you start engaging in the act of having sex and unwanted children. You will not want to be responsible for those crying, always-hungry, starving-for-food-and-attention little persons when LORD when you are in no position to take care of them. All Mighty LORD, give me the wisdom, courage, and understanding to teach my children the joy, responsibilities, and conscience of engaging in sex.

Help me show them the power of abstinence and being in control of their bodies. The Great High Priest, send your loving-kindness, wisdom, understanding, and patience for me to be comfortable with myself when giving the appropriate information to my children about the consequences of having unprotected sex. Go forth and multiply the earth; take stock; push for an education. Even take one or two classes in early childhood education or human growth and development before you have children.

Don't abuse them when they are seeking your understanding and attention. Ask the LORD for his patience. Mighty Father, show women and men how to refrain from abusing their children's bodies and minds "And ye fathers and mothers, provoke, exasperate not your children to wrath (anger)," (*Ephesians 6:4KJB*). "Do not aggravate your children, for they will become discouraged." (*Colossians 3:21NLT*). LORD, give me the wisdom, courage, and understanding to teach my kids the joy, conscience, and responsibility of sex.

Great High Priest, help us to care for our children. Go forth and multiply the earth. Misguided children themselves want to love and attention and look for love in all the wrong places. Great Father, the first commandment mentions love and brings the joy of the resurrection. You, LORD, who holds wisdom in your bosom, give me the good sense, courage, and understanding to teach my children the joy, responsibilities, and conscience of engaging in sex.

Help me to teach them the power of abstinence and being in control of their bodies. Great High Priest, look down on me with tender mercies. Go forth and multiply the earth. Restless children need friendship, patience, and understanding, ever loving Father, the joy of the universe, the infinite wisdom of joy and blissfulness. Precious LORD, give me the good sense, courage, and understanding to teach my children the joy, responsibilities, and conscience of engaging in sex.

Help me show them the power of abstinence and being in control of their bodies, Great High Priest. Look down on me with tender mercies. Go forth and multiply the earth, innocents. Suffer the children not to come unto God. Faithful witness, speak to my heart, sincerely caring LORD God of creation.

Selah.

84

NEEDS

LORD, fill all of my needs according to your riches in heaven. Fill me up, fulfilling all my needs. My needs met according to the Lord's loving-kindness; your grace is bountiful and generous. Angry and disappointed am I, with all of my past efforts and failures. Forgive me, Mighty One, who granted me lots of blessings and provided me with never-ending favors. I am renewing my request for brand-new favors.

Grant me new flavors. Grant me these favors in the name of our LORD and Savior, precious Lamb, Jesus Christ, who enriches my soul and blesses my cupboards, pantries, and entire home. Supply my needs according to your riches in heaven, so there is no need for me to beg or compromise my soul among men or women on earth. Mighty LORD, bless these new flavors you bring, to enhance my soul to more joyous, happiness, and contentment.

Keep me happy and close to you. You alone are my redeemer and my supplier. I will rejoice and be glad about humankind speaking hope and encouragement. You will be pleased with me in your temple. You will supply my needs for the world to see and hear forever, I give your name praises from here to eternity. My needs will be fulfilled to change hearts and spread love in your name, bountiful Father of the Universe.

Renew your everlasting might, build a pure temple in your name and your name alone, and leave the doubters and disbelievers behind in confusion and disarray. Blessed is the LORD God. God, Jehovah, bring them to shame, those who tried to waste my time, taking away my talents and joy to use for their purposes. Let them see themselves and place them at the bottom of my feet, those who took me for granted.

Lift me up and supply all of my needs according to your riches in heaven, forever praising and worshiping in your name. Keep me true to myself and your love for me, O LORD. Give thanks to the LORD, for he is good forever.

Make a joyful noise For the LORD is good; his mercy is everlasting, and his truth endureth to all generations. (*Psalm 100:5 KJV*) (*https:// www.biblegateway.com/passage/?*)

Selah.

85

THE JOY OF THE LORD

O LORD, make me know your delight with each breath that's inside me. He who is filled with joy at all times, even unknowingly. The grace of the LORD is right. His mercy will endure forever; serve the LORD with wisdom and understanding. Joyous and happy is he or she who is grounded in the LORD. He or she is a delight to the LORD and the angels in heaven.

The joy of the LORD magnifies and tantalize. Moon and the stars shine for him. The rock praises him. The faithful and genuine one, I pay homage to you, O Mighty One. Some try to steal my joy and confidence in you, not knowing that I have come from the LORD God, Jehovah. Know the LORD your God, and bring yourself under his mercy.

He will lighten your load; he will provide all your needs and replenish your soul with the joy of life. When things are not going right, give him praise and thanks. Don't wait for things to go bad before you call Jesus. Whether things are good or dreadful, praise him; he is the Kings of Kings. Serve him, the LORD of LORDS. You will have joy and confidence in your life.

Know that he is with you through all your trials and tribulations, in all things. Jesus promised never to leave you or forsake you. He is calling upon you to trust and obey, Listen to his quiet voice. "Make a joyful noise unto the LORD, all ye lands." (*Psalm 100 KJV*). (*https://www.biblegateway.com/passage/?*)
When friends let you down, make a joyful noise to the LORD.

If you lose your job and are hopeless, if you trust in him, he always makes a way out of no way. Call upon him in the middle of the night. He will make a way. Come; let us utter a joyful, happy noise to the LORD. He regularly makes a way out of no way, proclaims a joyful noise. To the LORD, He is the bright morning star.

Yahweh's infinite eyes watch over the souls of men. LORD the author and perfection of my faith, make a joyful noise, to the LORD, he oversees the souls of men. Make a joyful noise quietly in your heart. (*Selah*), O LORD, make me know your delight with each breath that's inside me.

For he or she that's filled with joy and hope at all times, even unknowingly, the grace of the LORD is right. His mercy will endure forever. Serve the LORD with wisdom and understanding. Joyous, happy, and confident are they who is grounded in the LORD. They are a delight to the LORD and his angels.

The joy of the LORD is magnified and tranquil. The moon and the stars shine for him. The rock praises him. Faithful and Genuine Father, I pay homage to you, O Mighty One. Some tried to steal my joy and confidence in you. With the help of the angels, you stood and surrounded my soul with protection.

All that I am comes from the LORD, God Jehovah. You must know the LORD your God. Come under his mercy, and he will lighten your load; he will provide all your needs. He will replenish your soul with the joy of life. If things are not going right, give him praise and thanks. Don't wait for things to go terribly; call upon him.

Whether things are good or bad, praise him. He is the King of Kings. Serve him, LORD of LORDS. You will experience joy and confidence in life. Know that he is with you through all your trials and tribulations. Through these things, he promises never to leave you or forsake you. He is calling upon you to trust and obey. Listen to his quiet voice.

Make a cheerful noise to the LORD, for his mercy endures forever. When friends let you down, make a joyful noise to the LORD. If you lose your job, he will consistently make a way out of no way. In the middle of the night, make a cheerful noise. He always makes a way out of no way. Make a joyful noise. He is making way for me right now.

"Enter into his gates with thanksgiving, and into his courts with praise: be thankful unto him, and bless his name."
(*Psalm100:4 (KJV*) (*https://www.biblegateway.com/passage/?*)

Selah.

86

BORROWING MONEY

LORD, mightier than ever, everlasting Father, show me how to earn and manage my money. Send good friends to show me the way. LORD, help me to forgive my creditors. O LORD, you are an excellent steward. The banks are calling me for their money, exceeding my credit limit, and owing on my student loans.

My house is in foreclosure; give me the strength to increase my money and control my spending habits. Cover me with your grace, and forgive my debtors. Wash away my debts in your blood. Show me ways to comply with my creditors. I know your precious blood was shed for me. Shine your light on me and my financial situation.

Give me the power to satisfy my creditors. Send wisdom from above and hand me a good favor to pay off these debts, satisfying my creditors. I tried finding a job, pawned my jewelry, and sold my blood to satisfy my creditors. I am at the last straw. Forgive my creditors, for they are charging me too much in the interest rate. "You shall not charge interest on loans" (*Exodus 22:25*).

The interest rate is making it difficult for me to repay these loans. I blocked out the phone numbers of my creditors, changed my name, and ran for cover, so they do not bother me. These debts are killing me and stealing my joy. Make haste; have mercy on me; rescue me from my creditors and this misery.

Call my lawyers; get me out of this nightmare. Ask, and it shall be given you; seek, and ye shall find; knock, and it shall be opened unto you: (*Matthew* 7:7(ASV) LORD, you did not hear me, now I am sleeping in my car.

Selah.

87

BREAKING UP WITH SOMEONE

He is the way, the truth, and the life. (*John 14:6 ESV*) Mighty God, the light of my life, I am not happy in this relationship. My partner wants me to compromise my faith. You sent you're only begotten Son who redeemed us from fear, negative communist infiltration, and confusion.

And not the enslavement of the mind, body, and soul of any man or woman, this relationship is unhealthy for me. This man has no intention of committing to me and marrying me. LORD, help me to set myself free. You were with King David when he won many battles over the Philistines.

You were with Martha as she balanced service with worshiping and trusting you, LORD, you were with the Samaritan woman as she drew water from the well. (*John 4:7 (ASV)*) Maybe he would see the light and change his mind and not come around me. But he keeps insisting.

We are always arguing, and his infidelity is haunting my soul. There is no peace in this relationship, only mind control, misuse, manipulation, and abuse. LORD, restore my soul to an earlier time when there was joy, peace, happiness, and confidence in my life.

Hold my heart deep in the palms of your hands. O LORD, I put my trust in you alone. Hold me through these disturbing emotions. Lord, I have to break up with this guy. I was looking for love and understanding from the wrong source. When you, O, LORD, was guiding me along, forgive me.

Precious Father, provide a safe place for me to lay my head. Give me a steady spirit, so I don't succumb to his temptations and violent threats. Protect me from this psychological mind-changing affair. This game is tearing away at my soul. There is not inner peace.

Furthermore, protect me from this silent partner who confesses to being in love with me. When we venture out to have fun, however, he looks at and discusses other women in my presence. All he does is try to distract me from taking my joy away.

Alpha and Omega set me up high in another place from this misery. My husband or boyfriend a silent control freak; bring peace and honesty to the heart and soul of this mate. And give me a clean exit out of this relationship.

Give me the strength to let go of this torture's pains.

I am being used and abused, physically and psychologically, the latter being the worst form of wrongdoing. LORD, he is messing with the mind or trying to destroy my body, mind, and soul. I know how real love is supposed to feel.

And this sure doesn't feel like love to me.

True love lifts up the soul, not pull it down.

Rise, O Heavenly Father, and save me. I beg you, for you are the Kingdom and Power and Glory. I will forever worship you in strength and truth.

Refresh my soul to find genuine and kind love again.

Selah.

88

TRANQUILITY

Mighty LORD, thank you for protecting me, day and night, your love awakens me to this peaceful day. How lovely and peaceful. LORD, keep your spirits around me at all times, never-ending and genuinely, guiding and protecting me through this day.

You are the author of tranquility, radiating joy, the inner joy that comes from within and flows from within. You give quiet confidence through your mercy and love, just like the lakes and the waterways continuously flow, stimulating the mind and soul.

Your love has brought tranquility to my life in ways no one would ever know. Gracious and loving Father of the universe. Thank you for these gifts and for gently and slowly streaming thoughts of positive energy. I am grateful your perseverance, give me the courage to nurture and partake of these gifts of life.

You bestowed on me the courage and joy, knowing that nothing is impossible with you and all things are possible with you on the throne. Let me be an example to those who are trying to find their way in this world. Lighten up their lives along the way, bringing them to a place of serenity and confidence in you.

O LORD Great Father, let them know to be still and know that you are God, all by yourself, when you do things the right way, the way in which the Mighty Father intended it to be. When things go wrong, his steady hands are there to scoop you up, disentangling any unforeseen complications and obstacles the enemies place in your way.

He created soothing and reassuring calming waters.

Be still and know the Mighty One who rules over the moon and stars. He may not come when you think you need him, but he is on time when you need him. His Grace is right on time when you call, all the time, whether rain or shine.

Selah.

89

FACING YOUR FEARS

I am walking through the valley of decision. I will Fear no evil; no weapon formed against me shall prosper! Take my soul, O LORD; let no man instill fear into my heart and soul. Mighty LORD, give me constant courage, day by day. Prepare the way for me, O LORD, as I go, removing any obstacles that may hinder my course, including myself.

LORD, you faced your fears on the cross and came out the conqueror. Fear cannot live in the house of the LORD, nor can it be injected into God's children by nonbelievers or obstacles. Circumstances and confusion cannot penetrate my soul with fear. Give me real courage, O LORD so that I can overpower the spirit of fear and doubt.

Stretch forth your Mighty hands to protect me from all fears. Some men and women lost, in their minds and afraid are pessimistic and try to trip me up with their insecurities and confusion. They do this to steal my mojo. Heavenly Father, let them not sidetrack me from my glory and ruin my success or circumstance.

You, all Mighty LORD, created me without fear. Let no incidents or men or women in this life or life beyond discourage me or steal my energy. The Mighty LORD is on his throne daily, strengthening his children in the way they should go. I will still listen to his soft, even-so-silent voice as he gives me the courage to face my fears.

He is listening to my prayers and quietly supplying my pure soul with the sincerity to face my fears.

Selah.

90

LONELINESS

Loneliness is the LORDS way of working on your behalf, making you healthy. Speaking to your heart, take the time to enjoy your solitude, for God is trying to spend time with you, reaching and enriching you through his Holy Spirit, preparing you for future battles. Spend time with the God of hosts. He is the light of the world.

Loneliness is the LORD working with you, making you stronger. His voice is quiet and still, Holy Spirit joy of the world. Take these lonely moments and turn them into positive experiences, spending time with your LORD. Let me see all of your splendor and glory, my portion in the land of the living.

Loneliness is the LORD working with you from the inside out, keeping you away from dangerous souls who will swallow you up and devour your soul. In times of weakness, and loneliness a void is created in your mind to make you feel less worthy of the LORDS blessings.

If you are not careful and become restless, your action and decisions can be harmful.

Mighty Savior, save me from those who will destroy me; guard me against this awful spirit called loneliness. LORD, take this moment to spend time with me. Send me honest, confident people who can understand and care for me, enriching my soul. All Mighty LORD, you are my secret dwelling place.

LORD, take refuge in my home, disputing all distorted spirits that may enter through my door. When I am lonely and in doubt send your angels to comfort and protect my mind. Let me take this time of isolation to converse with you, and rest on the LORDS mighty inner strength.

Find productive activities to fill the void. The thought of loneliness considers, you spending time with the Heavenly Father. Learn to control your mind if not you can head for a disaster in your mind. The LORD will speak to your mind of the service, or services he would like you to partake.

The LORD promises you through his words that he will never leave you or forsake you. Even if it appears as though he is not there, his loving spirit is always there to keep and guide you.

Selah.

91

GIVING BACK

LORD, make me know the principle of giving back. There are those who take and take all their lives, and at no time do they give back. They never know there is a principle called giving and receiving and giving back. Mighty Father, we would not get anywhere if we didn't give back to our friends, society, nature, and community.

LORD, you're the chief principal example of giving.

You sent your only begotten Son to die on the cross for our sins. Innocent Father of the universe, beloved son of God, an abundance of joy comes from giving. You gave your children nature and its beauty. We have to give to others.

If we don't know that at some point in our lives, then we are doomed. Let the spirit of giving engulf members of a world that's in crises. The cities, townships, nations, ghettos, suburbs, and communities— make them live in harmony with each other, sharing and respecting.

Helping and giving back to teach and assist others 'in the communities and will make life the best for themselves and others. Someone had to make life in a superior way for us, so why can't we create a life better for someone else? Make someone's life special. Life is a gift from God. It is special.

Giving back from your heart lifts up the spirits of the dead, lifeless, mindless souls lost in a society of despair, and makes life and civilization better and livable. Give what you have—time, money, talent, experience, skills. Whatever, you have, the LORD can use to build his kingdom and make it work for his children.

Mighty Father who rules the universe and wants the best for the children of humankind, the arm of the LORD wants you to look out for the unfortunate, hopeless, fatherless, abused and misused, old, sick, and weak. Do these things without robbing and stealing from the weak, helpless and the weary ones.

Love your neighbor; the strong must protect the feeble. However, the healthy must not destroy the sick. Show kindness to those in need; be polite. Show patience to the lost souls. In the process, you might save them by showing them the love and glory of God the Father, and you also could save yourself.

Selah.

92

FORGIVENESS

Only begotten son of God, give me the courage to forgive those who trespass against me in life and death. Let me not take misgivings and misunderstandings into my hands but instead turn them over to you. For you are the Redeemer, the judge, and the jury. However, give me the power to renounce and fight back, giving me victory.

Only begotten the Son of God, give me the courage to forgive those who trespass against me in life and death, Let me not take misgivings and misunderstandings into my hands but instead turn them over to you. For you are the Redeemer, the judge, and the jury. Even so, give me the power to disown and fight back, giving me victory.

Only begotten son of God, give me the courage to forgive those who trespass against me in life and death. Let me not take misgivings and misunderstandings into my hands but instead turn them over to you. For you are the Redeemer, the judge, and the jury. However, give me the power to relinquish and fight back, containing my emotions, giving me victory over this ordeal.

Only begotten son of God, give me the courage to forgive those who trespass against me in life and death. Let me not take misgivings and misunderstandings into my hands but instead turn them over to you. For you are the Redeemer, the judge, and the jury. However, give me the power to reject and fight back, giving me victory over greed and jealousy.

Only begotten son of God, give me the courage to forgive those who trespass against me in life and death. Let me not take misgivings and misunderstandings into my hands but instead turn them over to you. For you are the Redeemer, the judge, and the jury. Even so, give me the power to disown and fight back, giving me victory.

Only begotten son of God, give me the courage to forgive those who trespass against me in life and death. Let me not take misgivings and misunderstandings into my hands but instead turn them over to you. For you are the Redeemer, the judge, and the jury. Nevertheless, give me the power to repudiate and fight back, giving me victory.

Selah

93

NATURE

Thank you, Mother Nature, for being there for us through creation. Your never-ending love, patience, fortitude, and commitment to humankind are consistent with the timing of the LORD God. You were the still-dormant creature who lay in the darkness, patiently waiting for the voice of God to resurrect your soul. Your never-failing love and commitment to the heavenly Father are ageless and constant.

He tamed the darkness to work together in harmony with the light. Its nature at no time seems quiet, never-failing, dark, nature, not caring, cannot be tamed. Realms of colored sparks penetrating into the light, growing, watering, burning, blowing, always guarding, lifting up your children, and forgetting others, You, Mother Nature, were in the dark, stumbling around, waiting for the light to shine on your miserable existence.

The LORD breathed life and spoke the word light into your existence. The light manifested itself. Let there be light. It was unceasing and never-ending. Whatever instructions you gave at the start of creation, You, O God, created Mighty nature, obedient to you. The LORD blesses faithful to nature, persistently and forever loyal to the LORDS instructions, since the days of old to the present, fulfilling according to the book of scrolls.

You were and still are faithful, caring, carrying on, and dispensing undoubting energy to create. Excellent Father is proud of you. He takes pride and has fulfilled glory with your loyalty and commitment to his heavenly works. You are alone, Nature, with the Mighty blessings of all Mighty Father. You should be satisfied with the part the LORD gave you.

We love and honor your great nature, the mother and the keeper of the earth, the tides of joy and gratitude paying homage to you, so organized and orderly from centuries gone, never failing to serve humankind per the Mighty Father's instructions as he goes on his way. Blessed Nature—consistent and everlasting goddess of wisdom and truth.

O magnificent Nature, how diligently you shine. You will have a place in my heart continually and always, seeing, touching, imagining. O blessed Nature, how magically your love encompasses me. The LORD breathes life into Mother Nature, giving her his Mighty power to enter the light, the LORD God, Creator of heaven and earth. Fire, water, air, earth, light, and the resurrection, nature as calm and gentle as a lamb, also have the powers to be brutally harsh and unforgiving.

Selah.

94

DOCTORS

I need both conventional and unconventional medicines.
Conventional versus unconventional medicine—chant!

Yeshua of Nazareth, who healed the sick?
Yeshua of Nazareth, who healed the sick?
Grant us healing divinity through doctors.
In spite of how messed up this world turned out to be, no one wants
to die.

I need both conventional and unconventional medicines.
Conventional versus unconventional medicine—chant! Yeshua of
Nazareth, who healed the sick?
Yeshua of Nazareth, who healed the sick?

Grant us healing divinity through doctors.
Even though they are xenophobic and confused, everybody wants
compassion and mercy at the end of their lives.

I need both conventional and unconventional medicines.
Conventional versus unconventional medicine—chant! Yeshua of
Nazareth, who healed the sick?

Yeshua of Nazareth, who healed the sick?
Grant us healing divinity through doctors.
Despite they steal and abuse children, everyone deserves to live a
healthy life.

I need both conventional and unconventional medicines,
Conventional versus unconventional medicine—chant!

The children are dying from cancer and other strange Petri-dish diseases. We need both conventional and unconventional medicines. Conventional versus unconventional medicine—chant! Yeshua of Nazareth, who healed the sick?

Yeshua of Nazareth, who healed the sick?
Grant me divinity healing through doctors.
Yeshua of Nazareth speaks to every fiber in body
As I beg for forgiveness for poisoning blood with unnatural substance.
Distress me and detoxify

I need both conventional and unconventional medicines. Conventional versus unconventional medicine—chant! Yeshua of Nazareth, who healed the sick?

Yeshua of Nazareth, who healed the sick?
Grant me healing divinity through doctors,
When things get cloudy, they curse the LORD. However, they sit in limbo, waiting for the LORD to call their names.

I need both conventional and unconventional medicines, Conventional versus unconventional medicine—chant!

Yeshua of Nazareth, who healed the sick?
Yeshua of Nazareth, who healed the sick?
Grant me divinity healing through our doctors.
My body needs both conventional and unconventional medicine to function well.

A tower of strength, who was given the power to raise the dead, shows us health, mercy, and peace.

Selah.

95
TEACHERS

LORD, help the teachers to teach the children and stop playing with their young minds. Teach the children not to steal. Teachers speak the truth; don't hinder God's kingdoms. Teach the children not to kill and steal. Teach them not to bully other kids. Mighty Father, these kids are our precious cargo, brought here on earth to serve your Kingdom and glory.

Give the teachers the wisdom and courage to focus on the truth about your kingdom. Teach the children not to steal. Teach the children not to kill. Teach them not to bully other kids. O, LORD! Guide and protect our children's minds from misguided information; give them a sturdy mental foundation.

Mighty LORD, when night falls and morning comes, send your light. Teach the children not to steal. Teachers speak the truth; don't hinder God's kingdom. Teach the children not to kill. Teach them not to bully other kids. In part, we are responsible for one another's well-being.

It is not just loving them first but loving others as they love themselves, so your Kingdom fulfilled. Teach the children not to steal. Teachers speak the truth; don't hinder God's kingdom. Teach the children not to kill. Teach them not to bully other kids. Confusion must disappear from their minds so they can comprehend their schooling and life's purpose.

The truth revealed through the children. Teach the children not to steal. Teachers speak the truth; don't hinder God's kingdom. Teach the children not to kill. Teach them not to bully other kids. Teach the children not to steal from senior citizens. Teach them to respect, shame on you adults because you were supposed to teaching the children the truth. Then you expect them to respect for themselves and society.

You are the children's bridge to the community. God has entrusted you with their minds, hearts, and well-being. Burn in hellfire as you goes long teaching children the opposite of the truth.

Selah.

96

INDULGENCE

Heavenly Father, help me to know you are there. Let me indulge myself in your Holy Spirit. Be there for me in time of darkness and fear. Give me the courage to know that you are there for me. Kind and merciful Father, when my mother and father betrayed me, I turned to drugs and alcohol to ease the pain. Let me feel your loving, tender kindness and loving mercy. Keep me in your devoted realm. Selah! Shouting out to Jesus Christ for he is the LORD!

Engulf my soul with your love and courage; let me indulge myself in your Holy Spirit. Let the light from your Mighty Kingdom illuminate its radiant love inside of me. Rescue me from my indulgence [reader: name habits] and make me feel your gentle spirit. LORD, disciplines me so that I can break this habit. Father, bring rationality and tranquility to my soul. Rebuke these unclean spirits that are making it difficult for me to quit my negative habits.

Lift my human consciousness, balancing my purpose in life. Let me indulge myself in your Holy Spirit, thoughts, and actions; take away my disappointments. Anxiety and depression cause me to indulge in the bad habit (*reader name the habit*). You are God All Mighty. Only you can see beyond the minds of men. Mighty Father, my friends have detached themselves from me and have lost their human caring, nurturing instincts. They have replaced it with evil.

Mighty Father, they have detached themselves from the actual meaning of living, loving, sharing, respecting, and saving Africa and Israel from powerful men so your Kingdom can fulfill. O indulging the provocative spirit of evil, release, the minds of the evil men who forbid people of good nature to live in peace and harmony with love and nurturing their children.

Furthermore, the firm spirit of rebelliousness and confusion is present in the minds of young men governed by distinguished men, who turn them into psychopaths of destruction. They are indulging themselves in the art conformity through war and destruction. These unclean spirits are making it difficult for the world to live in peace, harmony, love, and understanding.

LORD, through god's sake, Mighty Father help, me to quit their harmful habits. I ask these things in the name of Jesus Christ, the Son of God. Holy Father, make these blessings available to all men. Drive out these unclean spirits, allowing them the ability to change from within and build their communities on your teachings. That instructs us to embrace love, kindness, and gentleness and to show respect to ourselves and fellow humans.

Selah.

97

GAMBLING

O Mighty LORD, I am seeking your mercy and guidance. Have mercy on me. My wife and children are upset with me; they are all disgusted with me, the spirit of confusion, greed, and wanting things. The easy way has taken hold of my mind and forced me into the arms of the casinos and the horse track to gamble and squander my hard-earned money.

My life is in shambles, for I have allowed the spirit of chance, uncertainty, and irrationality to enter my mind and soul. Send forth your Mighty Spirit of contentment and good stewardship to heal me. Send someone or something to guide me to a place where I can receive the help I need to overcome my gambling addiction. Rearrange me, O LORD, and be my help in this time of need.

LORD, I took money to spend for maintenance of my household and squandered it on gambling. Mighty LORD, hear my prayers. "I pray in your son's name, Jesus Christ." Intervene on my behalf and set me free from this addiction. My father is disappointed, and my mother is praying. I can't help myself, O Father. The urge for this game is defeating me. (*Reader name the* game)

I place my mind in your trust. O LORD, lift up my soul. Gentle Lamb, you alone has the power to redeem me from this awful, undesirable habit. It is like cancer in my mind that is slowly consuming me and destroying my family. Send your spiritual forces, and purge me, rescue me. Save me from this evil and unfulfilling habit, in the name of Jesus Christ.

Lord, when you deal with the devil you change but the devil doesn't. I give thanks and praise to you for my deliverance, All Mighty God.

Selah

98

LOVING YOURSELF

Heavenly Father, teach me; show me how to love myself. I feel as though no one cares; no one has time to understand me. They studied my weakness and shortcoming and used it against me to control me. LORD, I am experiencing problems with my self-image. I am confused and consumed with self-hatred. The media, my mother, and friends trust others over me.

The yearning for love and appreciation is destroying my self-worth and burning a deep cavity down in my soul. The establishment is daily confusing my mind with regards to my identity. I have no idea. What's considered beautiful, healthy hair, skin tones, anger, destructive behaviors, and attitude? Everlasting Father, a trap was laid, filled with distortion and confusion. I cannot love myself the way you instructed. Self-hatred has engulfed my soul.

Shine your light within my heart and soul and make me love myself the way you created me. The thoughts I think are lower than the thoughts of an animal. I have children out of wedlock without consequences. Meanwhile, I am verbal, psychologically, mentally, and physically beating and abusing these kids to death, until they end up in prison or on drugs, alcohol, or they turn themselves over to strange gods or bring an end their lives.

LORD, the beast of incest, has completely taken over my mind and soul. My virtues and intellect comprised. Teach me to love for me, acceptance of me, and me for myself. Engulf me with your tender mercies and fortitude; society has condemned me. They look down on me because I am different and love myself. They look down at me as if I was responsible for killing Jesus Christ. LORD, I cannot help myself. I love myself. I have to be me and cannot allow others to determine who I am and how I should live. My enemies have laid traps to block my way, making me want to hate myself. Only you alone, LORD, can save and lift me up from this madness. Lord, you taught me to love myself first and then others. Unconditional love, LORD, is the gift you give to yourself and your children.

Help me to love and appreciate me when others do not or have not loved me. *Akal ʽEsh LORD*, The keeper of the gate I will honor you for the rest of my life, giving you alone the praises. Search my heart and see a considerate, gentle, caring person who thinks everyone should be happy, contented, and respectful to each other. However, LORD, I looked around and saw those whose minds and souls are not right, they fight against the chosen ones.

They don't love themselves and need your divine intervention. Take the self-hatred and fear away from the minds of men and women. Fortify their minds to combat this self-hatred, so they too can live in joy and happiness. You are the supreme ruler of life and death. Men or women can never replace you or your love because they are helpless and fooled by the glitter and the powers of Life. Have mercy on them and help them.

Selah.

99

MORNING

Faithful God and gentle Father, morning gently opened up to a brand-new day. The sun is rising in the east and slowly coming into view. I have to face the morning and bring myself to start my day. My night filled with sleeplessness and haunting dreams.

Faithful God and gentle Father, morning gently opened up to a brand-new day. Help me to stay mindful of things at this moment. Keep my mind steady and my soul in perfect peace. You are my guide and protector.

Faithful God and gentle Father, morning gently opened up to a brand-new day. Send your reassuring spirit to calm my nerves. As I sort out my day, save me from worrying about the things I cannot change. Replace all my fears and with self-confidence and joy.

Faithful God and gentle Father, morning gently opened up to a brand-new day. As I usher in the new day, channel your patience, love, and grace into me. Keep the spirit of anger and concern away from my realm.

Faithful God and gentle Father, morning gently opened up to a brand-new day. Help me understand the people I come across. Let your love and joy engulf my soul, spilling over on the lives of others.

Faithful God and gentle Father, morning gently opened up to a brand-new day. Hold me with your soft hands and comfort my soul. Bring steadfast comfort and assurance. Save me from morning anxiety. Faithful God and tender Father, morning gently opened up to a brand-new day. Your light and confidence will take me through this day.

Selah.

100

CONFUSION

Dear LORD and Mighty Savior, my mind is experiencing great confusion. I have strange thoughts of ending my life. Every attempt I have made with marriage, friends, Mother, Father, business, and people has failed miserably. Trade and employment efforts have ended up at an impasse.

My wages are low, and debts are high. I have invested energy, time, and money in others and business ventures and did not spend quality time with myself. The creditors are calling and adding more and more stress to the confusion in my life. I cannot undertake this stress and these burdens. I feel at times as if the whole world is against me.

Others who cannot cope with their confusion are trying to saddle me with their confusion. My friends have all deserted me. Now it's hard for me to look at myself in the mirror and feels good about myself. Let me know, O Dear LORD, which way I should go. Stretch forth your Mighty hands to assist me.

Let me feel your love and understanding to block out these urges. If there is anything worth redeeming in my soul, then LORD, save me. Rescue me, LORD, from these depressive, suicidal thoughts. I filled my life with faith, joy, and hope; for my future and now my days are consumed with disappointing thoughts of the way my life has turned out.

Forgive me, Heavenly Father, if I have unknowingly or willingly sinned against you. Send your steadfastness, Holy Father. I submit myself to your will. My request to you is to replace my worn-out disappointing spirit, that's filled with discord and resentment, with a mind filled with new joy and lasting opportunities.

Turn my brand-new efforts into a complete success. Save me from these thoughts of confusion and suicide.

Selah.

101

DRUGS

Holy Father, help me to overcome this dependence on drugs and alcohol. Horn of salvation; unleash your powerful love and mercy. Send me healing for my mind, body, and soul. Holy Father, this strong negative spirit of drug and alcohol dependence is taking over my mind.

Has taken hold of my heart, and it's eating away at the core of my soul like a cancerous cell. I have lost all my earthly possessions and lost my livelihood. I sold everything I ever possessed to satisfy this demon who lives inside of me. Mother and Father have given up on me.

My friends have all forsaken me. Reach down from above and save me—save me from this misery. Day to day, I live with constant trauma; I can't seem to find someone to love and understand me. Mercy and more forgiveness, I ask of you. I put my trust and faith in your hands.

Author and perfecter of faith, my life is filled with hope that you will deliver me from drugs. The Redeemer of hope, my faith is in you. You said if I have faith as small as a mustard seed, you will honor. You said a little of faith is all you need to work with to make a change in someone's life.

Mighty one, make my taste buds and desires for these substances. Disappear, I use and misuse and look forward to abusing myself with these drugs. I use and misuse and look forward to abusing myself with drugs and alcohol.

Mighty one, make my taste buds and desires for these substances disappear. My dependence on these substances is starting to taste bitter in my mouth. And my soul is craving its intake. LORD, this habit will fade from my mind with the help of your intervention.

My thoughts at this time are so clouded and are taken over by the monstrosity of this addiction. It can't seem to detach me from its use. First and last, release me from this dependency and miss the call of death that's knocking at my door. Send your strong hands, and rescue me from myself and these negative.

These dreadful thoughts that subdue me to this chemical dependency don't turn my soul over to death. I will worship you in strength and truth and speak of your name to all who reside on the earth.

Faithful and genuine Father hears my prayers and comforts me with your assurance.

Selah.

102

UNDERSTANDING OTHERS

God, firstborn of all creations, give me the wisdom and understanding to help others without harming myself. Give me patience and endurance to recognize the failures and discontent in others. We all are different but are the same, in ways unknown. Bestow understanding in others.

Don't throw your love away to swine. You, O Mighty LORD, warned us daily in your words. The most Powerful Father who defeated death on the cross and is constantly watching over me. Take care of me, so I don't allow others to use and abuse me. Teach me to be diligent in all things. Shield me from the mistakes and misjudgment of others.

Light to the nations; keep me confident, knowing that you are in command of my life. LORD, you are the highest tower, my strength and hiding place. You alone have the authority to protect me in battle and give me victory. Overall, you are my high tower, fortress, and a tower of strength.

Bring understanding to others so that I can live in this world in peace and harmony. Heavenly Father quietly whispers in the heart and soul of your servant, replacing fear with understanding and blessings. "Blessed is he who comes in the name of the LORD; "(*Psalm 118:26(NASV*) (*http://biblehub.com/psalms/118-26.htm*) he or she shall have victory over all situations.

Evette Forde

"Fear of the LORD is the beginning of" wisdom and understanding" (*Proverbs 1:7 NASV*) (*http://biblehub.com/proverbs/1-7.htm*) Respect for oneself and others are the key to civilization and the future of humankind. Know yourself and your purpose in life. No one has the power over another and cannot subdue or force his or her will on others. LORD God of Host, send down fire and brimstone on those who for so long forced their will on others.

Selah.

103

SMILE

O, Dear LORD, keep this smile in my heart and on my face. Through all these trials and tribulations that come with life, keep me confident and thankful in your love, never failing me. Retain the joy in my heart and a smile on my face. Life has trials and tribulation, through these ordeals, it is not so bad after all, because God loves you, and he will take care of you. Smile, God loves you he always will.

He is always sending the sun and rain to replenish the earth, giving you food and light. He keeps you in perfect peace. In times of troubles, he sends his angels to assist you through the hard times. He gives you the opportunity to acquire talents and skills to make a living. Smile—God loves you even though jerks are messing up.

Smile—are lost. God loves you when you. He sends his angels to guide you. Back home, not one of his sheep shall be led astray. He will break down all boundaries to recover his lost children. The house of the LORD filled with joy and laughter, so smile. God loves you.

Put aside all your worry and fear of one another. God's sake is sufficient to carry you through. Look up and love the LORD. He is good. His mercy is everlasting; he will carry you through your struggle on earth. The light of the LORD is upon the earth, searching for true believers of the Word.

A smile is better than a frown. God loves you. His love is everlasting. Make a joyful noise unto the LORD. His loving mercy is forever. Put a smile in your heart and turn over all your worry and fear to the LORD. He is sufficient to carry your burdens; capable is he who rules the world and its inhabitants. When the going gets rough, and it's hard to smile. Take the time out to smile.

Selah.

104

ENJOYING LIFE

LORD, show how me how to protect myself from the life's doldrums and appreciate the simple things created by your hands. Let me enjoy life with vigor, curiosity, and adventure always knowing your strong hands are there to guide me, making sure no one steals my joy and happiness. Protect me from unhappiness and unhappy people, and help me to enjoy life among all of your creations.

Your endurance on the cross and resurrection has given me the rights to inherit joy, happiness, and confidence in your victory over death and so I enjoy my life. Blessed assurance knowing your love is mine and is sufficient to sustain me through this life. Problems come, and challenges go, but your love is everlasting and forever. LORD, keep me close to you, protecting my joy and happiness.

Sadness, discord, discontent, heartlessness, and unhappiness are all around me. Mighty LORD, keeper of the gate, misery likes company but finding joy and happiness come from you and you alone. Check yourselves before you wreck yourselves. The joy of the LORD is the tower of the tabernacle. Make a joyful noise to the LORD. His mercy is everlasting. Dwell at the moment and for the moment.

Life is too short and unpredictable. Live day to day; be kind to one another always. Try to find something nice to say to others, to extend a helping hand to those who are weak and hopeless. The LORD will open up the windows in heaven and pour out his blessings upon you. When you give, you may not reap the rewards from the people you assisted, the LORD will send a stranger to help you and give you your blessings. See the joy in your children and life, smile, and say hi.

To one another, make someone smile. See the love of God the Creator in the people you meet. Life is good and everlasting. You should be thankful you're still above the ground. Greet one another in the joy and happiness of the LORD. Say amen. Help if you can. You will find life's worthwhile. Thank you, Jesus, King of kings, and LORD of LORDS.

Selah

105

GOVERNMENT

King of Kings, the great Father, send intelligent men and women of wisdom and knowledge, with healthy hearts filled with courage, to carry us through these hard times of uncertainty and confusion. Pray for your government and the difficult decisions they must make daily. They too have to answer to the All Mighty God on behalf of his kingdom. Their powers belong to God. Pray for your government for the difficult decisions they have to make daily.

The King of Kings, the great Father, sends intelligent men and women with wisdom, knowledge, and healthy hearts to sustain and withhold past Constitutions that were once created by people of God. Keep these men's and women's minds rational, so they put God the Father first in every decision they make, honoring God the Father. Turn their deception into a constructive outcome for your children here on earth. Let these guys be a good example for their citizens.

Install in government leaders that their powers belong to God the Father. Pray for your government for the difficult decisions they must make regularly. The King of Glory, Heavenly Father, sends intelligent men and women with wisdom and strong hearts to help us through these difficult ordeals. Say prayers for your regime so that they will make rational, accurate decisions when governing our country, giving them integrity and power to solve the economy and the threat of war.

Pray for your government for the difficult decisions they must make every day. King of Radiance, King of Kings, LORD of LORDS, assist our government in making the right choices. As they pertain to the tent peg, the bow for battle, so they don't sell "us out for a few pieces of silver" (*Malcolm X freedom-rally-1960*) to make our lives miserable and unhappy. Pray for your government for the difficult decisions they have to make daily.

The King of Glory, Father, sends men of the spirit of old whose wisdom and steadfastness has kept us safe and from falling. God of the highest, be with us in this battle. They are forcing us to be weak and hopeless. Mighty LORD is resurrecting the powerful spirit of Sir Winston Churchill to carry us through these hard times, forgiving us for our past sins. Who the LORD has released from his or her transgression is free indeed.

Carry us through these daunting and challenging times. Pray for your government, their power, and glories; pray for the difficult decisions they must make daily. Mighty God of Hosts, give them the wisdom and strength to govern. There is light at the end of the tunnel, Creator of Israel.

"Success consists of going from failure to failure without loss of enthusiasm. If you're going through hell, keep going"—(Sir Winston Churchill)

Selah.

106

FEAR OF TERROR

Mighty LORD, LORD of the Universe, foreign forces have entered my world and have taken hold of the minds of men, leading them astray to make them evil and violent, causing them to perpetrate fear and doubt into the hearts and minds of Christians and other faiths. The children of Israel, the apples of your eye, are in danger.

Men in powerful places are deceiving and confusing, bringing harm and destruction to them and others.

Set forth your Mighty hands and preserve our minds. Prepare us to undertake this battle for our lives. Take hold of the task that's at hand, making boys into men; help us to be strong to resist these temptations.

Send the real spirits of your beloved prophets—King David, Moses, Meshach, Abednego, and Samson—to see us through this revolution of morbid ideas of violence and deception. LORD All Mighty; protect our families and us from propaganda, fear, and terrorism. Mighty LORD, your majesty delivers us from fear, and doubt gives us the courage to stand up for our ideals.

Keep us forever in your bosom; wrap and shield us with your shawl. Be with us through life and death, securing our souls for your coming kingdom. All Mighty God, the time is now for people of faith to come together and call upon the name of God to see us through these difficult times.

His faith and our confidence in him will see us through. Make us come to know you better in these trying times; keep us close to the sacred heart of Jesus Christ. Give us victory over evil and confusion. Put courage into our hearts; Give us your grace and protection. Clothe us in the whole armor of God—the great Mighty awesome God.

Give us the victory over evil. Make our minds strong to withstand the fear and destruction; in you, we place our trust. Prepare us to face this ordeal of entitlement by these foreign forces—those who decided to push you aside and put their ideas into play. Give us the strength, wisdom, and understanding to overcome these ordeals.

Selah.

107

BLESSINGS

Bless everything I do. Send divine help from above to assist me in every way. Fortify me so I can be a blessing to others. Give me grace; shower me with blessings, LORD of the universe, patience, and prosperity. Send the archer of good luck and blessing in every endeavor.

LORD, give me favor with those who are in high places of authority. Let me feast on the goodness of the land, and shield me from jealousy and envious spirits that roam the earth, seeking to pull down God's children. Take away the spirit of self-doubt and doubt by others who would prefer me to suffer on this earth.

Lift up my spirit when I am feeling despair. Send your mind of encouragement, warding off the evil eyes and minds of those who will take my gifts far from me if I let them. Help me to fight the good fight, making me the winner in all my misfortunes. Where there were failures, replace with success, and rule out all negative forces.

Who set traps of failure in my way? You, who made me intelligent, grant me power, wisdom, and understanding; let no man or women take these gifts given away from me. Send down from heaven spiritual blessings that none can take, daily trying to be blind from my destiny.

They wanted to take my place. Carry the flaming arrows and sword of salvation, blinding their eyes and their minds so that they do not hinder my growth and prosperity. Towers of strength, Lion of Judah, merciful Father, hear my prayer; respond to my petitions in a swift way so that my enemies marvel and are in disarray. What is in the dark brought to light?

Surprise my enemies and those who seek my soul for their selfish means. Quietly bless me in every way. Thy, will O LORD here on earth. Purposely bless me, for you alone have the power to enrich me in the land, blessed Father, LORD of the universe. When those throw stumbling blocks in my way, make a way out of no way for me to marvel the minds of my enemies.

Preserve me, keeping me steadfast in everything I do and say, repelling fear, anger, and doubt. Renew my spirit, the portion of my inheritance.

Selah.

108

CON MEN

Protect me from the modern-day con men, conning the minds of people. They dwell in the kindness of the sacred heart of Jesus Christ to devastate and take what is not rightfully theirs. Vigorously, like a thief in the night, fallen angels among us are cheating and lying, distorting God's anointed.

Make sure in these times that no man deceives you (*Mathew 24:4 Berean Study Bible*) (*the word of the LORD*). Protect your mind and soul, and guard your heart. Put on the general armor of God to protect yourself from these con men of the world. They regularly prey on the emotions, generosity, and vulnerability of God's anointed to distort God's children. Saint Michael, draw your sword once more to protect us from these con men.

Little do they know that the con games they are currently playing will come back to haunt them. They will pay for their evil ways. Money is the root of all evil and can't save their souls. Honesty and a little compassion are always the best policy. These lying and cheating con men of the mind, body, and soul rape the minds and hearts of the uneducated, generous, lonely, and distorted ones. God has a place for you in hell.

God, show no mercy on the souls of these con men and women. They lay in the dark, waiting to strike as fast as a cobra and slowly put their venom into your time, money, and energy, emotionally entering the space of the souls of men. They prey on them like wolves in sheep's clothing; they disguised themselves, preying on the unfortunate and vulnerable servants of God.

Stretch forth your Mighty hands, Heavenly Father, and safeguard us from this insanity. Have mercy on us, protecting our minds from these con men. When presented with a situation, they seize the opportunities and are willing to destroy others by taking someone or something away that does not rightfully belong to them.

LORD, they are ruining people's lives to benefit their con games. Show no mercy on them when they fall. Send your forceful angels to destroy them, never allowing them to see the light of day.

Selah.

109

PRISONERS

LORD, help me through these issues of the confinement of my mind and freedom. There is no one to help me, and I fail to realize I need to help myself. Loving Father of wisdom, give me the patience, knowledge, and understanding to deal with these issues—the sentencing and confinement of my mind and soul.

I pronounce myself guilty without a trial. LORD, I am doing jail time here on earth. My greatness, principles, and virtues are under attack. LORD, I am being made to feel guilty for nothing other than past misjudgments of ignorance that once filled my heart and wanting the people of the world to be free, happy, and healthy.

LORD, help me through these issues that are trying to confine freedom of my mind. Loving Father, give me the wisdom to deal with these matters confronting me; there is no one to help me. Give me the patience and understanding to organize my thoughts, mind, soul, and community. I have already dealt with myself.

Now the powers in control are trying to sentence and confine me here on earth. Save me, O LORD, from this self-hatred, guilt, anger, and confusion that are subjecting me and others to discrimination. Free my mind. LORD; help me through these confinements, loving Father. Return the wisdom, in my opinion, to deal with these issues confronting my life.

There is no one to help give me patience and understanding, to deal with my confinement, sentencing, and doing jail time here on earth.

My punishment is not for committing serious crimes but for misuse of the powers. I once had, ordered by supreme rulers, based on greed and political affairs.

LORD, help me through this confinement, loving Father. Mighty one who rules the universe with patience and reasoning, give me the wisdom to deal with these issues of prejudice confronting me and the inequality as it pertains to the distribution of wealth. There is no one to help me. Give me the patience and understanding to deal with the deterioration.

Of my constitutional rights, especially my freedom of speech, the confinement of my spirit, sentencing, and doing jail time here on earth. LORD, help me through this containment. Loving Father, these nations need to come together to correct themselves from their efforts to confine the minds, of their citizens.

To align themselves with the order and blueprint forwarded from the celestial sphere generously and gently bestowed unto certain species of humankind. Some species of humanity here on earth have taken the order of things out of context. They all need to connect themselves to the order of stuff to be in compliance with the Universe.

Selah.

110

NURSES

Stretch forth your merciful hands and guide these nurses. Mighty LORD, give them the patience to show kindness and love to those who placed in their care. Gracious LORD, who showed compassion and love to others in need of love and healing, send your light to show them the way. Your loving-kindness and wisdom are sufficient.

LORD, Light of this world, who's begotten Son died for them, Mighty LORD, give them the patience to show kindness and love to those who placed in their care. Merciful LORD who showed compassion and love, your loving-kindness and wisdom healed the sick. Allow your caring spirit to flow into these nurses to their patients.

The high, Mighty, awesome God, keeper of the gate, great LORD, give them the patience to show kindness and love to those who placed in their care. O, Kindhearted, LORD who showed compassion and love, your tender forbearance everlasting and faithful to your children; give them strength to carry out your will and be good stewards of your creation.

The Spirit of the LORD God, the rock of our strength, Mighty LORD, gives them the patience to show kindness and love to those who placed in their care. Merciful LORD who showed compassion and love, your loving-kindness and wisdom caused the blind to see. Dispatch your angels to watch over the nurses daily and always.

Grateful and loving God, thank you for having them choose the nursing career as their profession.

Selah.

111

OLD AGE

Your Majesty, you stayed with me in my youth. Precious LORD, you kept Sarah's blessing her in her old age. Make my mind free of concerns for things I cannot change. Gracefully give me peace and adorn me with joy and patience.

God All Mighty, watch over me, keeping me thankful and grateful. Continue to bestow on me wisdom and understanding. Bless those who bless me, and curse those who bring harm to me, Give me good health and long-lasting memory, contentment, and thankfulness.

Glorious Father, you alone knew me from childhood. You protected me in the stormy and days dark nights. You were with me and took care of me through abuse and confusion; you held my mind and protected my soul from danger, showing me your love and kindness.

When uncertainty and fear tried to lead me astray, you sent your angels to stay by my side, giving me the courage to live and continue to have confidence in and obey your words, listening to your still steady voice and trusting you, LORD. All Mighty LORD, you are the light at the end of my tunnel, forever shining brightly in my life, penetrating and keeping my soul safe.

Glory is to the Father, Son, and the Holy Ghost. Eternal kindness and wisdom caused the blind to see. Dispatch your angels to watch over the nurses, day and night and always. Grateful and loving God, thank you for calling these women and men to the nursing career let you love, patience and compassion shine through them.

Selah.

112

IDENTITY

God, the Creator and chief designer of all things, you formed me from the dust of the earth. You breathed life into the dust, renewing my soul. You have made me into a living human being and placed in my mind thoughts of good and evil. You gave me choices; you rule the universe with might and strength, great Father.

My friends try to imitate me. They take but do not give. The world decided to form my identity. At times, my life became confusing and disappointing. Keep me strong within myself. Your love continuously showers me with encouragement, beckoning me to continue in this life, always softly saying to me that I must unfailingly be myself and no one else.

If others cannot accept me for being myself, then move on. Heavenly Father loves me the way I am, from the tiny hair on my head to the soles of my feet. He is mine, and I'm his. He stops negative thoughts and means situations that hinder my way. The light of the LORD is constantly shining on me, showing me the way.

Back home to Crystal City, a place where there is no chaos, where order and peace reside. In spite of all the confusion that presents itself, his love and constant attention kept me safe and sound, making conscious decisions that bring joy and happiness in my life and blocking out all frustrations. His glory of strength forever will keep me in my identity. God, my Maker.

Selah.

113

DISAPPOINTMENT

LORD, when we obey your will, and disappointment comes knocking at the door, and it seems your grace has forsaken me, you alone know what lies ahead. Mighty Father, you know what's best for me. Maybe the things I requested were not meant to be.

Help me to cope with these thoughts of disappointment and despair; only you know what's around the corner. Look into my life, and if it's your will, make it content. Show me what's best for me. If this is not to be, then reveal yourself to me in your infinite wisdom, preparing success.

Provide me with patience to deal with these setbacks.

Father God let your great mercy and compassion engulf my mind, bringing comfort and reasoning to my soul. Let me see beyond these disappointments, opening new doors of opportunity for me to enter. Give me foresight into these possibilities; make me not be a quitter.

God, I patiently await your direction in these issues, letting neither man nor thought hinder me. Continue to hold me up in your heavenly realm. My heart will sing praise to you all day long, giving you all the glory, lifting up your name. Your hands are forever holding me.

Selah.

114

BUSINESS

Mighty LORD, my mind is absorbed with thoughts of business and prosperity. Help me to provide a lucrative service to members of my community. Help build this business from the ground up, and if someone or something hinders me, let your light of vengeance come down on them, casting them in the pits of hellfire.

You alone are LORD, all by yourself; send me productive thoughts and paying customers to patronize my business, enriching and edifying me. LORD, let me be a vessel that your words can be administered, and lift up my clients while protecting me from harm. I give you the honor and glory in everything I do.

I am destitute and longing for some success in my business attempts so that I can be a good provider. LORD, I would like to be an example for you first, O LORD, and to family, friends, and my community. Teach me the concept of charity and giving back to myself, family, friends, and my community.

Lord, my mother, and father have forsaken me, and I am left independently to take care of myself. Send speedy delivery. I am in need, O Dear Father! Send divine help from above to show me the way. Giving good favor makes me feel your presence near; overseeing everything I do and say. Let me not quit when the going gets rough.

Make a way out of no way, and send excellent helpers and business-minded associates who can help me to establish this new business, forever giving you the praise and glory, Forgive me, LORD, for tryIng to build a business without your blessing. The LORDS plans for man's prosperity are constancy and continually.

The Father of Prosperity cast down all evil spirits that may confront me as I do your will for enriching my life. Grant me your great powerful blessings of prosperity.

Selah.

115

THANKSGIVING

Faithful and genuine one, forever giving, Thanksgiving comes once a year. The rest of the year, the unfaithful people walk around complaining, grunting, forgetting that you're constantly on the throne. O Mighty LORD, you give them strength to wake up in the morning and eyes to see the sunshine or rain. Thank you for your loving-kindness and wisdom.

You're the glory of their strength, God, which always causes us to triumph in Christ. Help us to remember to thank you, praising and giving thanks, minute by minute, daily and weekly, quietly in our minds and souls as we partake in life's nectar. Let every voice say at all times, thank you, LORD, for all the right things you have done for the children of men.

The Blessed Creator, Ruler of the Universe, thank you for good and thank you for the terrible as we grow in wisdom and understanding, you send the wrong, so we all can appreciate the good. Thank you for your understanding. You are a jealous God because your major requests to us are not to love or serve any other Gods but you; worship (*you must worship the Creator himself and not his creations*).

Love God with all your heart and soul and love each other. Give thanks and praise to the LORD your God. Bring joy and thanksgiving to his tabernacle. Thank you for good; thank you for the bad, Disappointment doesn't last a lifetime for a child of God. Take my mind off the bitterness and place it in your illuminating light. Burn out the bitterness in my life with your love.

My heart will sing songs of thanksgiving to you, LORD, all day long until the rest of my existence. Lord, evil cannot reside in a place of love, joy, and the strength of the LORD. Thank you for me, thank you for my children, and thank you for life, so glorious and pure. When my time comes to return home to you, let my lips possess enough strength to say to you, "Thank you, thank you, thank you, LORD, God of Hosts. I thank you."

Thanks giving should be every day.

You must give thanks every day.

Selah.

116

ANGER

Faithful and genuine one, my life is out of control and is in a mess. Mother doesn't understand me. No one cares about me, including me. I am tired of punching the walls, cutting myself. My life is unfulfilled. I have attempted suicide several times, but not even that is going very well.

Hopelessness is my friend; only you alone, heavenly Father, can rescue me from this nightmare of alcohol, drugs, fussing and fighting with others, stealing from the church offering, cheating on my wife, not knowing if I have any children—my girlfriend says I am the father of her son.

My life consumed with anger; I have stolen the children's newspaper route money. I disrespected my stepson by lighting myself on fire in his presence. Prince of life rescues me from this hell. Forgive me for all this confusion; bring healing to my restless soul. Excuse me for these iniquities; bring peace and tranquility to my life.

Abused by my uncles for food, damaged for life by these acts of insanities, taking more than I give, buying stolen goods, using your earthly angels, manipulating, wanting this for nothings, drinking, smoking, doing drugs. Light of the world, Father of light, hear my prayer and adhere to my confusion.

I retire to a private place in my mind and ask your forgiveness— pimping out and taking advantage of your divine creation, using my strength to suppress the less fortunate and helpless, committing acts against you by several suicide attempts, destroying lives instead of enriching.

I could say to you, LORD, forgive me. I am not worthy of your kingdom. Just say the word, and my soul shall be healed. O LORD, hear my petitions. I bring them to your altar of life, leaving them in your care. All things are possible with you, LORD, who reigns in your Heavenly Realm.

For a friend

Selah.

117

HOMELESS

Majestic and Honorable God of the Universe, who commanded the light and kept my kids and me safe as we lay underneath the deep night skies, let your angels enclose and comfort me as I assist them with their homework. I am sleeping in the car with my children.

Because of an abusive, misunderstood, adulterous husband, who, with calculated evil, has taken over me and my kids' domain? With no one to help me, my children have to attend school and be taken care of properly. My children and I are homeless with no place to rest our heads. LORD, no one on this earth knows the situation but you,

O, LORD of this earth. With the wisdom of God, help me to find a safe place to raise my children. Send divine intervention of kindness and mercy to enrich us. Doing homework in the car with my children—have mercy on us. Guide me in the way I must go; protect my kids as they grow and learn. Each day no one but you knows the ordeal I face, day and night.

My husband walked out on the children and me, left for another woman. LORD, he abandoned us without a cent to our name, forgot his kids and the obligations. The burden is resting solely on me. He feels proud and Mighty because the children and I are suffering. It's all on me to provide for my kids.

The love you place in my heart is keeping me healthy and hopeful, as I fight this act of use, misuse, abuse, and betrayal. I am forever faithful to the powers of God All Mighty. Take hold of this situation with your sword of justice.

Selah.

118

TEMPTATION

Deliver me from temptation. Jesus Christ, the Son of God, a crown of thorns was placed over his head and lured on the mount. He was willing to obey the Heavenly Father. A great example for us to follow, There is none like Jesus Christ LORD and Savior blessed Son of God, who sits on the right hand of the Father. All the angels rejoiced in the LORDS faithfulness,

He inflames my soul with his Holy Spirit of resistance against this New Age religious, psychological intimidation that he thrust on his children. Help us to become weak in this godly struggle; hasten to deliver us from this temptation that we too may endure and withstand the powers of this temptation. You are my guiding light at all times, an eternal flame in my life, light of the world.

The gates of hell could not behold you, LORD, Mighty King of David. A crown of thorns was placed on your head, tempted by the devil and his angels. Those who we ought to fear, let not their intimidation and lawlessness bring tyranny to our hearts and minds. They ride upon the heaven, seeking and pretending to deliver salvation to souls.

They tempted you at the beginning and the end of your journey here on earth. The divine realm sustained you, protecting your mind and soul from earth's temptation. Deliver me from the trappings set by man, tempting and testing your faith here on earth. If you can turn water into wine and heal the sick, "come down from the cross and save yourself," they cried. (*Mark 15:30 (NIV)*)

Mighty Father who left heaven and came to us in the form of a man (eternal) to bring the message of life, love, joy, equality, respect, and rationality to this earth. He stamped out darkness and savagery from the minds of men. Your Holy Spirit reigns forever on this earth. Hold us together as we resist the temptations and the political traps set for your children. Let not the spirit of fear and doubt that has descended on us tempts us into submission.

LORD, your spirit is so powerful, pure, and true and lives on today in your children. Death could not hold you. You resisted temptation and parted the grave to reunite with God the Father and sit in heaven on the right side of your Father. Let me not be led into temptation. Surround me with the purity and tenacity to resist temptation.

Through the Holy Spirit, O LORD of Israel, he who allowed you to remove the stone from your natural resting place. The powers of the angels and the forces of the Crystal City descended to earth to set your mind free to return to the Father's the Heavenly Kingdom. Hallelujah, hallelujah, hallelujah, hallelujah, hallelujah, hallelujah.

Selah.

119

MOTHERLESS

Mother to the Motherless, she is the hope for all eternity, Virgin Mother of God. Your tenderness and caring, loving mercy have shown me compassion. Hold me together with your fortitude of love and your undivided attention. My mother has rejected me; she places her trust and faith in people she does not know—strangers and material things.

She has not entirely believed in the All Mighty God Father and his mercy, wisdom, understanding and love. Holy Mother of God, at no time, had my mother found the time to say to her children "I love you" and made them feel unconditional love. She only found a chance to criticize everything. They did, never embracing them or trusting them.

"Alligator eats its own," (*mother*) she consistently said to me.

Virgin Mother whose heart is kind and filled with love and adoration for her children, shine your light on me, so I don't make the same mistakes when it comes to raising my kids, dedicated mother of all, whose wisdom and understanding reached me, enriching my life. Your example of motherhood has taught and given me patience.

Virgin Mother of God, tranquility and gentleness lay in your bosom. Show yourself to me once more, blocking out all frustration and disappointment, confusion, and the insanity and burdens placed upon me by my biological mother. Surround me with your blessed assurance to cleanse and renew my soul.

Take these burdens away from my mind; help me not to adopt this attitude and example set forth by my mother to my children. In your Holy Mother and God the Father I trust. LORD, I put my faith and confidence in the powers of your spectacular mercy. Mother to the Motherless, Virgin Mother of God, who carried my soul and formed me in the womb.

Stretch forth your loving hand and guide me with wisdom, understanding, and patience; renew my soul so that I can continue to love my children unconditionally, making sure I don't eat my children and continue to love them in your grace always.

Cover my ears and blind my eyes to this ignorance, so I don't pass this self-hatred on to my children, steadily loving myself and taking the example from you, Virgin Mother, mother to the motherless. Assist me to come to the reality of the situation that I psychologically find myself in, as I long for my mom's love, trust, and understanding.

Holy Mother to the Motherless, through the power of the saints of God the Father, he gives me glory, virtue, and understanding when these strong thoughts of confusion and destruction enter my mind. As I struggle with questions of how or why my mother feels this way. Let your Holy Spirit engulf my soul and bring peace, salvation, understanding, and joy to my entire being.

Resting on your love, keep me in your bosom; continue to grant me unique and excellent favors.

Selah.

120

GENERAL LAWSUIT

Go before me, O Precious LORD, leaving no stone unturned. Send your guardian angels to pave the way to defend my innocence. Grant me favors of mercy as I stand before my accusers. Heavenly Father you are the Judge and jury, God who always causes me to triumph in Jesus Christ.

LORD gives me the victory through our LORD and Savior Jesus Christ, ever-loving father of the universe, forever faithful and suitable. Grant me favors of mercy as I stand before my accusers. Father of all things, judge and jury; make me humble, giving great wisdom and understanding to my lawyers, who always cause us to triumph in Christ.

Make this day, as I face my accusers, be filled with compassion and favor as I face judgment for my transgression again men and God. Examine me, O LORD, and grant me the favor of mercy, as I stand before my accusers. Heavenly Father you are the Judge and jury, God, who always causes me to triumph in Christ.

All of my friends have abandoned me; they left me to face the beast on my own. I place my confidence in your omnipresence. Send the spirit of Daniel in the lion's den. To assure me of your supreme confidence and your reassurance, grant me favors of mercy as I stand before my accuser's judge and jury. Sustain me,

God, the great Judge of all judges among men, My LORD, the keeper of the gate, the defender of Israel, the great Comforter, the one who grants favors. Who always causes us to triumph in Jesus Christ, our LORD, and Savior. I will continue to glorify your name, offering up burned candles, singing praises to your day and night until my time to return home to you.

Every day I will light candles in your honor to the day of my demise, Grant me favors of mercy as I stand before my accusers. Heavenly Father of all things, you are the judge and jury, God, who always causes me to triumph through Jesus Christ. Gracious, merciful God, and great King above all Gods,

Favorable One, Have mercy, blotting out all of my past sins, washing me in the blood of the Lamb, baptized in your spiritual kingdom, whiter than snow. Grant me favors of mercy as I stand before the accusers, Father of All Things, judge, and jury, God, who always causes me to triumph in Jesus Christ.

Selah.

121

ROAD RAGE

As I am about to put my key into my ignition today, let not the spirit of anger and rage enter my mind and soul. LORD, who works all things after the counsel of his will, anger, and anxiety has taken hold of me, repressing my thoughts. I am seeing red and cannot control this emotion. Heavenly Father, send your loving patience to penetrate my mind and soul.

Heavenly Father guards my mind against this cancerous evil. Emotions of anger and frustration let me not stumble and fall over exerting myself on the roads. Monitor my temper, slowing down my mind on the road today; put me under your tender loving care, turning my fury from negative toward positive. Gentle Jesus, who shows mercy and understanding,

To those who call on your name in times of difficulty, steady my nerves regulate my blood pressure and bring calm to my entire being, Mighty Father who works all things. After the counsel of your will, when I lay down to sleep, make my mind clear, resting in your blessed assurance, confidence, and patience, that when I wake the next day, my mind and soul will be grateful for life.

Have clarity and rationality surround me, so I have patience for others, bringing minimum road rage to this angry emotion. Search the ruins of my heart, Magnificent Father who works all things after the counsel of his will. Send me your spirit of patience and understanding to assist me. If there is a way for me to find another method of transport, then show me the process.

The Mighty Spirit of peace and control, furnish answers to this wicked spirit of road rage. Forgive me for not having foresight and oversight to find out the danger and anger that absorbs my soul. Your will is allowing me to live day to day, intimidating others on the road because of my selfishness and ignorance.

LORD, forgive me putting fear and anger in the mind of other road users and making their lives commuting early in the morning a nightmare of confusing emotions. Come to me, LORD of wisdom and patience. Aid me with this negative emotional feeling; be my counselor; protect my mind from this madness. I put my trust in you, O Dear Father, helper, and Redeemer. Selah.

122

DIVORCE

LORD, I am confused and distorted. My husband and father of my children have betrayed my children and me. Until death do us part, for better or for worse—that's what the preacher said. LORD, I worked hard to be a good helpmate and mother in this union, willing to give up my soul to keep this family together.

LORD, I see changes in my husband's attitude toward the children and me; the environment is becoming abusive and without love. Influential Father, give me wisdom and strength to continue in this union. Outside forces have taken hold of my husband's mind. Things are getting worse day by day, fighting and criticizing.

The spirit of lust and envy has made its way into my domain, where once love resided. LORD, I am concerned for the welfare of my children, all Great and most Powerful Father. I have taken them to a safe place where they do not have to see this kind of mistreatment and grow up in an unloving environment—to see and hear all this negative fighting.

Be by my side in every way, guide me through this turmoil, keep us safe, and send your divine spirit to guide me. I have to file for divorce. Forgive me, Father and great mediator. Plead my case and assist me to deal with this situation. Send your strength and loving-kindness to guide me through this; let me not lose sight of loving and protecting my children.

Help me stay in healthy and sound mind while I provide for my kids. Ever-loving Father, who made me with a healthy mind, sound spirit and heart, LORD, have mercy on the person who brought this disaster on my family. Let her soul never see the light of the day. Prepare for her a place in hell to be tormented by all of the hell's demons.

Let no one be present to help her in her time of need. Let me live in the moment, putting aside all discord with my husband and focus on my children's well-being. I am confused about divorcing my husband; send your divine intervention to guide me through this divorce, keeping me faithful to you and my children.

Selah.

123

ADVANTAGE

LORD, I call upon you, you who formed and created me with a sound mind and spirit. Others who put themselves in positions of authority have used their positions to take advantage of me, assuming I was of lesser value and weak. They took the opportunity to take advantage of me, threatening my integrity, using me for their gratification.

Shield me, O Precious LORD, from past and present perceptions and traitorous minds. Taking my kindness for weakness, LORD, help me to recognize the takers from the givers. Have mercy on them and shield me from those who took my inheritance and took advantage of me of my kindness.

Mighty One who made me with a sound mind and spirit, deliver me in a huge way. Shield me, O Precious LORD, from the tears of those who thought it possible to blame me for their unhappiness and overwhelming bad personal and business decisions. They are full with self-hatred, daily gossiping, and slandering.

My name among strange men, misjudging me, and taking advantage of me—shield me, O Precious LORD.

Give wisdom and help me put on the armor of the LORD to withstand the deadly mind games and ignorance that come from not blessing the day. God gave them the gift of being a part of his establishment.

And the powers for them to live and create, unless the evil doers take advantage of the servant of God, punish them and bring them beneath my feet. Shield me, O Precious LORD, giving me the patience and understanding. Let not your servant go astray. LORD, because of these obstacles and stumbling blocks.

Let me be set aside from their intentions. Evil punishments, putting them to shame, send your angels to protect and guide me. LORD, help me to make good, steady decisions to compete and win in the world with regards to further raising my children. Keep me knowing that you are my priority in every way.

God the Father, who sees the hearts of men and looks down on their intentions, renew my spirit, placing in my heart the spirit of the intrepid, ever-loving Father, who made me with a pleasurable mind and spirit. LORD! Have mercy on the takers. They try to trick my mind, taking advantage of my hospitality, interpreting.

My kindness for weakness, rewarding evil for service, kind gestures, and wonderful deeds, biting the hand that feeds them, "Father, forgive them for they know not what they do." (*Luke 23:34*) Be my defender in all things.

Selah.

124

MISUNDERSTOOD

Heavenly Father, your confidence, and wisdom have kept me from falling. You have guided me from childhood, adolescence, adulthood, to senior citizen. Foolish minds seem to think something is wrong with me. They believe I am arrogant and overly self-confident, not knowing that my confidence comes from you, LORD of Hosts.

LORD, I am misunderstood, LORD of perfection and knowledge. Maintain me, keeping envious eyes and haters from destroying me. They camp around me, taking my words and kind gestures for granted, thinking that they can use trickery and silent psychology to enter my soul and lead me astray, causing destruction to come into my life.

They are without hope, lost, and confused without the answers. Holy Spirit of promise, when others pursue destruction and glorify evil and trickery and partake in the demise of others, protects me from their bad karma. Glorify those who bless me; curse those who fight against and curse me without cause. Shield my feelings; protect my integrity,

LORD of perfection, virtue, knowledge, and wisdom. LORD, as you walked the earth, you were misunderstood and paid the price by dying on the cross, but you rise again, defeating death. My virtue confidence, courage, wisdom, perfection and knowledge come from knowing you. LORD defeated death.

Heavenly Father, you ordered my steps and sent me on my way. Giving me wisdom and knowledge, placing big dreams in my heart, giving wisdom and knowledge and foresight to fulfill those dreams, let me not be bothered or moved by those whose purpose is to confuse, steal my ideas, and defer me to take my place.

You are the God of hosts who protects your servants' dreams from the destructive minds of others. Hide my dreams from those who will try to deny me the help I need. Their will is to deceive me, causing my demise and failure, not making my dreams into reality. They will attempt to discourage me and change my direction by replacing my integrity with their agendas.

Their intentions are to steal my dreams and decrease my luck, and chances to make my journey out of poverty a difficult one. Intervene, O LORD. Intervene. O, LORD, making them in disarray and confused. Steady my course; anchor my ship in calm, prosperous waters, making.

LORD, make my harvest a bountiful one, horn of my salvation. You, LORD, are my house of my defense; hide my dreams; distract them long enough. Give me time on this earth to turn my dreams into reality.

Selah.

125

FACE-BOOK AND TWITTER POSTINGS

Mighty LORD, all I do is post my every movement and aspects of my life on my Face-book and Twitter pages. I am losing sight of my real self, caught up in this vicious medium that invades the mind, preoccupied and blinded with the actual reason for this carefully thought-out information-collection media. Created to spy on and collect information on subscribers and end-users and used for tagging citizens.

Mighty LORD, all I do is post my every movement and aspects of my life on my Face-book and Twitter pages. My mind cannot think fast enough; my thoughts and feelings are not my own. I don't have time to rationalize my emotions, thoughts, and actions, wanting the whole world to know what I am thinking and doing. I don't communicate in person with my fellow humans and only post the things.

I want to show off on this medium. LORD, put in my mind an intelligent, rational thinking process perspective. Making eye-to-eye contact is a thing of the past because the spotlight is on Face-book and the Twitter screens. Help me, LORD, to seek out new ways of communicating without my life being under this destructive scope. Mighty LORD, all I do is post my every movement and aspects of my life on my Face-book and Twitter pages.

My boastfulness, stupidity, and confusion computing has engulfed my mind. All I do is post every detail of my life on Face-book and

Twitter. My friends are bullying me, spreading false rumors and sharing personal messages about me for everyone to see. My boss knows about my fetish and my religious belief, my anger, and pain. They found out about my God-fearing affiliation and what I am thinking about and doing about my belief system.

O LORD, save me; anger and confusion have taken over my mind and soul. Mighty LORD, all I do is post my every movement and aspects of my life on my Face-book and Twitter pages. My mind is wandering around, giving out more information, free information about myself, more than I need to. This medium is furthermore taking me far away from you. Mighty LORD, all I do is post things on Face-book and Twitter pages.

Help me to find time to converse with you, O LORD. I am experiencing sleep deprivation. I stay up day and night, computing, and my mind is in a state or revolving, mindless, worrisome emotions. Neglecting my family, I am losing sleep. Wet bags are forming under my eyes. Save my mind from this unconscious state of nothingness. In you, I place my trust, Mighty One, who conquers and controls all temptations.

Rescue me from my computing urges and posting aspects of my intimate thoughts. This invasion will lead to singling out end-users for their ideas and views. Promoting a modern-day La Rafle du Vel' d'Hiv: La rafle du Vél' d'Hiv, the French police round up of the Vel' d'Hiv.

Selah.

126

IMMIGRATION

Blessed LORD, keep me as I prepare to embark on another country, a dangerous trip, migrating to another country. Give me favor with authorities. Send caring people in my path because the odds are against me. I put my confidence in you, all Mighty Father. Protect my efforts, removing all obstacles. That may come my way.

LORD take care to protect my family left behind help them to understand the reasons and purpose for making his decision and embarking on this venture. Bring about swiftness with the process of gaining citizenship. Grant me the finances to afford a lawyer. Protect me from victimization.

Make me understand I must be vetted (investigate) for illness and lawlessness, open up my mind to receive wisdom and understanding to learn new things. Assist me to be a good citizen. Let your light shine on me so that I can be an inspiration to others. Send your spirit of adaptation, and use new customs, cultures, and languages.

Give me favor with the right people to find work and housing. Come to me, O Father of Hope. With patience, defend me from loneliness and those who will try to exploit me. Sharpen my intelligence, so I can overcome those who may sidetrack me and hinder me from my blessings.

You alone, LORD, have the power to give me sincerely the desires of the heart. Let me be fearless against those whose hearts are as hard as a stone, which will attempt to discourage me and take from me without giving anything in return. Place in me the heart of a lion, forever and steadily, staying truthful and faithful to you in all ways.

Your voice, O LORD, called me out of darkness into Magnificent light. Slowly shine on me; surely bless my efforts, minute by the minute, day by day. Immigration officers can be intimidating. Let them grant me the perfect favor, finding no faults within me as I pursue my dreams.

He is God ascended. LORD, you are the Highest Ruler of the mountains and meadow, whose eyes are constantly open, standing guard over me, granting me a good favor; I am forever indebted to you, LORD of the Universe.

Selah.

127

FAVOR

Give me a favor, O LORD, who awards favors, grants me favor with influential people. So that your will be done in my life, take me to a private place where I can mature and grow intellectually, gaining recognition by the world. Grant me the joy of prosperity to forge ahead and fulfill my dreams.

Favorable Father who said, "Ask, and it will be given to you, seek, and you will find; knock, and the doors shall be open" (*Matthew 7:7 (ASV)*). Be the one, O LORD, to intervene in my circumstances, granting me real favors. Put a song in my heart, confidence and substance in my soul. Grant big favors to me, the offspring of King David.

Be swift to expose and beat down those whose intentions are dangerous and fruitless for me. And their desires are out of line with your will for my life. Dispense divine blessings, and have mercy on those who hindered me in the past. Glorious Father, one who's Mighty Spirit was with Moses as he parted the Red Sea, take away all doubts and fear within me.

Raise me up out of this depressed state of mind. Turn defeat into victory for the entire world to see; let my success in life be an example to those who are lost and hopeless and for them who took my kindness for weakness, and others, who took from me what was not rightfully theirs. Let the haters, and the downward trotters put to shame, heavenly Father.

LORD of light and power rules the universe with the hands made of brass and whose might have the authority to turn past failures into success with more than expected. Shine your light of success on my path, descending on me like a Mighty volcano. Whose flame scorches out old failures, despair, disappointments and replaces them with the new birth of hope, faith, and success.

Give me your blessing of favor on my endeavors.

So let your Mighty strength takes hold of my bleak circumstance and traps of deceptions set by my mother and friends, stealing my blessed energy, leaving me to die. Heavenly Father, who resurrected from the dead, stretch forth your vigorous hands, saving me, setting me high, so I can look down on the fools and say,

What was meant to be evil, the LORD God turned into good and prosperity of his beloved servant? Favorable Father, grant and fulfill all my dreams. My confidence and every effort rest in you, O, Mighty LORD of the Universe.

Selah.

128

THE LORDS ANGER

The LORDS anger is upon the earth, making men stronger in their faith. The Mighty God of salvation and mercy, who is slow to anger but swift to react, is setting people apart, seeking out his servants, preparing for the day of battle—the battle over good, bad, and evil. He is searching the minds and souls of men and women, trying to find peace and love.

He is seeking men and women of firm conviction who are willing to put on the armor of God, defending God's kingdom. The wrath of God, the God of the Universe, will be felt by those who are constantly deceiving and provoking and misleading the children God, pretending to be the chosen ones while destroying God's creation.

The LORD of righteousness keeps Israel. He will not slumber. The LORD, keeps Israel, He will not slumber. His anger is continuously displayed on the earth, shamed and displeased with the way men have turned their hearts and souls against him. He is a right-on-time God of Faith and true Jehovah God, the Father. Don't let the sun go down with anger in your hearts.

He speaks to you daily, warning of false prophets. Don't be deceived by those who preach peace and wage war on the earth. Don't turn your minds away from the authentic God who has anointed us. Giving us life, who will be in the LORD's army? Who will fight for the one true living God, gather all his children together, and put on the whole armor of our God?

He alone does great wonders and establishes us in the power of Jesus Christ, our LORD, and Savior. The wrath of God dispensed on earth. He is searching the land for ruined, deceived, and broken hearts that were betrayed and misused to reestablish his kingdom on earth. Be meticulous and know that the LORD your God is all powerful and patient.

His wisdom, knowledge, and understanding come from being patient, giving you unconditional love. When he is fed up with your rebellious ways, he will turn you over to your transgressions, therefore blocking you from the sun and the tree of life.

Selah.

129

LORD, I NEED A FRIEND

The LORD warns us about trusting, commanding us to be careful and reminding us not to trust anyone. LORD, I need a friend like you. LORD, a good friend, one who will not be jealous or overshadow me. LORD, I need a friend like you.

LORD, I am lonely and need a friend, someone I could confide in without his or her being judgmental. LORD, I need a friend like you. I never really could get along or trust anyone until I met you. LORD, I need a friend like you.

LORD, make me your friend. LORD of the meek, stable, faithful; LORD, I need a friend like you. Beyond betrayal, honest, trustworthy, everlasting, some say they are my friends when they deceive me and betray like a snake.

LORD, I need a friend like you, and I want you to be my confidant, hope, associate, minister, and teacher. You are my true friend, and the spirit that keeps me alive, hopeful with joy and happiness.

LORD, I need a friend like you. Mighty LORD, who dwells within me, what a wonderful, delightful friend you are to me closer than a brother or sister. Better than a mother or father. What a friend we have in Jesus Christ. LORD, I need a friend like you.

Selah.

130

BREAKING SPELLS

Break this spell of evil placed in America by her enemies. Israel and America shall rise again to fulfill the glory and goals of the Lord. Break these chains of jealousy and confusion that has embedded itself around this nation. The struggle between good and evil will be fought. The blood of our enemies shall overflow from the rivers, streams, and seas. The Mighty LORD is upon his throne and is taking notes on those that oppose him and his laws.

The Great LORD, if he decides to return to this earth today, will face condemnation, damnation, and be killed again. For far too long, we allowed Government leaders to take the name of the LORD out of everything, including Christmas. The public school system does not permit Christian children to say prayers in the classroom.

In prominent places and churches, the crosses are covered to cater to other religions. You are forbidden to show the cross or wear the cross. LORD, On April 16, 2009, before President Obama gave his speech on economics at Gaston Hall George Town's University, Washington DC.

All religious symbols and the monograms representing Jesus Christ were removed or covered up, with a piece of black-painted plywood. The LORDS name can't be mentioned on sidewalks of our city's streets. His children banned from singing praises in the public squares of Toronto. LORD God Almighty, In America, there is even a problem with them singing the anthem.

The kids are prosecuted for worshiping Jesus Christ and God the Father, Keeper and Father of Israel and America. The Living One Always, fire and destruction will come from your mouth to devour your enemies. Fetch, the Holy Water from the springs of life, to break these spells of ignorance.

Throw some of the Holy Water of life on these treacherous, dark creatures of the universe, who daily worship the God of deception. Losing their identity, turning their backs on the Heavenly Father, the spirit of confusion and despair sent by these fallen angels has consumed the universe, blinding the minds of men and women.

The Highest, All Mighty Father, defender of Israel and America, sends your signs from above the heavens, making them afraid; let them hide in shame. The spirit of culpability has devoured their minds and souls. These fallen angels are trying to lead your children straight into hell. LORD, let the battle for good and evil commence.

Those who just live to destroy your name, hatred has consumed their minds, soiling their souls, making men and women go crazy, delusional, without love or fairness, respect or tolerance, meriting condemnation. O, Mighty One has mercy on them, their days numbered.

Mighty LORD of Host, alone can righteously judges and restore. He has the mercy and power to break these spells.

Selah.

131

FRUITFULNESS

Majestic Father, bounteous provider, beautiful Savior, Holy Spirit, the hope of Israel grants me fruitfulness. Let my cupboard filled and ran over with the depths of your love, bountiful Father; provide for me. Be a lamp to my feet and light to my soul; help me to prosper as my mind progresses in you.

Let my cup be full and ran over, and again, send your Holy Spirit to give me confidence. Dispatch angels to camp around me. Make sure I do the things that I need to do, which will allow me to prosper, LORD. I am in need of your blessings of plenty; give me the power to experience a bountiful harvest here on earth.

Bring plenty of rain and sunshine to nurture my efforts; get me an abundant harvest of riches, like you did for King David which no one can compare. You are a God of prosperity. Make a place in heaven, calling my name to the angels, beckoning them to assist me in my efforts to change from being an introvert to an extrovert.

Let me sharing my talent with the world, and reaping the rewards. LORD Shiva came to my aid. You are not a God of small means, but a God of bountiful plenty. O heavenly Father, who always delivers my blessings on time and generously provides life in a productive, plentiful manner, opens the windows of heaven, sending property now,

LORD of Israel shall provide my needs and the needs of my children always. LORD, I beg you.

Selah.

132

JESUS, MAKE ME YOURS

The LORD is the Bread of Life, the one that comforts me. He is gracious.

Jesus, make me yours, he who led his people through the wilderness.
Jesus, make me yours, he who led his people through the wilderness.
Jesus, make me yours, he who led his people through the desert.

The one who is in the midst of Israel, the All Mighty God, one God,

Jesus, make me yours, he who led his people through the wilderness.
Jesus, make me yours, he who led his people through the wilderness.
Jesus, make me yours, he who led his people through the desert.

Faithful, loving Father, generous LORD God, the good sheep,

Jesus, make me yours, he who led his people through the wilderness.
Jesus, make me yours, he who led his people through the wilderness.
Jesus, make me yours, he who led his people through the wilderness.

Holy One whose heart is full of grace and sunshine,

Jesus, make me yours, he who led his people through the wilderness.
Jesus, make me yours, he who led his people through the wilderness.
Jesus, make me yours, he who led his people through the wilderness.

"LORD, God of Abraham, Isaac, and Israel, (*Kings 18:36-40*) (*https:// www.bible.com/bible/1359/1ki.18.36-40.icb#!*) Forever willing and genuine,

Jesus, make me yours, he who led his people through the wilderness.
Jesus, make me yours, he who led his people through the wilderness.
Jesus, make me yours, he who led his people through the wilderness.

The LORD, whose spirit walks among us in the midst of the earth?

Jesus, make me yours, he who led his people through the wilderness.
Jesus, make me yours, he who led his people through the wilderness.
Jesus, make me yours, he who led his people through the wilderness.
Jesus, make me yours,

He who led his people through the wilderness,

Jesus, make me yours, he who led his people through the wilderness.

Selah.

133

THE LORDS ASSURANCE

Jesus, you are mine, pleasant feelings of confidence. Unthinkable gift, blessed is the LORDS assurance, unspeakable gift. Marvelous gift, blessed is the LORDS assurance, unspeakable gift. Indescribable gift, blessed is the LORDS assurance, unspeakable gift.

You sent your Son to die for my sins, hallelujah, and hallelujah. Wonderful gift, blessed is the LORDS assurance, unutterable gift. Unimaginable gift, blessed is the LORDS assurance, unspeakable gift. Beyond-description gift, blessed is the LORDS assurance, unspeakable gift. Lift Heavenly Father higher.

Lord, your love is sufficient to hold me forever in your care. Indefinable gift, blessed is the LORDS assurance, unspeakable gift. Indefinable gift, blessed is the LORDS assurance, unspeakable gift. Unutterable gift, blessed is the LORDS assurance, unspeakable gift.

Good things cometh from the LORD your God. Marvelous gift, blessed is the LORDS assurance, unutterable gift. Abundant gift, blessed is the LORDS assurance, unspeakable gift. Inexpressible gift, blessed is the LORDS assurance, an incredible gift bestowed on the children of men.

Selah.

134

HELP FROM ENVIOUS EYES

Mighty Father saves me from those who would kill me with jealousy in their minds. My strength and fortitude come from the LORD my God. My confidence and joy come from the LORD my God. To destroy me or take away from me, you will have to go through the Heavenly Father, the advocate for the poor and needy.

Save me, O Precious LORD, from the crab-in-the-bucket syndrome. Others that are of low self-esteem find ways to keep me at the bottom of the bucket. For each time I try picking myself up to take my place in the universe, leaving, breaking from the pack in the bucket, that dreadful spirit of envious eyes that resides.

In lives bucket of hopeless and despair. The LORD reached the bottom of the bucket, and he held on to me. Their intentions are to keep me back in the bottom of the bucket with crabs. Help me, O LORD, to break free and avoid this nasty, destructive spirit call, envy, and jealousy. Save me, God of the universe, from this crab-in-the-bucket syndrome.

Bless those who honestly bless me, and curse those who despise me for being me. Take away the pressures of feeling guilty for the many blessings you have provided me. Make me strong in your Spirit to withstand the evil forces of envy and jealousy. Let your Holy Spirit surround me, blocking out the spirit that steals joy.

And secure me from the negative powers of envy and jealousy; send your angels on time to deliver me, taking my soul and present situation to a higher place, where no one can prevail over my many blessings. Whoever the LORD sanctifies, no one can curse. Let not your heart is troubled for the suffering you undergo and endure at the hands of the non-believers.

The ones who put their trust in silver and gold while building their houses on sand, I put my trust and confidence in the All Mighty LORD God, builder of the Universe. Save now, all-sufficient God. I beg you, open up a big blessing for me. LORD, protect my mind and soul from envious eyes. Shield me.

O Great One, who looks down from above, prying into the subconscious mind of men and women. Shield my mind with your Holy Spirit. Protect my efforts from those who would prefer my soul went downward into the pits of hell with them. Make haste to protect me with your Mighty sword. Protect me, LORD, from the haters.

Selah.

135

REJOICE IN THE LORD

Rejoice in the LORD, for he is good. His mercy is everlasting. Make songs filled with love, praise, and adoration of the LORD God. Jesus Christ, our Savior, our LORD, is worthy to be praised. Sing and dance make merry; be joyous in the LORD of the universe.

Come before his Mighty throne, saying to the LORD, "Thank you, LORD, for everything." We bring to you from our hearts and souls, songs of joy. Our lips say to you. "This is the day the LORD has made. Let us rejoice and be glad in it." (*Psalm 118:24(NKJV*) you kept us through the night, sending your angels to watch over us while we sleep.

Your faithfulness to us is forever. Rejoice in the LORD, all angels in the heavens and children of the earth, fishes in the sea, and birds in the air. Rejoice in the LORD. He shelters us from the storm, sending manna from the heavens to nourish our bodies and his Holy Spirit to nurture our souls.

Sing praises to the LORD God, Creator of all things, from the dark depths of the oceans to the outer limits of the universe. Let everything that has life praise the LORD, triumph in the LORD, and I say rejoice in the LORD. He gives you the power to become rich. His patience and grace await your soul, saying to you, rejoice in the LORD.

His mercy will endure forever

Selah.

136

FREEDOM OF THE MIND, LORDS HELP

Universal God and Savior, confusion and evil are the devil's work, who resides in the minds of men. Release their minds from tension, fears, and doubts, replacing with positive and good behavior, Heavenly Father.

Keep their minds free from all this modern-day drama and confusion, which exists on the earth today. Help the children of men to achieve freedom of the mind. Let all those who call upon your name delivered from the confinement of the mind.

Teach them to be cautious, guarding their minds and hearts against the bad noise of this world. Make sure that no man deceives those, and keep their minds free from fear and doubt. The LORD of Hosts commands us to have no fear.

The devil is busy roaming the earth, seeking out the souls of God's children to humiliate, set apart, confuse, and use them. The ultimate goal is to destroy men, women, and children, turning them into child soldiers, martyrs, sex slaves, child porn, confusing and corrupting their minds.

LORD, with matters beyond their imaginations. They force their twisted ideas and self-hate upon these innocent minds, those that belongs to the LORD, imposing their views and reckless behavior, confusing the minds of the fragile and helpless.

Holy Father, bring freedom to the spirit of those subjected to these. Unconscious by those blinded by this dark evil spirit of collective selfishness that has engulfed the minds of men and women.

The Author of Eternal Salvation, send good examples exposing the false ideas perpetrated by the prophets of the earth. Liberate the minds of our children from this modern-day hell and madness in the land that always fight for the minds of our children.

LORD thy God the buckle and shield for those who trust in him, witness to us through your Holy Spirit, saving us from this misery. He will give us the victory, so we can free our minds and live in love and harmony with each other to create a sustainable world.

"Finally, brethren, whatsoever things are true, whatsoever things are honest, whatsoever things are just, whatsoever things are pure, whatsoever things are lovely, whatsoever things are of good report; if there be any virtue, and if there be any praise, think on these things. Those things, which ye have both learned, and received, and heard, and seen in me, do: and the God of peace shall be with you". (*Philippians 4:8–9 KJV*)

"In the name of Jesus Christ, our LORD, and Savior, we have the capability to create a better world for everyone." Unto him is glory in the church by Christ Jesus throughout all ages, world without end". Amen (*Ephesians 3:21 KJV*)

Selah.

137

HELP FROM DISCRIMINATION

All Mighty Father, you are my help in time of need, when men of greed trampled my soul, and I become weary and confused and doubt stepped. Your Holy Spirit protects me, giving me the courage to continue. You're my everlasting Father of love, who cherishes me in my darkest hours; help me.

Beloved Father, LORD of the universe, maker of all men, help them to see through life's obstacles of hate and discrimination. Emancipate my mind from this ignorance, instilling in all men that they were created equally among themselves. Some intentions are good, while others are bad.

Give wisdom, knowledge, and understanding to earth's custodians, who don't see things clearly and who have, because of this ignorance. Betrayed the entire human race, causing pain, hurt, and unnecessary suffering to God's creations uneven the scales of life by invoking the spirit of greed and madness,

Unleashing their anger on God's children, Holy Father, fight the fight daily over the earth's resources, unequally balancing the wealth of the earth, Heavenly Father, protect our children from discrimination. Jesus Christ, the son of a righteousness God. The evil doers use violence, treachery, and deception to instill fear, guilt, and shame in the minds of the children of God.

They use their power and strength to fight against us, by attacking our minds, souls and physical bodies.

These geared toward bringing harm to other members of the human race because of the color of their skin. Hopeless, honestly, and intelligently, the children of God are not responsible for their skin. Color does not make them slaves.

Heavenly Father did not make their skin black for you to turn them into slaves. Holy God of Israel, this is making it difficult to love their fellow humans. Emancipate the minds of those who are responsible for this constant economic genocide. Heavenly Father, you cannot send your Son again because he already came and was crucified.

By the same unbelievers who are perpetrating hatred, violence, embarrassment, and low self-esteem against the brotherhood of men. It is time to send your band of angels to dispense reasoning, wisdom, and understanding and truth in the minds and souls of those blinded by greed. God of Moses,

If they learned to love themselves and not be dissatisfied, we can bring back love into your world, and open their minds to the thought that all men are created equal and judged by their actions and color.

Selah.

138

JUDGE ME, O LORD

Judge me, O LORD, so I can come up clean and worthy. Let not the minds of men judge me as I live on this earth. Judge me, O LORD, for you alone; know what exists in my heart and soul. I depend on your good favor and loving-kindness to live today. Today I am forever present in your counseling, relying on your still quiet voice that governs me.

Judge me, O LORD, and daily wash away my sins, for others, have taken the liberty to judge my actions. You O LORD are, the Mighty Savior of the world, said, "Judge not so ye may not be judged" (*Luke 6:37*). "Fight against those who fight against me" (*Psalm 35:1*). Have mercy on those who do not understand that judgment belongs to the LORD our God.

The author and finisher of our faith, (*Hebrew 12; 2 KJV*) who gives life everlasting, Judge me, O LORD, superior person, Jesus Christ, the one who was judged for all the wrong reasons and found not guilty by Father God and his angels in heaven. Atonement sacrifice for our sins, you spent time on the cross. Lamb of God, with the outcasts of society, suffered pain and was humiliated by those who could not understand your purpose on earth.

They felt threatened by your confidence in the Heavenly Father. Judge me, O LORD, for you alone have the power to judge and praise to you. Many may think that Jesus is not the only way to salvation and heaven, and he is a fictional character, or they can disguise themselves as the present-day God of all things, waiting to destroy the believers in Christ. Every knee shall bend, acknowledging Jesus is LORD and God.

Judge me, O LORD, for others have taken it upon themselves to judge me, clouding and to confuse the minds of others into thinking that killing without cause or purpose and compassion is an honorable thing to do. Punish them according to your Mighty Judgment. Be swift to dispense your wrath. Upon the evil ones send thunder and lightning;.

Discharge fiery objects from the skies and vast water to places where there was none, overshadowing them. Bring the fear of the LORD King Jesus Christ into their hearts.

Selah.

139

THE LORDS VENGEANCE

The LORDS vengeance is swift. He is not afraid to pour out his vengeance on the earth. Choose to serve him in spirit and truth. Close your eyes; turn away from the suffering and pain. The LORDS vengeance is to the children of men who have committed sins against the Heavenly Kingdom. He sends judgment from his Mighty Tower, slow to avenge.

He will send his angels to keep you in perfect peace, blessed and only ruler, LORD God of Hosts. Let not yourself be bothered by your enemies and the pain and suffering caused by sin. The LORD said, "Vengeance is mine" (*Romans 12:19*). In time of trouble, call upon my name of the LORD, and "he will keep you in perfect peace" (*Isaiah 26:3*).

Gracefully bring your tears and hurt to the altar, and I will wipe away your tears with my beautiful white garment. Through the secret heart of Jesus Christ, he will send his angels to keep you in perfect peace, glorified and just ruler, LORD God of Hosts. The LORDS vengeance is being powered out on the earth. Turn away from all the mortal sins committed against the heavenly kingdom.

LORD, you are the Blessed and only Ruler of the Universe, LORD God of host's peace and understanding cometh from the LORD, through eternity. Thunder and lightning, like a roaring lion—he is silently roaming; he will send his angels to keep you in perfect peace. Blessed and only Ruler, LORD God of hosts He will send his angels to keep you in perfect peace, blessed and only ruler, LORD God of hosts.

His patience is extended through eternity, waiting for you to change your way of thinking. The time is soon approaching when there will be no time. It's essential that we change our way of thinking. Christ of Israel has his fiery arrows pointed at his enemies. His sword of correction and salvation is ready, willing, and waiting to avenge his adversary, that daily fight against his Kingdom.

Selah.

140

ROWDY NEIGHBOR

Precious LORD, stay by my side today. Give me the patience to love my neighbor, the strength to relate, and the wisdom and knowledge to cope. Send your loving-kindness and patience to guide me through this ordeal. Be my protector against my rowdy neighbor.

My neighbor is rude and unforgiving. Love thy neighbor, LORD. Shield my mind that I may control my anger. Help me to deal with this situation and manage the constant, daunting provocation that comes from the family next door.

Dispatch your Angelic forces to calm and control the noise and confusion. Use me as your vessel to administer your grace and salvation to these troubled, lost sheep. Silence my mind, giving me the energy to deliver your love to my rowdy neighbor. Let your light shine through me.

Bring harmony and peace of mind to this uncontrollable situation, LORD. Give me the wisdom and knowledge to come to a peaceful solution, finding true friendship and cooperation from these strangers who are my Rowdy neighbors.

Prince of Peace, Father of creation, God of love and harmony, synchronize your blissful presence. Be the mediator. Bring cooperation and calmness; help me to surrender all egos and forge together to enjoy the peace and joy that comes from within.

LORD, bring the light of your love to my neighbors; LORD, your will be done on this earth. O Mighty Father, any reason if this request can't be fulfilled, then go forth and relocate my rowdy neighbor.

Selah.

141

JUDGMENT DAY

The last war is at hand; give me the greatest favor on judgment day. See us, O LORD, as we see ourselves.

O Faithful Father, judgment day is at hand. O Faithful Father, judgment day is at hand. Many souls have lost their whole minds and are bent on stirring up discord among citizens.

Allow us to walk in the garden of life with you.

Allow us to be in your presence, sitting at your side.

O Faithful Father, judgment day is at hand.

O Faithful Father, judgment day is at hand.

Let us behold your magnificent splendor and mercy.

Let us be with angels and saints as they pay homage to you. O Faithful Father, judgment day is at hand.

O Faithful Father, judgment day is at hand.

We say to you, "O Precious LORD, our souls belong to you". Preserve our eternal souls, chief magistracy. O Faithful Father, judgment day is at hand. O Faithful Father, judgment day is at hand.

Mighty Father, let us endure these tragedies without falling into Satan's trap laid for us. A trap filled with pain and suffering. We cannot go wrong with you in control of our minds and souls.

Keep us aware, sharing the wisdom, love, and understanding you give us among ourselves and supply us with the strength and forbearance to fight on. Faithful Father, judgment day is at hand. O Faithful Father, judgment day is at hand.

When this fighting is over, and the victory is ours once more, then you, LORD, will say to his soldiers, "Well done, good and faithful servant. You have been faithful over a little; I will set you over much. Enter into the joy of your master." (*Matthew 25:23 ESV*) O, Faithful Father, judgment day is at hand. O, Faithful Father, judgment day is at hand.

Selah.

142

JESUS SAVES

Evil men cast down, and God lifts up.
Daniel in the lion's den, for God's name sake,

Jesus saves, yes; he saves, he who keeps you; I will not slumber; we thank you for your goodness.

Jesus saves, yes; he saves, he who keeps you; we thank you for your goodness.

Jesus saves, yes; he saves, he who keeps you; we are grateful to you for your goodness.

Like you tested the faith of Shadrach, Meshach, and Abednego in the furnace for God's name sake.

Jesus saves, yes; He saves, he who keeps you; we thank you for your goodness.

Jesus saves, yes; he saves, he who keeps you; we thank you for your goodness.

Jesus saves, yes; he saves, he who keeps watches the sparrow can watch over you; thank you for your goodness.

Like Moses parting the Red Sea with unquestioning faith, for God namesake.

Jesus saves, yes; he saves, he who keeps you; we thank you for your goodness.

Jesus saves, yes; he saves, he who keeps you from harm; thank you for your goodness.

Jesus saves, yes; he saves, he who keeps you; we thank you for your goodness.

The Samaritan woman at the well, for his name's sake,

Jesus saves, yes; he saves, he who keeps you; we thank you for your goodness.

Jesus saves, yes; he saves, he who keeps you; we thank you for your goodness.

Jesus saves, yes; he saves, he who keeps you; we are grateful to you for your goodness.

He who raised the dead and healed the sick, for his name's sake,

Jesus saves, yes; he saves, he who keeps you; we thank you for your goodness.

Jesus saves, yes; he saves, he who keeps you; we are grateful to you for your goodness.

Jesus saves, yes; he saves, he who keeps you; we thank you for your goodness.

Jesus saves, yes; he saves, King of kings, LORDS of LORDS, and the Glorious Father.

Jesus saves, yes; he saves, he who keeps you; we thank you for your goodness.

Jesus saves, yes; he saves, he who keeps you; we thank you for your goodness.

Jesus saves, yes; he saves, he who keeps you; we thank you for your goodness.

Selah.

143

BE WITH ME ON MY JOURNEY HOME

All Mighty God, you stood by me through trials of physical and mental abuse, misuse, marriage and divorces, and childbirths. You stayed with me in the dark from the beginning of time to the end and brought me into the light at the time of my conception.

Through the dark tunnels of my mother's womb, you promised to stay with me from the cradle to the grave. Be with me on my journey home, forever and always. You have been my guide through times of uncertainty.

Living Father, your steady hands shielded me through all my personal failures. The courage you give me to live through these failures is magnificent. Your love and understanding have held me upward and brought me joy.

Be with me on my journey home, forever and always, through the darkness of the night, sleepless nights, and pain of worrying. You have given me many blessings, blessed confidence, peace, and your joy to enjoy.

Strengthen my heart, devoted Father. You were with me from the beginning of time and stayed with me through it all, Faithful Father, LORD of hope, who forever took the sting out of death. Be with me on my journey home, forever and always.

Mighty One, Alpha and Omega in you, I put my trust in you, continually until the resurrection. You promise your never-ending love for me, through thick and thin. I did not put my faith in this world and its trappings when the world was unkind.

You comforted me. I looked for love in men and women, and they were without. Be with me on my journey home, forever and always. Precious LORD, be with me, stay with me on my journey back to you.

Selah.

144

A PRAYER FOR SOMEONE SPECIAL

Mr. Rob Ford, former mayor of the City of Toronto

The LORD sent you on this earth, giving you power and charisma. You were sent to give hope to children and those lost. The arena is different with you out of the game, and the city already feels the confusion and pressure of your instants for caring about the people.

You paved the way through trials and tribulation. The All Mighty LORD only knows you were trying to accomplish good things. When the way became rocky and gray, The Mighty LORD, in all his wisdom, sent his angels to keep and guide you. The God of old, today, tomorrow, and forever, will be there to guide you in time of need,

Call upon the God of mercy in his powerful light. He will respond. The Mighty God will send his good angels to lift your spirit, and to surround you day and night. Your love for the City of Toronto and Torontonians showed in your dedication.

May the God of Truth and Light hold you in his bosom and cover you with his wings, dispensing his grace, love, and mercy, blocking and shielding "You will not be afraid of the terror by night, Or if the arrow that flies by day". (*Psalm 91:5 NASV*)

Gently ask the All Mighty God for a speedy recovery, renewing your mind, strengthening your health. Through the Holy Spirit, to work

Evette Forde

on behalf of the poor and disadvantaged, Good things for you in the future, through the LORD and Savior Jesus Christ.

All Mighty God of Abraham protects you.

Selah.

145

RUNNING FROM THEMSELVES

O LORD, some are searching to find themselves. They are running up and down all day long, visiting churches daily, especially on Sundays. They attend the Catholic Church. They cling to the Holy Mary, holding her hands and garment, and they appear to be seeking favor from the black saint and Jesus Christ.

(*Holy Saints Forever*) The deceivers' make the sign of the cross to Jesus Christ and say "as Salamu Alaykum," and act holier than Holy. When they come out of the church and get on the streets of America and Toronto, Ontario, they drive without mercy, impolite and intolerant. It appears inhuman. In the malls, they stare at you directly in your face. LORD an unpleasant look on their faces.

And act as though anyone who doesn't look like them is an intruder to the malls and should not be there. When exiting the malls, apartment buildings, and elevators, they do not hold the front doors open behind them as a kind gesture to their fellow men.

Mighty LORD, we live in a multicultural environment in Canada and soon to be America.

America and Canada, our societies are not created one religion or culture having dominance over another. LORD, the establishment is telling us to watch what we are saying. And how we are saying yet, they are rediscovering themselves through some other religion. While the teaching of Jesus Christ, as embodied in the New Testament, and Holy Bible emphasizing Jesus Christ as our Savior (*Christianity is being subdued*).

Christians and the Canadian and American experience being undermined, yet, on the other hand, they are dissing the hopeful, uplifting, fortitude Canadian and American experience and its religion. Mighty LORD, the Canadian and American experiences slowly replaced with a strange unknown experience. The Canadian and American experience built on Freedom of Speech and Expression and Religious Freedom for all. Respect for life and one another.

The new cultural wave filled with no respect for the poor and needy, impoliteness, racket, mistrust, in-depth corruption, hatred, no peace, any tolerance, savagery, unclean customs, pollution of the mind, and no respect for women. Some of the leaders and fellow Canadians and Americans are compromising the integrity and have lost their national identity. Powerful LORD, Mighty LORD, things are getting a bit frustrating.

Selah.

146

SUMMERTIME FUN WITH THE LORD

Precious LORD, who formulated the seasons, thank you for creating the summer, an opportunity for us to venture outside of our homes to enjoy the sun and have some fun, soaking up the sunshine, clearing our minds, enriching our souls,

In your infinite wisdom, you have placed all of these elements for us to partake of, especially the summer sun. We can feel your love and adoration for us, with the bright yellow, energetic sun, beaming from the sky, smiling down on us.

O LORD, the sun brings tantalizing beams of streaming energy, joy, laughter, contentment, and growth. I am mesmerized; your sacred heart, the heart of Jesus Christ, opens up with joy and immense energy. Only fools would assume that you were not here on earth among us, nearby.

LORD, I am, said the LORD, who elevated himself from the dead. I rose from the dead for you to enjoy the summer fun. See my face, feel my energy flowing from the heavens, have fun, and take your worries to the foot of the cross the sacred heart of Jesus has the power.

Live all lives in harmony with each other; live in love that beams from the heavens. LORD, my heart is open wide for you to see my soul. The love of All Mighty Father is holding you up today, day and night. Have fun.

In the summertime, partake of this love.

The son sitting on the right hand of the Father knows each one of you knows in your heart that the father's intended and purpose for you all was to love one another; you have taken the LORDS love for granted, pushing him aside. LORD, give me the glory to have fun in the summertime.

Feel the rays of my sunny love as it touches your skin, for when the moon turns to sackcloth, my love, you will no more feel my face. You will no longer see. Live for and within the teaching of the New Testament.

Glorify your LORD and Savior Jesus Christ; let no man or woman put his words asunder. Fight the good fight.

Selah.

147

THE BLACK MADONNA

Virgin Mother, your descendants, is in a heap of trouble living in the twenty-first century. They are walking around town, thinking that slavery was wrong. They did not receive compensation for past injustices. Mighty, Mighty God, in the prelude of things; the authority was forced to remove the yoke of slavery from around their necks.

Massa, done removed the shackles from around their feet, leaving them indigenous to themselves. Heavenly Father, while they engulfed in the belly of mental and physical bondage, they failed to observe and learn from their slave masters about the ways in which the establishments that governed them did business.

They have also failed to see the way in which people responsible for their enslavement go about loving themselves. God the Father of creation, instead of the children of the black Madonna living in America and around the world they should learn to love themselves and the United States of America.

Black Madonna, Virgin mother, your offspring's needs to take charge of their destiny. Adopt the laws and norm of the land by not burning the flag. Respect themselves, county, anthem, and the police. Apply the positive they have learned from their former slavery masters to enrich themselves, LORD, remove the curse from their minds and have mercy on the children of the black Madonna.

They all have developed hatred and disrespect for themselves, frustration, confusion, and deep anger. Your kids did not take the time to organize themselves, their children, homes, and communities. This intolerance for themselves is eating away at their integrity. Powerful, all Mighty God,

The ways they treat themselves and their kind are appalling, while their children are practicing every kind of unholy act against their bodies, minds, souls, families, and society. Black lives matter; yes, black lives matter. It does matter. All lives matter and must matter to you. First, your life must be important to you before it matters to someone else.

Virgin Mother speaks to the honorable Father Godhead on behalf of your children because they are still wondering around lost in the universe.

Selah.

148

THE WHITE DOVE

Peace is with you always and forever. The white doves shouldn't be taken lightly; pray for peace. The Holy Spirit is making himself known to men today. He disenfranchised with the way the house of people is operating and administering to the children of the saints. (*Abba Father.*) The spirits of darkness attacked the two white doves.

Holy Father, in his infinite wisdom, understanding, and sheer disgust, is about to dispense retribution for the acts committed against his kingdom. He is preparing and commanding his saints in heaven to show no mercy to humankind.

The Mighty One, who is the real King of Kings, LORD of LORDS, the one who cannot be bought or sold, has previously passed judgment on the earth. Persons of the earth are feeling his wrath and are already preparing to flee their cities and villages. He has commanded his saints to unleash the full force of the spirit of greed.

The All Mighty God is using the spirit of greed once more and has sent a foreign entity to use their wealth and camaraderie to drive out, shake up, distort, deceive, fear, confuse, frustrate, challenge, demolish, slaughter, and bring mayhem to present-day governments around the world and their citizens.

Greed has engulfed the minds of these government leaders around the world. Their morbid policies of evil are apparent in the lives of their citizens. They have no regard for human lives, God the Father, and his laws. LORD, they are making sure their pockets are filled with the spoils of their deceivers, while their citizens are paying the price for their greed and evil ways.

These leaders camouflage themselves with their rhetoric and deceitfulness, making promises they cannot keep while pleasing their cultural (*goons)* to bring more disaster to the children of God. The white doves—do not underestimate the powers of the white dove. His Holy Spirit will once more rain on earth to destroy the wicked.

The white doves are not to be taken lightly when the black crows attack. Watch out for the pope!

Selah.

149

THE PLAN FOR PROSPERITY

God's plan for us is to prosper properly. Everlasting God, your blueprint for humankind was not solely based on their having and worshiping materialism. Your plans for us were not for us to worship and destroy nature (*not to worship his creation*) but worship the Creator himself. Enjoy don't destroy. He is a jealous God.

The oppressors are all running around lost and in disarray, angry and displeased. All the material goods they have stored up for themselves have not brought them any joy or happiness. Mighty God, you put them in the Garden of Eden to enjoy and protect.

The evil doers, they became obsessed with the creation and forgot the Creator, his presence, and request. You cannot blame the catastrophe which took place in the Garden of Eden on the woman who resided with Adam. The episode with the snake in the Garden was because man became blinded by the light of God.

They are living in darkness. Blinded by the material things that God established, they have replaced the Creator and worship the creation. His will is for you to prosper as your soul advances. The prosperity of the soul is enrichment, and it is stronger than the material blessing.

When God the Father observes in you that you have mastered the law of prosperity, "he will give you your heart's desires". (*Psalm 37:4 NASV*) He is a loving and giving God of the universe who wants his children to prosper and live happily. Prosper as your soul prospers in

God the Father, Son of Jesus Christ the Holy Ghost (*Ruling Father of all*).

They came to the planet earth to live in peace, joy, and happiness. They got blinded by the shiny light of materialism, exasperated the land, and fought the yellow, black, and red tribes for their inheritance given to them by God the Father.

And they were consumed by the materialism here on earth, so they walk the earth with a frown, injecting everyone around them with their poisonous venom of greed and destruction. *The end is in sight.*

Selah.

150

SILENT WATERS FLOW DEEP

Honorable LORD, I call upon you. You never seem to speak. You kept your voice for me in my darkest and deepest moment of wanting and fighting to gain something worthwhile here on earth. When I became stuck and lacked experience and knowledge, not knowing you, I still called out your name. "Abba Father," help me, Abba Father, your gentle still, noiseless voice. Spoke to my soul.

LORD, you were silent while teaching me. Not at any time did I understand your silence so that you could teach me; never could I figure out why. Within these trials and tribulations, I wanted you to speak to me. "Help me, LORD," I called. "Can't you see I want and am hurting? Stretch forth your Mighty hands and do something. Forgive me and remove the curse of my ancestors.

Time is running out on me. Can't you see?" Your silences were even more intense. "Be still and know I am the LORD your God" (*Psalm 46: 10 NASB*) seems to be silently administering to my soul. My mind became drunk with your silence, as I listen to your gentle voice.

As you slowly teach me, showing me, asking me, talking to me, whispering to me, holding me, comforting me, guiding me, supplying my needs, confiding in me, protecting me, giving me courage.

Being my personal God and Savior, allowing me to have fun, giving me confidence, protecting my integrity, giving me wisdom and knowledge, sturdiness, everlasting joy, love for my fellow men and women, and shielded me from disasters and held me through death, my silent partner.

Yes, peaceful waters flow deep in the LORD. Yes, you answered me and delivered me, giving me freedom of the mind and soul, living an undercurrent, wanting only what your love has provided for me. Yes, quiet waters flow deep down. I pay homage to you that still small gentle voice, who always speaks to me, so gently and so right. Silent water flows beneath.

Selah.

151

REALM

Mighty LORD, the heavenly kingdom was broken when men and women of ill faith disguised themselves as a confidant of the LORD and used their authority and positions of power to perform acts of sexual misconduct on our children, as they destroyed their dignity and self-esteem and stole their innocence.

Mighty LORD, you gave them the willpower to tame their sex sentiment. Instead, they turned themselves into beasts without logic. Spiritual Father of rationality and consciousness, they descended and preyed on the innocent minds and bodies of their unblemished victims.

Heavenly Father shows no mercy on those who disguise themselves as trustworthy subjects, gaining confidence and unleashing their valetudinarian human predatory spirit. It has genuinely converted their souls to the point where they break the oath of the covenant.

LORD, when they perform these tasteless, meaningless act of sexual deviancy on the guiltless minor' lives. Send your spirit of revenge to slowly pluck away at their souls. Your will is to leave them with nothing but misery and obscurity, so their souls judged according to your divine covenant. Heal their minds.

The Powerful universe, deal with them as your will intended. Comfort and bring rationality the spirit of the children who unfortunately became victims to these subhuman entities. Let the victims know that these acts perpetrated on them were not manifested in the LORDS plans for their lives and are ungodly.

These acts of evil done by the fallen angels of the Universe whose intentions are to defy the will of God.

Selah.

152

TREACHERY

The job of the politicians is to deceive the masses. Mighty Father, you conquered death on the cross by the hands of the politicians. The best thing for the black man living in America and Canada is to find his identity and stick with it. Those who govern do not have the ordinary people's interest as their priority.

Those who governed the wealth of this world used their power, wisdom, and understanding to subdue and misuse the masses of people worldwide. LORD, open the eyes of your people and the ones whose souls trapped in life's darkness. Mighty LORD, the entire economic system,

And the intellectual powers you have bestowed on humankind have manifested itself into the dark pit of fathomless greed. This greed has taken over the minds of men and women, causing them to make use of God's children. They took the sons of God for granted by using and abusing them.

Their aims are to deceive and confuse them to bring about the destruction of the Kingdom of God. LORD, they have accomplished this through their fraudulent nature and managed to invoke the spirit of perfidy, unleashing this spirit on their follower. Their treacherous indulgence has only served to betray the trust of the masses.

Father of the universe, they are manipulating and violating the allegiance of faith and confidence of the poor trusting people,

Selah.

153

SODOM AND GOMORRAH

LORD, it is strange in the way we came to accept and have unveiled the chained-up evil spirit of sodomy. The powers are supporting and have legalized this agenda in America and Canada without properly educating the public of the health risks.

Mighty LORD, the president, has even gone so far as to unveil the rainbow colors in front of the White House. In my opinion, it was done to let us know that a sodomite resides or was living in there. This act sends a dangerous message to young people.

Where is the surgeon general in all this? Isn't it his or her job to warn the people of the consequence of their actions as it relates to their health and the health of others? Did they not put warnings on cigarette boxes, indicating the health risk and smokers' fate if they continued to smoke cigarettes?

Mighty Father, then why are LGBT promoting this lifestyle without cautionary health hazards? LORD of the universe who healed sickness and diseases of the minds, bodies, and souls of men, administer your angels to redeem these misdeeds that have logged themselves in the minds of subjects. Set the minds of men and women free to conquer this unhealthy lifestyle.

The cities of Sodom and Gomorrah destroyed because of the despicable things that took place there. The Dead Sea—nothing grows or can live there. Sodomy is not an alternate lifestyle. It is a sin performed against the mind and body. It is a style of death!

Selah.

154

POWER PLAY

The world's leaders are in a power-play situation. Winner takes all the wealth and power. And all of God's children suffer in poverty and go to hell. Death and anguish on the horizon. The veil of evil lifted, and the drums of war are silently beating.

The intentions of the evil doers are to manipulate and subjugate the weak and unintelligent. LORD, controlling the world's resources on the ground and in the air has made men insane and without love—so mad that they do not know what to do with their wealth and power.

The earth filled with abundant resources. Men of greed and manipulative spirits have become intoxicated with the world's wealth. They are manipulating the minds of the children. Their small minds are in a state of war of ideals and morality.

Fear and tension surround the arena. And life has become unbearable to some, just hanging in there. Mr. Opportunist you can't fight against nature. How much do you want to pull from the air, sea, and ground? LORD, you have destroyed, your brothers with greed and consumption in your day-to-day activities only ripping off your fellow men.

And the environment you have created wealth by raping the earth and everything that's on the earth. Your living conditions have turned you into mad men and women, drunk with consumption and greed. Time is running out. Have you prepare your underground bunkers.

The fat lady is starting to sing. The LORD is showing your iniquity to the world. The establishment is exposing their dirty laundry to the public. The trumpet sounded. Wake up; it's too late, if not for yourselves then for your children. The LORD of Hosts is still on his throne.

"Power play, power play," some says in their hearts. "There are no gods." Well, God individually lives within each of you. Surprise! You are only fighting against yourselves for your evil righteousness, cannibalizing your inner selves, revolting against yourselves and hating you. The joke is on you all.

O Mighty men and women, what are you planning, masterminding for the last applause, the final curtain? Is it World War III?

O Mighty men and females, what are you planning, masterminding for the last applause, the final curtain? Is it World War III? The joke is on you all.

O Mighty men and women, what are you planning, masterminding for the last applause, the final curtain? Is it World War III?

Selah.

155

FOR THE MASSES

Many of the world leaders do not believe in the words written in the Bible. The masses of people's minds are being programmed to accept things that are not conducive to the will of God. They are like sheep led to the slaughterhouse. Their minds and souls are being twisted to advance this evil.

Many seem to think that the powers of God are not sturdy enough to withstand the devil's powers. O LORD, their freedom is slowly being taken away from them, as they are punished severely, for exercising the laws governing the United States of America's Constitution. (*Yahweh,*) protect and sharpen the minds of the people, removing the veil from their eyes.

LORD, take them to a safe place where they can be comforted and care of by souls that are kind and loving. The governmental powers that are in control have no souls and are empty with the darkness of their transgressions. People pray for your government leaders that they would put the needs of the above their greed.

This mindless, soulless psychological disorder is in their minds. They do not believe in the one and only true God of the universe. This destructive spirit will wreck others who trust, believe and follow them. LORD, seal the minds of your beloved children, making them aware of the situation and danger they face.

Give your faithful followers the wisdom and provisions to flee to safety when the banking and Internet services malfunction and the evil minded people rise. As the red flag of destruction and confusion raises its head in the Western nations and around the world, make us aware of the seventy-two hours' notice.

The children of God can relocate from the cities and seek safety on higher ground. Save us from the cages. They are planning for them. Mighty Savior, who calms the seas and gave victory to King David, forgives us for past sins. And bestow your diligence on the masses of people and bring us the victory over confusion and tyranny.

Selah.

156

"HOES" AND PROSTITUTION

What is the difference between the politician and the average street walker? The LORD doesn't see much difference. They both are selling their souls and integrity for dollars. The Democratic Party in America is one of the biggest run "hoe houses" in the world.

They have been pimping out the underprivileged members of the black and white communities for years and years. They have solicited the black politicians, entertainers, pastors, and the sleazy black community leaders to help them influence and pimp out their communities' parishioners.

They use the black community leaders and the black professionals or the ones who thought they had made it to corral the remainder of the black community, confusing and keeping them impoverished. Good and mighty LORD. Precious Jesus Christ, the black leaders of America like Jesse Jackson and Al Sharpton the established so call black professionals, black stars in Hollywood and high-paid athletes.

They are having a difficult time financially organizing themselves and their communities. O, Mighty LORD, the Back-to-Africa Liberia project established in the 19th century, because of the lack of insight and the results tribal wars and ignorance. Even that project was a failure. The revenues and fame they receive from their professions not entirely redistributed in a positive way in the black communities.

LORD, the show must go on. It's clear that all they are doing is prostituting themselves in the white man's game. The black communities are not gaining and are not learning anything positive in this game of life. While they are performing on the world stage, unconsciously or consciously, they forgot why they are in these positions of power. Almighty God is frowning on them.

It was their responsibility to educate and bring themselves together. What shame and disgrace will come to the leadership in the black communities? The black establishments continue to push the white man's agenda and are subjecting members of their communities to killing and keeping their black community down.

Their minds poisoned to a point where they are harming themselves. LORD, there were both white and black overseers in the day of slavery. The role of the white and black superintendent was to make sure the masses of blacks stayed in line and carried out the economic side of slavery, while psychologically destroying their minds.

Like the role of Stephen, played by Samuel L. Jackson in the movie Django Unchained. Today the Democratic Party in America is prostituting them, and the black community leaders are pimping out members of the black communities, leaving them confused and ignorant.

Selah.

157

THE MOTHER-IN-LAW

God, do not send me a meddling mother-in-law who is demanding, controlling, and intrudes into the lives of her son or daughter and that person's spouse is what the Bible calls a "busybody" (*Timothy 5:13*).

It comes at a time when a man and woman leave their birth families and are raising their brand-new families. They both are responsible for loving and protecting each other and their new family. God bless them and keep them together.

You are the mother-in-law. The LORD has entrusted you with the opportunity to raise your children. Not to use and take over their lives, but to give them room to grow and become men and women.

You cannot infiltrate their marriage to create havoc in their lives. This action is an assault on the sanctity of marriage and violates (*Genesis 2:23–24*). Assist them sometimes with something like babysitting, house sitting, or in some cases taking your grandchildren to school, the park or shopping at the mall.

However, when it comes to the bond that was created by God between your sons-in-law and daughters-in-law, this relationship needs to be respected. This kind of irrational behavior on your behalf can only bring friction and destruction to this union. Boundaries need to be set and respected, regardless of the resistance you encounter.

God has given you the boundaries, bothersome nosey mother-in-law. Mother in law all you are doing is creating problems for your children by destroying the marriage, making their lives miserable. Use your wisdom and understanding; your job is to nurture the marriage and the relationship and make sure they stay happily in love.

Selah

158

BOOTS ON THE GROUND

The LORDS powers are still operating in the land of the living. The time will soon come when men and women in the United States of America and Canada will take up arms and go to war. Brace yourselves for this dilemma.

Meanwhile, there is suffering and despair in the ghettoes of America and Canada. The political atmosphere in America and Canada is just about ripe for an Arab Spring uprising revisited.

LORD, boots on the ground; how about putting boots in the classrooms of America and Canada? Instead of using taxpayers' money to finance wars and bring refugees from other countries into the ghettoes of your cities, use the money to educate.

The people and reconstruct these rundown schools and neighborhoods that exist in the black communities. Busing black kids to schools located in better areas was not the answer to the education problems in the past.

Creating good schools and implementing stern discipline in the neighborhoods where the black children live was a better solution for educating the black children. Where is the present-day Mr. Joe Clark Public school administrator born 1939? Mighty LORD,

I am tired of seeing the majority of black men and women in utterly confusing, out-of-control, adverse situations. This difficult problem exists in the homes and communities and is cause for concern by the black leaders, like Jesse Jackson and Al Sharpton.

O, Mighty LORD, the black sportsmen, and women, teachers, media, colleges and university professors, lawyers, mothers, fathers, professional and ordinary members of the black communities, all of you need to get it together. And give this new generation of black children something substantial and confident to work with and look forward.

Put your boots on the ground to protect our young people. The good LORD is listening and watching adverse actions of the ones who were anointed to lead the black people. The political climate and economics are against you all. They are pushing you of your out to make with safe cities

The other races of people are trying to keep their acts together. It is embarrassing to see black leaders and principles misrepresenting their people and leading them in the wrong direction. Their communities are out of control. They cannot cooperate for the common good of the children and communities.

Mighty LORD, blacks haven't made any progress since the last Civil Rights Movement March and The Million Man March on the Mall in Washington, DC, and black lives matter. These young men and women should be taught to have spiritual and economic elevation, not racism.

LORD, help them to put their house in order and stop placing the blame and problems on the white race. White people are not your problem. LORD, lift the minds of the black people and bring deliverance and morality to their souls. Band them together as a monolithic group.

Have them not destroy themselves and their communities. Stomp out the destructive eggs in their communities, and help the progressive black people who are trying to shine your light on the ignorance portrayed by the unconscious black people.

Selah.

159

PRAISES FOREVER

Praises forever God, the LORD, His mercy will endure incessantly.
Praise forever the LORD with the stomping of feet. Praises forever
with your heart and soul, Praises forever with your going out and
coming

Praises forever at breakfast, lunch, and dinner times,
Praises forever in happy times and sad times.
Praises forever, in limited times, through all times,
Praises forever, whether things are good or bad,

At all times praises forever, to the LORD.

Praises forever; he lives in your hearts and souls.
Praises forever even if your heads are being cut off,
Praises forever; the wicked know him but choose to rebel.
Praises forever, God of Abraham, Isaac, and God of Jacob,

Praises forever, perpetually, you are fatherless; he is the Heavenly Father.
Praises forever, eternally, LORD of the Universe,
Praises forever, incessantly, for he is good. His mercy is everlasting.
Praises forever; to him in the days of your youth and days of old age.
Praises forever, God forever and continually, in sickness and good health
Praises forever, in life and or death,
Praises forever, God perpetually,
He is God, Eternal.

Selah.

160

SING PRAISES

LORD, you said, "No weapon formed against me shall prosper" (*Isaiah 54:17(NKJV)*).

You were the one who said, "Love one another" (*John 15:12*), and we disobeyed. You were the one who said, "Thou shall not Covet Thy neighbor's goods" (*Exodus 20:17*), and we disobeyed. You were the one who said, "Honor your father and mother" (*Deuteronomy 5:16*), and we disobeyed. You were the one who said, "Thou shall not kill" (*Exodus 20:13 NKJV*), and we disobeyed.

Sing praises with harps and trumpets, rap, rock and roll, soul, soca, country music, opera.
Sing praises from the valleys low and mountains high.

You were the one who said, "Thou shall not worship false Gods" (*Exodus 20:2–6*), and we disobeyed. You were the one who said, "Thou shall not have any gods besides me" (*Exodus 20:3*), and we disobeyed. You were the one who said, "Thou shall not bear false witness" (*Exodus 20:16*), and we disobeyed.

Sing praises to the abundance of life and the King of Life, God the providing Father.
Sing praises from the valleys low and mountains high.

Heavenly Father God manifested and delivered through Jesus Christ and the devotional book of scrolls, which contained his organized plan for humankind. Sing praises with harps and horns, rap, rock, soul, soca, country music.

Sing praises; the morning dew saw your face and adores you.
Sing praises of your loving-kindness toward humankind and creation.

The providing Father you, LORD, took the sting out of death and dying (*1 Corinthians 15:56*) and told us you would be with us in all things to the end. We are not to be afraid of death or life's circumstances. You were the one, who said,

Sing praises to the abundance of life and the King of Life, God.
Sing praises of your loving-kindness toward humankind and creation.

"Thou shall love thy neighbor" (*Mark 12:31),* and we disobeyed. You were the one, who said,

Mighty LORD, "Furthermore we have had fathers of our flesh which corrected us, and we gave them reverence: shall we not much rather is in subjection unto the Father of Spirits, and live"? (*Hebrew 12:9 (KJV) (https://www.bible.com/bible/1/heb.12.9.kjv#!-)*

Sing praises; the morning dew has seen your face and adored you.
Sing praises; you are the star who shines at night.

"You were the one who feeds the multitudes (*Matthew 14:13–21)* and turned water into wine" (*John 2:1–11 KJV*).

Sing praises; the soft, gentle sun rises in the morning. Sing praises; the light quietly whispers your name, and the darkness is afraid.

You were the one who said, "Love your brother" and sister. We disobeyed. You were the one who gave us life, and we are destroying it. You said to parents, "Do not exasperate your children" (*Ephesians 6:4*), and they disobeyed. You said, "Look toward the light" (*John 8:12*). Your words of wisdom and blessings bestowed on us, and we neglected it.

Sing praises; you are the gentle lamb who lies down with the lions. Sing praises, let the dead burn the dead.

In spite of our disobedience to you, O Mighty LORD, you presently have us living underneath your loving grace. God gives us this grace period, enough time for us to repent. Embrace us and kept us together. If men cannot praise you, LORD, then the stones under the earth shall praise you.

Sing praises; he comforts you in time of mourning.
Sing praises; he loves you even though you don't believe.

Father, have mercy and forgive us because we disobeyed your words. LORD, like Job, trusted you in our agony and despair; we give you praises. We sing praises to you for our deliverance. Sing praises.

Selah.

161

GLORY CHANT

Let the angels in the heavens victoriously sing forever and ever, amen.
Glory to God in the highest,
Glory to God in the highest,
Glory to God in the highest

Let us bow down to the King of Kings, LORD of LORDS.
Glory to God in the highest,
Glory to God in the highest,
Glory to God in the highest

"He is the heir of all things, the" (*http://www.sacred-texts.com/chr/tbr/tbr024.htm*) faithful and living God of integrity,
Glory to God in the highest,
Glory to God in the highest,
Glory to God in the highest

Residing head over all things, you are the beginning of the world without end.
Glory to God in the highest,
Glory to God in the highest,
Glory to God in the highest,

The resurrection and light, cleanse; his kingdom will be established on the earth.
Glory to God in the highest,
Glory to God in the highest

Glory to God in the highest,

Let the angels in the heavens victoriously sing forever and ever.
Glory to God in the highest,
Glory to God in the highest,
Glory to God in the highest

Let us bow down to the King of Kings, the LORD of LORDS.
Glory to God in the highest,
Glory to God in the highest,
Glory to God in the highest

"He is the heir of all things, the" (*http://www.sacred-texts.com/chr/tbr/tbr024.htm*) genuinely living God of integrity.
Glory to God in the highest,
Glory to God in the highest,
Glory to God in the highest

Residing head over all things, you are the beginning of the world without end.
Glory to God in the highest,
Glory to God in the highest,
Glory to God in the highest

The resurrection and the light, cleanse; his Kingdom will be established on the earth.
Glory to God in the highest,
Glory to God in the highest,
Glory to God in the highest
Glory to God in the highest

Selah.

162

SUNSHINE

Powerful Father, Wonderful God, I see your handiwork. Mighty Father God, I see your precious sunshine and feel its splendid glory here on earth. God, I feel the rays and warmth of your sunshine, absorbing its energy into my veins. Your faithfulness to men and women is never-ending and consistent.

Mighty Father, Splendid God, I see your handiwork. Mighty Father, marvelous God, I feel the rays and warmth of your sunshine. Wisdom and foresight you give, planting nurseries of flowers, watching them as they slowly grow and blossom into multitudes of colors and life.

Mighty Father, Supreme God, I see your handiwork. Grand Father, Splendid God I feel the rays and warmth of your sunshine. Wisdom and foresight you give us to plant a variety of foods, flowers, treats, and the beasts of the field that lay down their lives each day to nourish us.

You are gently stretching forth your wisdom toward the soil and injecting life into our existence.

Watching the plants and flowers as they slowly grow to feed and nourish your children, Mighty Father, splendid God, I see your handiwork. Forceful Father, Grand God, I feel the rays and warmth of your precious sunshine.

LORD, you are providing air and water and sunlight, the winds carry the seeds; everything is so beautifully designed and orchestrated.

Mighty Father, splendid God, I see your handiwork; it's picturesque to me. Active Father, wonderful God, I feel the warmth of your sunshine.

I pay homage and worship you first, in all things, O Mighty LORD, glorifying you and your sun, basking in your handiwork, giving you all the praise always. LORD, you are the sunshine given to men. They took your intense sun and turned it into distortion.

Their thoughts and deeds filled with comprising deceitfulness and destruction—why LORD? Why, LORD, have men become noncompliant and bitter toward you? Is it because you did not save them from hurting themselves when, all along, they were supposed to check themselves and protect themselves?

Selah.

163

PRAISE THE LORD

Praise the LORD, for he is wonderful.
Praise him in laughter and tears.
Praise him from the mountain tops and valleys below. Praise him in the synagogues, mosques, chapels, streets, sidewalks, schools, and churches, walking and lying down.

"Praise the LORD for all he has done:" (*Psalm 111 CEV*) (*https://www.biblegateway.com/passage/*)

"Praise the LORD for All He Has Done." (*https://www.biblegateway.com/passage/*) (*Psalm 111 CEV*) for the children of men when you are feeling impoverished, quietly lock Jesus Christ in your hearts and souls, and praise him.

He will send his angels to show you the way. Praise him, in your cars, offices, complete parts of your homes (*kitchen, bathroom, and rooftops.*)

Praise him, for he is good. His goodness Is everlasting. Praise him, for he is the bright morning star.
Praise the LORD in silence with loud noises, shouting
Honor him in your hearts and souls.

You must dance the dance of life, especially when you are still in the land of the living. Praise him in good times and bad times.

Praise him in the light and darkness, mornings and evenings.

Praise him for keeping you safe while you sleep at night and for waking you up in the morning.

Praise the LORD, the light of this world, for he is everlasting.

Praise him for waking you in the morning and sending you on your way and for keeping you all day long.

Praise him. He is the beginning and the end.

Praise him; he joyously rose from the dead and was peaceful and solemn. His spirit still lives within us.

Praise the one who said, "Let there be light" (*Genesis 1:3 NASB*), and the darkness disappeared. The light was pleasurable and everlasting. It is good. Praise him with your heart and soul. All living things praise him.

The LORD is consistently rearranging from the beginning of time to the end. Always, praise him, O Ye Faithful Souls.

Praise him for anointing his disciples, commissioning them to create the books of the New Testament. Because of the LORDS blood we are presently living by the principles bestowed on us, written in the new book of testament and not by the old book of testament.

Praise him. LORD of wisdom and understanding,

Praise you for anointing your beloved disciples, inspiring them to create the New Testament. Glory and wisdom always and forevermore, lift their spirits and souls up to you. LORD.

Praise you. You are one with the Father, Son, and Holy Ghost.

Selah.

164

SING PRAISES TO THE LORD

The stones scattered on the earth and underground have the powers to praise the LORD. Everything that breathes has the authority to worship him. Sing praises to the LORD with all instruments. Sing praises unto him, LORD God Jehovah, for he is LORD. Sing praises to him who looks on in silence as men ruin their lives, along with the planet and all decent things.

The joy of *Yeshua* is our strength. His love will never cease. *Yeshua* rises with the sun each day to watch over his chosen ones. Sing praises to him. Honor him in truth and love. Sing praises to the LORD, the King of Kings, LORD of LORDS. Sing praises to him, the LORD, for his mercy is everlasting and spirit worthy. Sing praises to the LORD in the dawn of the mornings and when you lie at night.

In spite of all that's happening today, he is on his throne. Men and women have come a very long way with the help of the LORD and his divine patience. His journey here on earth is drawing to an end, but this world will continue to exist without men. It is noted in the scriptures—the Holy Father said, "World without end." (*Ephesians 3:21KJV*). Amen.

The father's time is at hand. Sing praises to the LORD, for he is good. His mercy will endure forever. Sing praises to him, the LORD, with your every breath. O LORD, we beseech you and sing praises unto you. The birds in the sky sing praises to the LORD. The beasts in the field sing praises to the LORD. The fishes in the ocean sing praises to the LORD. Praise him, all nations, and the LORDS eternal spirits. Bow to him.

Life will never end. However, the duration of men will end. Sing praises to him, the LORD. Sing praises to the LORD. Today people's sin has become natural. Sing praises unto him, the LORD. They have accepted sin as though it was right and natural. "The World without end" (*Ephesians 3:21KJV*). — This World will continue to exist without men and women. Put your confidence in the LORD Jehovah.

He will lift you up to meet him in heaven. Your soul renewed. Sing praises to him, the LORD. Sing praises to him, the LORD. Sing praises to him, the LORD, Sing praises to him, the LORD. Sing praises to him, the LORD, and sing praises to him, the LORD. Sing praises to him, the LORD. Sing praises to him, the LORD, and sing praises to him, the LORD.

Sing praises to him, the LORD. Sing praises to him, the LORD, and sing praises to him, the LORD. Sing praises to him, the LORD. Sing praises to him, the LORD. Sing praises to him, the LORD. Sing praises to him, the LORD. He is consistently showing mercy to the children of men.

Selah.

165

SING PRAISES

Sing praises; make joyful noises unto the LORD. Sing, all you nations, Sing praises on the earth, in the sea, air, and on the mountaintops, Sing praises with joy and thanksgiving, for he is King of Kings, LORD of LORDS.

Sing praises with guitars, cymbals, flutes, drums, harps, bagpipes, steel pans, and voices. Sing praises in the bedroom; sing in the bathroom, kitchen, hallways, and all. Sing praises in the car. His loving-kindness is forever. He is God in the flesh.

Sing, sing, sing, sing, and sing praises, for he is good. His loving-kindness is forever, sing. Don't wait until it is too late to sing. Don't wait until you are cold. Sing praises while you can. Sing quietly; sing praises. Don't wait until you become affluent or sick. Sing praises to the King of Kings, whether you are poor or moneyed.

Sing praises if you're sick and while you're healthy. Sing; Sing praises unto the LORD, for he is good. His mercy is forever. Sing, sing and sing. Sing in the synagogue and churches, temples, mosques, shrines, parliaments, Congress, and your home and car. Sing, sing and sing. Sing praises to God, your Maker.

He is the God of the covenant. Sing; Sing praises unto the LORD, for he is good. His mercy is forever. Sing, sing, sing, sing, and sing praises to the God of Abraham and the God of Israel. Sing; Sing praises unto the LORD, for he is good. His mercy is forever. Sing, the children of men. In the sea and on land, look up toward the stars. Sing praises unto the one who removed the stone.

Sing, sing and make noise. Sing and sing hallelujah in the mornings to see another day. Sing, sing and sing. Sing in the evening, for his loving-kindness, is always. He came out of the grave and descended into heaven. Sing, sing, and sing in the dark; sing in the light; sing in the silence of your soul.

Selah.

166

PRECIOUS LORD

Precious LORD, the Lions, is at our gate once again. The children of God face misery and pain. Their enemies are as many as the grains of sand on the seashore, and they are from all sides. Give us the wisdom to resist.

Precious LORD, men, have gone crazy with ideas of destruction and intolerance for your name's sake. Hate has once again engulfed the hearts and souls of men and women in an infuriating, cynical way and has entered into our schools and governments.

Precious LORD, they disguised their thoughts, intentions, and deeds in different ways to deceive and confuse our children, forcing their bad intentions with aims to conquer and control the minds and souls of others. You, O LORD, anointed King David, sending him into battle and giving him the victory.

Precious LORD, whose strength and wisdom are as bright as the morning star and who is quick to respond, promise your children never to leave or forsake them, even onto death. Send your angels to protect us when we faced bullying from the rest of the society.

Precious LORD, we are once again defenseless, weak, and confused. Our leaders are scattered in the wind, mindless and hopeless, distorted and living in fear of the evil that men are perpetrating here on earth. LORD, your children.

Are still fighting each other and finding it hard to join and collectively agree upon who the real enemy is or to perfect ourselves. Men in power have lost their minds, apologizing for everything they say with fear of offending.

Precious LORD, send your divine intervention. Our world today is filled with a multitude of deception and confusion. Words and actions demonstrate using fear to downgrade and rapidly stifling your name (*Jesus Christ, Son of God*). In the United States of America mentioning, your name is a misdeed in the colleges and universities.

LORD, while others are allowed to threaten and take the lives of others as they call on the name of their God without being ostracized. They distort and confuse your children as they lose sight of the real issues. Precious LORD, men, have organized plans to destroy your name and teachings on earth,

Your enemies are knocking at the doors of the minds and souls of your children, trying to replace tolerance, confidence, and love for you with fear, doubt, and disbelief. (*Elohim, Elohim, and Elohim*), takes aim of the hearts of our enemies and reverses their bad intentions of evil.

Precious LORD, seal us with your blood so that our minds and souls can find satisfaction and stay steadfast to you. Help us, LORD; be with us when we go to war to fight for your name and ideology. Lead our minds to a peaceful place where men can't destroy it. Blot out our past sins and return us once more to the (*Garden of Eden*).

Selah.

167

PRAISE

Everything that has breath praises the LORD.

There is life among stones above and below the ground.

If you don't praise him, the stones shall praise him.

Everything that has breath praises the LORD. The fishes in the sea shall praise him. Everything that has breath praises the LORD. The animals shall praise him.

Everything that has breath praises the LORD. The babies shall praise the LORD. Everything that has breath praises the LORD. The blind shall praise the LORD. Everything that has breath praises the LORD; the sun shall not smite me by day or the moon by night. Everything that has breath praises the LORD.

"The fool says in his heart, "there is no God." (*Psalm 14:1*) (*http:// biblehub.com/psalms/14-1.htm*). Surely only a madman can come to this conclusion. Merely a fool shall not see the mercy of God. Fools don't possess the heart of God. Fools take things for granted; praise the LORD. The day will come when all fools shall seek Father God's mercies.

They are not aware of this in their present state of mind because they are blinded by all the power and material stuff here on earth. When their days turn to night, and their wealth, psychology, and manipulation cannot help them, on judgment day, it will be away from them. LORD, you are still waters that flow during the night.

They should be quietly asking God for mercy. God, show them mercy; bring their souls to you before their final hours. O Mighty God, the world is filled with violence and deception. Come back to earth or send your angels to give us peace, tranquility, and joy. If this is impossible—and we know all things are possible with you.

Re-create the minds of men to control their spirit of greed and angry and jealous emotions. Hate and violence have taken hold of their minds and followed them around. Pour out your Holy Spirit on men so that they will reach for you in joy, install in their minds praises of the LORD. Praising him who creative thoughts above and beyond rational creation and endless love for the children of men.

We praise you for the miracles you would perform on behalf of your kids' secure future, in the name of the LORD Christ God, Jehovah, and his Holy Spirit. LORD, shield us from this violence and anger. We solemnly and quietly praise the LORD. Love and respect each other. Praise the LORD. We fill this world with love.

Selah.

168

PRAISE THE LORD

All the animals of the world shall praise the LORD.
The dead in Christ shall praise the LORD; praise the LORD. The wicked shall praise the LORD; praise the LORD.

Fishes in the sea shall praise the LORD; praise the LORD. Beasts of the field shall praise the LORD. The rocks on the ground and beneath the earth shall praise the LORD. The birds in the sky shall praise the LORD; praise the LORD.

The children shall praise the LORD; praise the LORD.
Parents shall praise the LORD; praise the LORD.
Praise the LORD for he is good; his mercy is forever.

Praise the LORD for he is the light of the world.
Demons in the hell cannot stand the sound of you uttering praises to the LORD. Praise the LORD, praise the LORD, and praise the LORD always.

Day and night, praise the LORD; praise the LORD.
In times of trouble, praise the LORD; praise the LORD.
Praise the LORD, for he gives you the desires of your heart.

Praise the LORD, for he is the Alpha and Omega.
Everything that has breath shall praise the LORD.

"Praise the LORD for all he has done" for the children of men. (*https://www.biblegateway.com/passage/? (Psalm 111 CEV)*)

Praise the LORD, summer, winter, spring, and fall.
Praise the LORD, for he will bring you authentic victory over all things. Praise the LORD in the face of adversity.

Selah.

POEMS

1

HAPPY BIRTHDAY, SON

I was up late, composing a "happy birthday" poem for you.

Birthdays come only once a year. You brought joy
and strength when you entered my life.
I knew some day I would receive a son, the best son ever.

The day you were born and given to me was
Indescribable,
I am secretly delighted and pleased with you, son,
Always and forever,

In particular, I feel happy, proud, and strong to know I had the
opportunity to birth a son —dreams answered by the universe,

One the day you were born, I felt the emotions of
Contentment and joy, I looked forward to a future
of raising you, loving and understanding you,
sharing wisdom and knowledge with you.
How pleased and astonished.
I thank the gods for giving me you and the
opportunity to be your mother.
Fighting to protect, love, teach, and keep you was difficult.
Son, words cannot describe how proud I am of you.
Having to share you with the world has left me in a
state of disarray and hurt, but I kept on trusting.

*I guess the gods knew I had to let go so you
can grow and become yourself.
My soul reaches out daily through the universe,
sending you all the love, love, love.*

*May the Gods keep on watching over you, protecting you, giving
you more wisdom and knowledge, and relaying my love to your
heart, Mum is hoping someday; time will bring us together again.*

*So we can catch up things. Spending time with each other to
share fun discussions over dinner and have a little food fight.*

*Love you, son, always and forever.
Love you, only love, only love, hope you are having a great day today.
Happy birthday*

Always and forever, through thick and thin, I love you
—

2

INCANDESCENT ETERNAL FLAME

Incandescent Eternal Flame Light my way with your eternal flame.
Fill me with your soul.
Keep my mind alive with your vibe.
Make me know me through you.

Breathe wonderment into my lungs and give me love again.
The love of life, love of you,
My ride through the halls of the blind,

Give aid to the halls of the blind.
Give me the gifts of your beauty without the glitter, without
the string of conformity but with the bow of unity.
Unify two into one, like the moon and the sun

Eclipsing the world of indifference forever,
Illuminating, the luminescence to an invisible state,
As we journey this secular plane,
Maintaining the unbreakable until the universe
Collapses,
Trying to absorb this light,

3

WHY

Why does the sunshine, even if it doesn't want to?
Why do the birds keep flying, even went they don't
Want to fly?
Why do we trample each other daily?
Why do we lose our innocent, childlike minds?

Why are families not together?
Why do we not smile and greet one another?
Why does everyone walk around so seriously?
Why do you have to explain a joke?

Why don't people know that they did not come on this
earth to stay, but to go back to the kingdom?
Why are all the fishes disappearing into the sea?
Why is the Arctic ice melting?
Why can't we judge men by the content of their
hearts and not the color of their skins?

Why is there an abundance of fuss about
having to be politically correct?
Why are the kids so angry?
Why do we fight each other?
Why do we think twice and lose our faith?

Why are we afraid of each other?
Why don't we love each other?

Why do we even bother?
Why are little children coming with adult sickness and diseases?
Why are we losing our freedom of speech?
Why! Why! Why! Why! Why! Why!
—

4

THE GAME IS ON

The game is on to win.
The game is on to win by any means necessary.
Fight the fight of all fights.
The game is on to win.

You have to con your brothers and sisters.
Fight the fight of all fights.
The game is on to win.

Watch me; execute the game, silent manipulation,
fight the fight of all fights,
The game is on to win.

Savagely, psychologically, secretly, they fight against each other.
Fight the fight of all fights.
The game is on to win.

Take off your invisible war paint.
Fight the fight of all fights.
The game is on to win.

The game is on, the fight, the fight to win by any means necessary.

—

5

FLOWING RIVERS

Flowing rivers' waters brings me backward to you.
Flowing rivers' waters brings me back to the love
I once knew.
Flowing rivers' waters washes away the pain.

Flowing rivers' waters, so tranquil and so new,
Flowing rivers' waters, gliding between rocks,
Flowing rivers' waters, the trickling sounds of
your water renew the mind and soul.

Flowing rivers' waters, that's unhurriedly gliding toward the sea.
Flowing rivers' waters, filtering, purifying my love,
Flowing rivers' waters, sparkling in the sunshine,

Flowing rivers' waters, glittering between the leave,
Flowing rivers' waters, winking and smiling
With pleasure,
Flowing rivers' waters, quenching thirst,

Flowing rivers' waters, racing across the sea
Flowing rivers' waters, returning me back to you,
Flowing rivers' waters, winding, curving,
following, making its way to the sea,

Flowing rivers' waters, I see your sparkly face.
Shimmering, gliding on the water surface,

Sparkling, twinkling, blinking in the eyes, hands, and minds,
Wondering, where does the sun go, beyond the river's edge?

Reaching for, touching the red sun as it slowly
follows the steadily flowing rivers' waters.
Vanishes beyond and beneath the water's edge,
—

6

LAUGHTER

Laughter is the soul's way of healing.
Laughter pleases the mind and soul with joy.
Laughter has a sense of humor.
Laughter exists in heaven.

The Kingdom is a place of joy and laughter.
A laugh a day keeps the psychiatrist away.
Laughter is for you. Laughter is for me.
Laughter is your face's way of exercising.

Laughter for is for boys and girls.
Laughter is for the wealthy and the have-nots.
Although the rich don't laugh,
Laughter is for the big and the small.

If you have to explain a joke to someone,
Ninety percent of the time,
They don't have a sense of humor—run.
Run for your life, for those are the ones who
are coming to cause your demise.

Some get it, and others don't.
You did not come on this earth to stay but to go back.
Don't be an old fogey.

Laughter eases life's disappointments and its pains.
Laughter is good for you and me; don't take yourself too seriously.

Laughter, laughter, laughter,
Laughter, laughter, laughter,
Infuriate me with your joy and laughter.

—

7

THIS LIGHT

This light, of from heavens,
This light makes us shine this light,
This makes you mine,

This light, radiating into my mind and soul,
This light which shines in the world,
This light that brings peace and joy

This light that looks down on this world,
Light which protects,
This light which sparkles in your eyes,

This light without darkness,
This light which men tried to destroy,
This light never-ending and everlasting.

This light loaded with energy.
This light welcomed you into the world.
This light was penetrating into your mind and soul.

This light, penetrating from heaven, dancing, moving,
gliding, stagnant, penetrating into the entire galaxy,
Electric lights descending and ascending through the universe are
touching the earth, sending jolts of energy into your heart and soul.

Igniting your mind, making your mind extend to galaxies planted
throughout the universe—yellow, blue, red, rims circling Saturn.

This light, exploding planets, moving, gliding, never
ending, and orbiting alongside each other,

This light, transcending while humankind still struggles
with self, through time and space not really in control of
anything, but their minds chasing after nothingness,

Galaxies unfolding, watching, and waiting, LORD,
Peep from the heavens into the universe.
Look up; stretch forth your eyes toward the heavens
connect your mind to the unknown universe.

—

8

MORNING DEW

Morning dew sparkles on the tall blades of grass.
The morning dew, tranquil, slowing and gently
vaporizing on the shrubs and small grasses your fresh
moisture fills my life with hope and joy.

Morning dew, the first thing I see; how pleasing it appears to me.

I woke up at the early light and opened my eyes to see the virgin
morning dew, its mist and glorious presenting grace to the earth.

Inhabitants slumber, silent, as they surrender their wills through
the night and welcome the morning with grace and tranquility.

The morning dew, you are slowly, gently spewing out
from the sphere. You cover the earth's vegetation.

The precious morning dew, like fresh mist entering my

Mind adorning it with brand-new curiosity,
and imagination the savannah grass

Sparkling with gratitude and hope,

Hope for the new day and beyond.

The morning dew sparkles on the blades of grass.

Morning Dew discharged from the ground and heaven,
steadily ascending, descending, and renewing the earth.

Moisture that filled my life with hope and virgin joy;

Morning dew, the first thing I see.

My feet wet from the mist as I stroll through the grass,
as the morning dew reminds me of who I am.

Speak to me, gracious morning; talk to me through

The silent sound of the morning, making my day a
Joy.

The countryside's gleaming with the gently roaming mist and the
morning dew, covering grassy surfaces, moisturizing, speaking
to the tall grass, plants high in the air and flat on the ground. I
welcoming the morning dew into a new morning, Green meadows
scattered as far as my eyes can see, from earth to eternity.

Morning dew sending his love on his creation, early

Morning dew resting on the plants, kissing the
faces of the animals in the fields,

Morning Dew sparkles on the shrubs, leaves,
blades of grass, and the treetops,

The morning dew was lying still covering the long green grass, gently
nurturing moisture that filled my life with graceful joy and hope.

Morning dew, the first thing I see on the horizon.

—

9

YOU HAD ME, MOTHER

You had a daughter, and what did you do?
You had a daughter, who loved you.
What did you do? You had me.
Putting strangers ahead of me, never trusting,
You had me, Mother.

I am ashamed to know you did not love me.
It is ashamed you did not trust me; everyone strange and everything
seems to be better than me, Teacher, you wanted me to be.

Nurse, you wanted me to be, you were my example. I
have to be me. I cannot be what you want me to be.

I was born to be much more.
You had me, Mother.
Carried away with hope and dreams of your loving me
unconditionally, distorted, losing time with life, longing for your

I always wanted your love and approval, wanting to
please, to love to understand, to help, to comfort. I have
to be who I was created to be; you don't love me.
You had me, Mother.

Confusion all around; you had me, Mother.
You were my first betrayal, the worst betrayal, biggest betrayal.
You had me, Mother.

Love and honor your mother; at times it's hard to do.
Lift you, Mother, when you were down, but you
want me to walk around with a frown. You're
Trying to put me in the ground, you
Had me, Mother,

Good luck, Mother, good luck; hope one day
you will learn to love yourself.
Trusting strangers, over me, I think first, Mother, you must
fully invest in yourself; that's where you must start.

From within you, toward yourself, then you could.
I have conveyed that trust on to me.
God wants you to see I did not have you mother, but you had me.

—

10

HAPPY BIRTHDAY

The Mighty LORD in his splendor and glory decided
to send you on this day in the spring.
What an excellent time to make that journey, in time,
When winter releases her grip on the earth
and spring gently enters the sphere.

The beautiful flowers, plants, and birds, every
living thing, dances with thoughts of receiving the
blessings and splendor as glorious as the sun,
The gods are happy and pleased with this great delight.

On this occasion of spring, this brings forth new life,
Let us dance and sing while we welcome spring. Your
heart is filled with the glee of life's conception;
Your thoughtfulness and caring soul filled with concern for others.

God has a special place for you in his universe.
Your knowledge, gentle kindness and love took for granted and
misunderstood by others, and the underdog to your sister. Just don't
Take yourself lightly. Keep your hope up.

Your turn to shine will come.
The Blessed day your birthday, bless your life; love
has a way of sometimes showing itself in strange
ways. Only the Holy LORD knows the way.
Do not give up; there is a smile behind the rainbow.

Look up in your mind and see the sun. Be contented; smile.
The blessed LORD will show you the way; he will show you
the way. May the Mighty LORD, in his entire splendor
and glory, keep you, on your birthday and always?

—

11

FATHER WAS DRUNK

My father was intoxicated.
I loved him. My father was drunk.
He destroyed the furniture; I loved him.
My father was drunk; he beat my mother.
Father was drunk; Father was intoxicated.
Father was drunk; Father was stoned.
My father was drunk.

The devil made him do it.

I loved him; he was my father; my father was drunk.
He slept with my sister. My dad was drunk.
Mother is jealous, Father. She hates, and sister.
Who's to blame? I am confused and afraid.
Father was drunk; Father was stoned.
Father was drunk; Father was drunk.

My father was drunk. However, he kept a good job.
At times, I feared him, could not understand him.
Silence grips him, always deep in his thoughts.
Silent as a crocodile coming up to take air and bite,
Honor your mother and father. I loved my dad.

Father was drunk; Father was intoxicated.
Father was drunk; Father was stoned.
My father was drunk. Hold and behold what my mother
was thinking. She thought he would change his ways.
(Come around)

You're not thinking, Mother. Were you not
there? Where was your head, Mother?

Did you not think he would stop beating and abusing you and the
offspring? Run, run for your life; there is no one there to protect you.
Father was paralyzed, intoxicated. Father was drunk.
Father was drunk; Father was drunk.
My father was drunk.

Honey, I am home. The doctor gave me two months to live.
Better cut back on my drinking.

He was the star around his friends, worked unyieldingly.
Worked hard, Father, hold back your anger;
Don't let it explode. Control your anger.
Control your desires, Father.
My mother made him drink.

Father was drunk; Father was stoned, hammered.
Father was drunk; Father was intoxicated.
My father was drunk. However, he was functioning when inebriated.

Save me, save me, save me, O Mother.
For I don't want it to be my turn; don't you care?
Draw the line; do not destroy.

Help me overcome my fears, fear of you and Mother.
Father was drunk; Father was inebriated.
Father was drunk; Father was inebriated.
My father was drunk. A drunk who loved me,

—

12
BEATINGS I RECEIVED

Don't beat me, Mother and Father.
I can learn! I need your love, patience, and understanding;
Try to understand. I can understand.
Don't beat me, Mother, Father.
Girlfriend, boyfriend, whoever,
Stepmother, Stepfather, whoever, whatever,

The beatings I received, can't say it did me good.
The beatings I received merely made me sad and unfortunate.
The beatings I received only made me confused.

Control your frustrations; control your life.
Learn to communicate with me.
Love me, listen to me, and tell me you love me.
Talk to me; lead by example.
Why not talk and communicate?

The beatings I received, can't say it did me good.
The beatings I received, at most, made me sad and bad.
The beatings I received only made me confused.

I am reluctant myself, to live.
Ashamed to enter my school, be a part of learning.
Scared to ask questions, to make mistakes, to
think, to love, to receive love, to fail.
Introverted and confused, afraid of my universe.
The beatings I received, can't say it did me good.

The beatings I received merely made me sad and sick.
The beatings I received only made me confused.
O Grandma, tell your daughters, do not beat.
Grandma, where are you, Grandpa?
Aunties, tell your sisters, don't beat me.
Talk to and lead your children by examples.
Make references they would understand and learn.

The beatings I received, can't say it did me good.
The beatings I received just made me sad and bad.
The beatings I received only made me confused.

Talk to me; listen to me when I speak.
Observe me when I am silent; something may.
Be wrong. Go with me when I am afraid;
talk to my teachers. Fight for me.
While you are trying to find ways, show me that
you care; your needs would provide.

The beatings I received, can't say it did me good.
The beatings I received just made me sad and bad.
The beatings I received only made me confused.

The world is equipped with the methods to beat
me down; reinforce me with confidence.

—

13

IGNORANCE IS A CURSE

Oh! I am wondering what I should do.
The world is looking at me in a different light.
They perceive me as being ignorant and angry.
My brain is smaller than the rest; my skin is too black.
Having illegitimate babies, too many babies without
black biological fathers to raise them,

Ignorance is a curse.

They say, "Send them back to Africa."
All the other races of people are smarter than me.
I am violent and unorganized, too loud.
I can't learn, can't comprehend, too slow.
Undetermined, no morality,

Ignorance is a curse.

My skin is black. My hair is nappy.
So what, so what, so what? My hair is nappy.
You pick and pick and pick—why?
Soft and loving targets are the black Americans and Africans.
Why don't you go and pick on someone your size?

You turned around and brought troublemakers to your
shores, making it harder and bringing more poverty to the
black communities. You have a situation on your hands.

369

You can be compared to the monkey thieves—
to be observed and feared.

Ignorance is a curse.

Your print media bosses and electronic media producers
display blacks as dumb and unproductive.
Murderers and confusion riots, mayhem in the black
community are all you see on the evening news and other
programming schedules, depicting annoyance.

Out-of-control black women in frustrating situations,

Ignorance is a curse.

Your media depicts black men and women in
adverse situations, while you hide
Your own faults and those of other cultures that you

Favor, all other members of society
Are portrayed as docile, rational, and intelligent manner,
Computer experts, doctors, etc., they appear to be doing.

Ignorance is a curse.

Something constructive and pleasing to everyone,
While you Internet and television portrays black folks in an angry,
irresponsible, weak way. Then they con us with Obama, who
was ignorant to the United States of America's Constitution.

Ignorance is a curse.

We contribute to everyone else economy, making their economies better
and advance them to become middle-class citizens. By the way,

*We contribute to everyone else economy, making their
economies better and advance them to become wealthy or
middle-class citizens. In the meantime are you going to pay
us for the free labor, the acre of land and the mule?*

Ignorance is a curse.

*Give us something to work with, an apology, some
respect; give our kids proper education, a computer,
free education, and some more respect.*
*John Philippe Rushton and his theory of variables—what's
up with his variables analysis? Was this man a madman?*

*He used his position to spread misconception about
the black and white students and impinge on their
lives. There are variables in every race.*
He besmirched these people's lives by practicing bigotry.

Ignorance is a curse.

———

14

THE TALL SHIPS ARE IN THE HARBOR

I can see the line of tall ships. The Redpath Waterfront

Toronto tall ship's festival is in town; watch them, as they slowly sail into the harbor gliding, entering into the harbor. The tall ships are in the harbor, paying a visit to you.

The tall ships are in the harbor.

Formation, formation, formation, formation, formation

Docked in the harbor, how magnificent their sails sway, orderly flapping around, as they ruffle in the wind, proud and majestic, beckoning. The tall ship festival is in the harbor; the tall ships are in the harbor.

Formation, formation, formation, formation, formation

Lots of flags, colorful flags, nations' flags adorned my bows, giant spectacles; people on board, cleaning, organizing, and waving. Come on board and join me, they seem to beckon. Come on board; buy a ticket and get on board. Smiling faces of captain and crew.

Come in out of the summer sun, and step inside my Cabin, See how I shine? The tall ships are in the harbor; the tall ships are in the harbor.

The sparkly blue water, shimmering in the sunshine,

It is a lovely day for sailing, sunglasses, food basket, and sandals. Adults and children are gathering around, curiously looking, and watching the tall ships with splendor and glory in their eyes, wanting to come on board. Get a ticket.

Formation, formation, formation, formation, formation Come on board; imaginations are high. Where have you been, around the world? The tall ships are in the harbor; the tall ship festival is in the harbor.

Formation, formation, formation, formation, formation

The tall ships are in the harbor; the tall ships are in the harbor. I have to wait for the opportunity to see them make their yearly pilgrimage to the harbor, waiting patiently, longing to be surrounded by their sometimes weary presence.

Formation, formation, formation, formation, formation

Formation, formation, formation, formation, and formation

My imagination is on high alert. What parts of the world lakes and sea shores have they visited? Someday I will be going on a voyage with them around the world.

Just you wait and see.

———

15

CARNIVAL

It's time for fun; Carnival season is here.
A time to let down your hair down and have fun,
Enjoy your life while you can.
Three hundred sixty-five days in one year.
Let's have some fun; let's get down.

The carnival,

Stress and joy are released, disappear.
Beautiful costumes line the streets.
All happy people sparkling, having fun;
The grave cannot hold them.
Life cannot keep them down.

The carnival,

The spirits of the ancestors are dancing.
They are dancing with their offspring, enjoying the
sun. Parade, parade, parade yourselves.
The Gods are happy for joy and happiness rules.

Oh you onlookers, how good it will be and feel when you are a
part of something as great as this Just set you free and attend the
carnival. Play in the celebration, jump and dance in the sun.

Mothers, fathers, cousins, neighbors, world spectators,
designers, men and women, best behavior, creative
spirit of the Almighty Father's blessings.
Creativeness and joyfulness are all on
Parade

Your imaginations produce joy and life, breathing,
Loving, enjoying, musicians, drummers, steel pans,
Calypsonian, trumpets, feet moving, voices singing,
Waists gyrating, revolving, the carnival
bands are coming down the road.

The carnival,

Freedom for one day, free for one hour, freedom for a
lifetime, the splendor of life, love, and peace.
Rivers are flowing, life's glowing.
We are entitled to express ourselves, breathing life,
Celebrating life and the carnival,

—

16

I WANT TO BE BLACK

The whole world likes to pretend they love me, especially
when they want some of my creative energy.
They criticize me and cheat me in every way,
creatively lying within them.

They are waiting for the next big creativity
or new swag or slang or hipness.
To come from my creative spirit, but they
criticize and intimidate me all
day long. I am tap dancing as fast as I can.

Black, I want to be black.
Black with respect from others,
Black with a higher income,
Black with morality

Take my soul away, and take my skills away.
Dehumanize me, my children; trust yourself.
I look within you. I have nothing to hide, nothing to fear.
If you trust yourself, you will trust others.

Black, I want to be black.
Black with respect from others
Black with a higher income,
Black with morality,

My economy, economy, my young people are hurting in this economy.
For jobs, respect, trusts are stereotyping.
Everyone seems to be better than me.
Let me live like everyone else; let me be free; let me
be equal. The ladder is so hard to climb.

Black, I want to be black.
Black with respect from others,
Black with higher income,
Black with morality,

my forefathers suffered because of your greed
and highly sexual deviancy.
Master of disguise, facade at all times,
and you're trying secretly and sincerely to make me your bitch.

Black, I want to be black.
Black with respect from others,
Black with a higher income.
Black with morality

everyone got paid and respected for your bewildering,
deviant ways. Work for me for free; say you're going to
pay me. Where are my mule and my forty acres?
At least give my kids respect, a high-grade computer, and a
proper education. Stop the manipulation of our minds.

Black, I want to be black.
Black with respect from others,
Black with a higher income
Black with morality

Colorless and running from myself, living in the suburbs, have
to find a friend to hang out within the ghetto—maybe a girl

or boyfriend, looking for drugs or comfort, losing my identity.
My life turned out to be a sham and filled with hatred.

Black, I want to be black.
Black with respect from other,
Black with a higher income,
Black with morality,
Overall setup is economic, and realizes you have to suffer
some so that others can get ahead. Unfortunately, you had to
pick on me. Every move I make, you try to take the air out of
my lungs, economically and educationally oppressing me.

Your media are still playing the game of divide and conquer.
When will you wake up to yourself?

Black, I want to be black.
Black with respect from others
Black with a higher income,
Black with morality,

—

17

MY SISTER IS A LESBIAN

I am a woman; watch me, love.
Strong, intelligent, and determined,
In the beginning, I was accused and supposed to be the
one who encouraged Adam to take a bite out of the
apple, was not allowed to vote, and treated as chattel.
I worked without pay; my sister is a lesbian.

Voting, for me, was prohibited.
Struggled with you for this opportunity,
I was your wife, mother, sometimes father to your children,
sister, therapist, and babysitter. Psychologically, I believed
in you and your dreams and forgot about my own.
My sister is a lesbian.

I educated your children, put up with your mother,
Gave you pleasure, showed you understanding.
I nurtured you, held you when you cried, infidelity.
I helped you take care of your mother and bore your children.
My sister is a lesbian.

I have been abused, raped, accused, and taken for
granted. Sexually exploited, burdened, subservient,
Lied to, manipulated, and scorned, but yet to be emancipated.
Subdued and discriminated against in the workplace.

Evette Forde

What about the glass ceiling, lesser pay, belittling, not allowed to vote? Your inhumanity and discreetness have turned me into an aggressive, infuriating, annoying, and monster freak.

My sister is a lesbian.
My sister is a lesbian.

—

18

LOWER EXPECTATIONS

He has low expectations, longing for someone
to share his lower expectations.
Oh, my, how quaint; he wants a lover to dump on;
however, he wanted someone to stay in the gutter.

A person without ambitions, even though it does
not matter; she does not have time for him.
He wants a lover.
Maybe he can pretend for a while to be someone else.
So he can conquer her love and then, lower
expectations, higher expectations.

Put the charms on her until she is mesmerized by his
persistence, taken her out to dinner and flowers.
Say the things she wants to hear, while all the time,
deep within his soul, putting her under,

All he wants is to capture her soul and move on to
the next target. He has nothing to offer her.
He is using up her precious energy. Has he secretly wants
her to be his slave, conning the pants off her.

As he, uses her low self-esteem to wear grind her down and wear
her out. Intruding on her spirit of adverse lost love with your
efforts, stolen, slowly preying on the vulnerability of a woman,

Evette Forde

Psychologically wishing and wanting her to be barefoot
and pregnant, slowing playing with her mind.
Maybe she would come around; in the meantime, he
is only trying to pull her down to his level.
Lower expectations, higher expectations, she has no time for him.

—

19

BABY FATHER DEPORTATION

My baby father got deported;
What am I supposed to do? Have ten children?
I am going through changes.

My friends and cousins are laughing at me.
What am I supposed to do? My baby's father got deported.
Only misery is facing me. What was I thinking? Lock
the children in the closet, the suitcase, starve them.

Oh wait; I could beat them, punish them for being born.
Maybe my mother can help me; I will put the burden on her.
What am I to do? My baby's father got deported, Wait a
minute—my boyfriend wants me to love him more than
my children and give him the baby's bonus money; he
also wants my full supply of attention and money.

Patience and love—
The patience and love, I have for me and my child not for
him. He wants me to take the love money and attention.
I have for myself and my child and give it to him. How
did I get involved with a deportation baby father?

The food is not enough. Anger fighting, hey! What about
school, society, and maturing? I have to return to school
and take care of my child, for my diploma, or work long

> *hours. This effort will take discipline and extended time*
> *for me to achieve. O should I abandon my child?*

> *All my love is for myself and my children. He wants me to give all*
> *the love and attention to him and not my children. His mother*
> *did not show him love—when he was a child; what a shame*

—

20

THANKSGIVING DINNER

November is Thanksgiving, giving thanks
for turkey, stuffing, and apple pie,
Thanksgiving dinner, O Lord; my family is over.
Where are the turkey and the stuffing?
No, son, it's not the time for the mistletoe.

Grandma has a problem. She is missing Grandpa.
Where are the dinner rolls? Did you buy the cranberry sauce?
Fix five pounds of mashed potatoes. My friend
is invited; she is always famished.
Oh, no; don't put the hot sauce in the gravy.

How many chairs are available?
Hey, the guys from the shelter are coming over.
Yes, they are coming over for Thanksgiving dinner.
Hide the silverware and the wine.
The dinner is ready; you better call Freddy; fix a plate.

Where is the stuffing? What's in the stuffing?
Who is going to carve the turkey? I will.
Oh my, God, the turkey bags are still inside the turkey.

Maybe a Canada goose,
Oh, snap! The bird is stuffed with its parts still
inside the bag, along with the stuffing!

Evette Forde

What a Thanksgiving dinner party.
Oh-oh, I am in trouble with my husband.

Had a good laugh with my children;
Off to Grandma's for dinner we go.
What a blast of a Thanksgiving dinner party.

—

21

GRAVY TRAIN

The gravy train, stop the gravy train,
Stop the gravy train while I fry my brain.
Stop the gravy train; I am going insane.
Where are my kids—on the soccer field?
What would they think about me?
Be aware of the examples you are showing.
Confusion and betrayal conveyed. I feel ashamed.

Bet your dollar! The children felt it and are confused
and disappointed with your actions.

Stop the gravy train, the gravy train; the gravy train,
Stop the gravy train, while I fry my brain.
Stop the gravy train; I am going insane.

Lead by a good example; we are not afraid, only made
a fool of self. Oh, no big deal. I can manipulate.
To protect and serve, they cannot get me.

Show some respect for law enforcement.
Hey, they have to protect and serve all.

The gravy train, stop the gravy train,
Stop the gravy train, while I fry my brain.
Stop the gravy train; I am going crazy.

All a political game; they are all insane.
Father taught me to mingle with and play with the voters'
minds. I didn't have to go that far. Did you help the poor?
Your actions did not help the black community.

You only made matters worse.
The gravy train filled with sadness and pain; stop the gravy
train, Stop the gravy train, while I fry my brain.

Stop the gravy train; I am going insane.
Using and abusing powers; only care about yourself.
Everyone looked up to you; sure fooled poor folks.

Even did some canvassing for you; nearly got run
over and assaulted in the parking lot by one of
Your opponents,
Of what, Four more years, four more years, four more years!
For all your selfish gains, you have made it difficult for your
brother to advance his career and help the citizens. Bad
decisions were on your path; hang your head in shame.
Others were expecting something better from you. The
city is hurting; too much taxing and spending,
The hard-working commuters need safe and reliable transportation.

Hope you get your act together, clean up your stuff,
and return to help the people of the city,
What a gravy train? Stop the gravy trains.
Stop the gravy train, while I fry my brain.
Stop the gravy train; I am going insane.

What a crock of poop.

—

22

I WANT TO BE AN AFRICAN DRUMMER

Love the African women;
How can I find me one of them?
One who will have lower expectations of herself and
serve me. Those days are long gone and far away.
How can I find one of those African women?
They won't come to me, so I go to them.
What a night, what a night in glory land.

All those African women; want one who can beat the
African drums with me. Where can I find an African
woman? I will have to do some African drumming;
I want to be an African drummer.

The African drumming—
What is involved in the drumming?
Stay up late at night, moving into the early hours
of the morning, summoning Papa Legba.
I want to be an African drummer.

Beat them drums, boy beat them drums.
Wake up the devil, beat them drums, beat them drums.
I want to do the dancing, the African dancing, to see the colors.

Why is the rabbit appearing every time you are near?
My man wants to be an African drummer.

*I want to wear my Afro if I can, white sugarcane
plantation outfit, with the three-quarter pants.*

*Splash on my Florida water to attract the African women
Meet the African women and use an aphrodisiac with them.
Disguised as women; don't know if I am a man. It might be the curse,
Pretending, wanting it all.*

*I can't travel out of the country to find a subservient
African woman to worship Me., My skin is pale; lost
my way. Can I pledge allegiance to two religions? Give
up myself and my religion; don't know if I should serve
Jesus Christ and the three kings or Papa Legba.*

*I don't want to be a contemporary abstract drummer;
I want to be a Voodoo African drummer. Late-night
Drumming, sacrifice the chickens and drink the blood.*

*I want to be an African drummer, drumming for the soul of
African women; maybe the ones in the ghetto will do.
They will give up their souls willingly and sell them cheap,
Papa Legba.
Summon Papa Legba; Jesus Christ died so that there is no
more sacrifice. God! Jesus Christ himself is on his way!*

—

23

LEGALIZE IT NOW

Food, food, I got the munchies.
Mellow me, mellow me out. I need to come
out of this reality and clear my head.
My mother doesn't want me to smoke it,
But I still conversely buy it.
How will I satisfy these munchies?

Where is the agriculture, the food? Why not plant food
to satisfy my munchies? Grown-ups set up medicinal
clinics, using my doctors to write a prescription.
Listed on Wall Street legalizes it now, and I would
Buy it. Let us smoke it. Did you get a toke?

The government said it was illegal to possess. Until they realized,
they can get their cut of the profit. I am hungry all the time. Why
not plant food? Lots of vegetables and fruits instead; my mom
put a lock on the refrigerator door. Smoke it; man, the hunger
and high it brings. Legalize it now, and I would buy it.

It paralyzes my speech and takes away self-esteem.
My goal-oriented skills calm me down, and it opens up my appetite,
way the out the task and slows my motor skills and sense of reasoning.

Smoke, smoke so that the government can make a
profit off of it, the agriculture farmers are penalized.
The food prices in the food store are sky high.

Legalize it now, and I would but it.

It's the hunger and high it brings.

Legalize it now, and I would buy it.

—

24

WHEN THE TIDES COME IN

Tumbling waves rolling onto the shore, moving-
away waves, slowly, briefly,
Momentarily moving, leisurely, motionless, is rolling onto
the shores. Those moving tides slowly beckoning,
Sand beneath my feet, elements of previous life.
Seashells lying on the sand,

At the edge of the sea, when the tides come in,
Calm waters stimulate your body and mind.
Bring tranquility, opening your mind, as the tides come in.

Overhead, the sky is blue and delightful.
Hover over the gentle sea, with the breeze, filled with
hope. When the tides come in, refreshing smell of the
sea, the fresh smell that exists from life beneath,

Birds delight in the air, flapping their wings with grace and
Thanksgiving when the tides come in when the waves come in.
Looking way out on the ocean; look at the ocean,
unfortunately, mysteriously rolling way out.
There. Can I walk on its surface, reach out my hands?
And hold it? Venture to reach and touch the end of
The horizon, sailing, canoeing, windsurfing
When the tide comes in,

I am looking at the waves as they glide along on
The top of this weaving, wobbling surface,

In the far distance, appears like the table's edge;
Would I fall off the edge when the tides come in?

Calmly moving, reassuring when the tides come in,
The sweet taste of saltwater, touching my lips,
My tongue licking my lips, tasting salt,
As the wind gently absorbs the water on my mouth,
Leaving particles of salt on my lips, when the tides
Come in.
The salty particles sticking to my lips and the wind
Touching my face drying on my lips, laughing at my
Thought,
Wondering, where does this magical life arise? Above
And beneath, filled with joy and fantasy, when the
Tides come in when the tides come in.

—

25

BLUE DREAMS

Oceans, water, oceans, water vast and lively,
How good and pure is your life. Excellent, magnificent life,
Spreading across the earth, pulsing, driving, gliding,
Beautiful sea creatures big and small filled a comfortable life.
Various shapes and colors are sharing enormous amounts
of space. I close my eyes and wonder; close my eyes and
sleep. Sleep on the sleep of death, deep sleep, and great
Sleep. Blue is the sky, the way above so many
distinctive shades of ultramarine;

Different shades of sapphire in the waters and the sky.
Come to me from the deep-blue seas; come and play with
me while I sleep. Come to me in your graceful glory.

Look into my eyes. I see your eyes as they look
at me. Close my eyes and wonder.
Close my eyes and sleep. Sleep on the sleep of death,
deep sleep and deep sleep. Blue is the sky.
Prepare my chamber, my underwater chamber.

Design and build my chamber with clear, sturdy glass, see-through
glass, glass that I can see my sea creatures through. Come on, boys,
Gently lower me down into the deep-blue depth of the blue
waters; see the mermaids engaging with the creatures of light.
I Close my eyes and wonder; close my eyes and sleep.
Sleep on the sleep of death, deep sleep, and deep sleep.

Evette Forde

*Blue is the sky. Cry for me; how peaceful it would
be, holding hands with the azure ocean.*

*Creatures beneath like me, carrying on with life, live,
give, love cuddles; your presence was known.
Sleep, sleep, sleep on the sleep of life and rest
your weary mind against my bosom.*

*Dream the dream, the dream, and the blue dream.
Comfort and assurance this blue dream brings.
I close my eyes and wonder; close my eyes and sleep.
Sleep on the sleep of death, extensive sleep, and deep
Sleep. Blue is the sky.*

As blue as my blue dreams,
—

26

ICY MORNING

The still night, long and cold; all living things
Needed a place to hide, Nature's doing its thing.
Holding the earth, gripping the earth's core,
With a harsh but gentle grip, unheated and
Purposeful,

Oh, how chilled the nights, waiting the icy mornings.
Icy morning brings out the shovel and fastens your
heart; time to face the frosty morning. Hold your
blanket tightly, take a sip of whiskey; go to bed,
Warm up yourself tonight to face the icy mornings.

Oh, how cold the nights, waiting the hot chocolate mornings.
Icy morning, white is the night surrounded by the
dark, glorified by the stillness of winter, gently.
Snowflakes, coming into the morning light, creatures
on the prowl, while icicles are forming.

Oh, how cold the nights, waiting the icy mornings.
Icy morning, flake by flake, slowly descending from
the sky; tiny flakes falling from the sky,
Accumulating, piling up, adding up inch by inch,
How many inches today? Light a candle through
The night, welcoming icy morning,

Oh, how cold the nights, waiting the frosty mornings.
Icy morning, layers, layers of cloth, and how

Evette Forde

Many layers of clothes do I need?

Put on my boots, scarf, hat, mittens, and oh, make some hot
Chocolate, Cuddle me from the icy cold mornings.
Warm up the car; sprinkle the salt on the pathway.

Oh, how cold the nights, waiting the icy mornings.
Icy morning,

—

27

KALEIDOSCOPE OF COLORS

*Colors in great varieties, unusual colors, invaded
the earth, stimulating and scintillating.
Longing to see more and more colors, pleasant, tranquil
and peaceful, all living form and colors found in living
things. Earth, what is this earth without colors?*

*Who is this life? What is this life? Where is the source of its beauty?
Where is he or she or it, or what searching and
Wondering existence, meaningful life, depths of this hollow world?*

Kaleidoscope of colors,

*Colors Piercing, look, slowly moving, gently penetrating
the sphere, whose hand is guiding, protecting, and holding
with loving patience? Welcome to the garden, the garden of
life, magnificent life, filled with colors, bright colors.*

*Penetrating your mind and mesmerizing your soul,
paintings, and colors no one can duplicate or come
Close, contrasting such a well-planned, designed
Landscaping layout,*

*Kaleidoscope of colors,
The thickness and richness of the greenery spreading out for miles,
Oh, behold, for miles and miles, as far as
Your eyes can see.*

The significance of blessings, touch it, feel life,
Happiness, and joy in creation. Possessing life,
Beauty, feast your eyes; allow your senses to absorb,
Energies coming from infinity, top bottom,
Left the side, right side, center, circle, dark, light,
fathomless, colors, impenetrable colors.

Kaleidoscope of colors,

Painful efforts of love and joy came together to present these
colors. As nature takes its time crafting and speaking words of
positive, noiseless efforts, formulating entirely in an instant and
insightfully closing one's mind and soul, breathing a kaleidoscope,

Of colors, mixing and pouring purposefully,
Seeing, knowing, and bringing silent joy and
peace to the spirit of humankind.
Behold the handiwork of our Savior's hand; take
care and protect the handiwork of our
Savior's creation,

Kaleidoscope of colors,
—

28

THE BRAZILIAN DANCER

The Brazilian dancer, dancing in the moonlight,
Her body moves to the beat of the samba.
Swaying hips, moving hands, smiling faces,

Dance; Dance the dance to the gods, your ancestor.
Dance; Dance the dance to the gods, your ancestors.
Dance; dance the dances to the gods, your ancestors.

Worshiping through dancing and joy, gladness, lifting up
Spirits,
Through dance customs of colors entirely carved
Bodies,
Organized rhythm, feet shuffling along the street,

Dance; Dance the dance to the gods, your ancestor.
Dance; Dance the dance to the gods, your ancestors.
Dance; dance the dances to the gods, your ancestors.

The loud beat of the samba, men and women,
Young and old, welcome spectators, anticipation high,
Wave your hands in the air, voices rising and singing,

Dance; Dance the dance to the gods, your ancestor.
Dance; Dance the dance to the gods, your ancestors.
Dance; dance the dances to the gods, your ancestors.

Swaying and chanting, happy people,
dancing, are swaying to the music.
The sounds of the samba drums move your head.
Stamp your feet, shuffle your feet to the beat.

Dance; Dance the dance to the gods, your ancestor.
Dance; Dance the dance to the gods, your ancestors.
Dance; dance the dances to the gods, your ancestors.

African Voyage way across the sea, Brazilian dancers,

They memorize me.
We meet at the edge of the river, awaiting the dance.
Beautiful colors adorn the heads of women, men.
White trousers,

Chanting and singing. Listen to the beat;
attractive men and women together
Happily
Dance; Dance the dance to the gods, your ancestor.
Dance; Dance the dance to the gods, your ancestors.
Dance; dance the dances to the gods, your ancestors.

—

29

SNOWY MORNINGS

Snowy mornings, how milky and fluffy,
Delicious particles falling from the sky,
Very and playful streaming in the air,
My dog loves it, loves to play and roll around in it.

Snowy mornings, how bleached and wooly,
I woke up this morning, looked out my window.
Suddenly, I am surprised looking out my window and to
see a bed of natural fresh early-morning snow, surrounded
by the sight of a winter wonderland, how intriguing.

Snowy mornings how white and fluffy,
Where are my boots and coat and scarf?
I must go outside to smell and touch, shake.
The heavy-laden white snow hangs from the tree branches. As
they wait for instructions to slide, slice right to the ground.

Snowy mornings, how white and fluffy,
The school is out, and the kids are pushing down
the bleached unpigmented snowy hills.
Children making snow angels, frolicking in the snow,
My nose and ears are frozen and fingers numb.

Snowy mornings, how white and fluffy,
Where is my webcam, had to capture this winter
wonderland? The foxes and rabbits love the fleecy
sight. They run and play in the fresh snow.

Snowy mornings, how white and fluffy,
Soft and velvety, hot chocolates are on the table.
I must warm up inside, have a hearty breakfast.
Mum says, "You must clean the driveway,"
Snowy mornings, how white and fluffy,

—

30

DANCING

I love it, dancing.
I have to do it, dancing.
It is the only way to go.
Some people do not dance.
I cannot hear the beat of the music,
Some search for something else within the music,
Music made for dancing.

I love it, dancing.
I have to do it, dancing.
Listen, hear the music and dance.

Dancing releases the stresses of life. Spirits love it
dancing, why! People, why can't you dance?
It is because you are too caught up with life's burdens,
And forgot your soul, your soul? Passionate dancing,
Is it because you are too caught up trying to exploit a situation?
Dancing, I love dancing under the stars that light the
nights, dancing during the day under the warm sunlight,
feet moving, hips swaying, take a boy or a girl.

Take your girl, dance in the streets together, Mama,
Papa and dance!

Dance to the oldies, dance to the new, listen to the music,
sway to the beat, shuffle your feet to the beat.
Why don't you, raise your hands in the air.'

Hips, moving to the beat, the people's Spirit lifted to
the heavens. Reaching the mind of God, movements,
orbiting, gliding toward the galaxies,

Dancing, dancing, dancing, dancing to the beat,
Dancing in the street, dancing to the tubas, drums, guitars, steel pans,
Listen to the music, open your ears, and relax your mind.
Dance, dance, dance to the music.
Music and mind made for dancing. The Lord loves dancing.

—

31

TURN OFF THE LIGHTS

Turn off the lights; it is killing the environment.
Conserve energy; it is destroying the planet.
Al Gore says to turn off the lights, yet his lights stay
on, adding brightness to his night skies.
We are indigent and need our lights to stay on; his selfish thoughts
and greed, all and them some of his very own lights stay on.

Snake oil salesman, reading from the manifesto left
Behind by his forefathers, titled "How to Screw and
Mislead the Majority of People." Misleading only to
fill his pockets; please, turn off the lights of greed and
manipulation that exist in your mind, Al Gore.

I am poor and cannot turn off my lights.
Why, why should I turn off my lights? My children have
to do their homework and play, read books at bedtime.
Jobs, we need more jobs to feed our families. We need
good-paying jobs and cannot turn off the lights.

What am I supposed to do, turn off my lights?
As it is I could hardly see already—save the
Environment; no one is saving me. Humankind worked
Long and hard to invent the energy of the
electric lights and give it to the world,
Why should we turn off the lights? Thomas Edison,
Through the wisdom and power of God, turned on the light,
Some still live in darkness while others have so,

Much, they don't know what to do; they are playing
the fool, telling others to turn off their lights,
Drive smart cars, useless trash, and buy smaller trash cans.
The Antarctic ice is melting, CO_2, plants eat CO_2.

Gore wants you to turn off the lights.
While he quickly fills his pockets, light up the world for all to see;
shine the lights in valleys, mountaintops, and harbor fronts.
Turn on the light in the villages and countryside.
The earth has been forming and reforming itself
for ages. Turn on the lights in your minds.

Turn on the lights.
—

32

DIAMONDS

Diamond, they are a girl's best friend.
Diamonds hidden deep within the ground,
People are suffering for the love of diamonds.
People are suffering for man's love of diamonds.

Digging and shoveling, sweating and moaning,
Conflict, dying, family's displacement, corruption,
People are suffering for the love of diamonds.
People are suffering daily for man's love of diamonds.

Conversations and deals are being made for the sale of diamonds.
Dig mister, dig, and dig for less, dig through for food, for
no pay, can't feed your families, digging for diamonds.
People are suffering for the love of diamonds.
People are suffering for man's love of diamonds.
New York, Rome dealers, England, and around the world,

Diamonds bright in the night skies,

Cry, cry for diamonds; makes loud noises.
People are suffering for the love of diamonds.
People are suffering for men's love of diamonds.
Finish digging, boys, quickly, dig fast and long and
Dirty; doesn't trust you, turn your
Pocket out before you leave the pit; can't have you
Steal the diamonds, even though the diamonds
belong to you and your family.

Evette Forde

The people are living in poverty and despair, and there are diamonds under the bottom of their feet. The oil is bubbling up from the ground, so many resources around them, while other nations gather together to explore and exploit. Wake up; wake up; it might already be too late!

Come with me to see the faces of the suffering.
Masses suffering for the profit, sale of diamonds,

People are suffering for the love of diamonds,
People are suffering for man's love of diamonds.

—

33

I LOOK LIKE AN AFRICAN

Looking like an African, everybody is an African.
Africa, the cradle of humankind, she is forever exploited and
taken for granted. She is always giving and never receiving, givers
and takers. All the takers took from the continent of Africa.

Modern-day slavery, disrespectful, carding,
Unwed mothers, no fathers—where are all
grandmothers, grandfathers? Men, say something.
Do something, protest in the streets, in Parliament, in
Congress. Speak up, come out, time to stand together and
fight these evils. Fighting each other and destroying properties;
build your communities. Where is the birth control?

There are flies and mosquitoes on the faces of
Your children; mothers alone are raising children.
Suffering, where is your dignity and honor? What are your
priorities? Your enemies are at the gates once more. They
are conning you again while they fill their pockets.

Speak words of blessing over your children, day and night. Hear
them when they talk to you; talk to them; listen to them. Don't let the
environment and the circumstances trick you. It is about economics,

Education, and respect, teaches your children about money and
responsibilities, collectively gathering yourselves and resources.
Pull together; protect your talent and your creativity,
And don't sell yourself short.

Where are the acres of land and the mule? Never
Delivered—well, at least give each one of our children a
computer and free education for five years; don't give our
kids discarded computers with mercury still inside.

Don't give us any more diseases, AIDS and Ebola, to hold us back
forever and make us look bad and hopeless on the world stage.

Black men, black people,
Spend time and money; you're assisting countries in
Asia, creating a vast amount of middle-class societies
all over the world, while your media portrays

Africa and the African as dumb and illiterate,
Making them come off as beggars and thieves on the world
stage. Stand aside if your deep-chocolate black; your media
makes us out to be unworthy and nonexistent.

Those other nationalities look productive and cohesive, good,
and upstanding. The media messes with your minds and
heads by misrepresenting people of color. Unfortunately,
I don't see myself in a positive light on the TV.

Black men! People!

Disrespect your women. When the master gives you a little
piece of the pie you turn around and marry your slave master's
wives, making your women poor, angry, and in disarray.

Be careful of these new gods you're serving; it is only a trap to
conquer your souls and those of your children and brothers.

Their intentions are to deliver you back into the
slavery system. You, black men, organize
Yourselves; take off those blinders,

Black men, black people.

Don't get conned in this game of thrones, this chess match; your present
situation and your children's future depend on the decisions you make
today, your actions. Respect yourselves, and others will respect you.

There are strength and power in tightness and unity.
The world is watching you; stop your black person is and
fight for what is right. Stand up for your dignity.
Don't give up!

___

34

FORGIVE ME, DARLING

Forgive me, my darling. I told you it would not work.
Forgive me, my darling, for I don't love you anymore.
Forgive me, darling, for you tried tricking me into liking you.
Forgive me, darling, splashing on Florida's water to catch me.

Your far-left views have left you in a quiver.
Forgive me, my darling. I told you it would not work.
Forgive me, my darling, for I don't love you anymore.
Forgive me, darling, for you tried tricking me into loving you.

Forgive me, darling, and splashes of Florida's water
to catch me. Love of confusion and drama.
Forgive me, my darling. I told you it would not work.
Forgive me, my darling, for I don't love you anymore.
Forgive me, darling, for you tried tricking me into loving you.

Forgive me, darling, splashing of Florida's water to
Catch me, lacking the strength to fight.
Forgive me, my darling. I told you it would not work.
Forgive me, my darling, for I don't love you anymore.
Forgive me, darling, for you tried tricking me into loving you.

Forgive me, darling; you splash of Florida's water
to catch me. You want more for less.
Forgive me, my darling; I told you it would not work.
Forgive me, my darling, for I don't love you anymore.
Forgive me, darling, for you tried tricking me into loving you.

Forgive me, darling, splashing of Florida's water to
catch me. Too many unsupervised children,
Forgive me, my darling; I told you it would not work.
Forgive me, my darling, for I don't love you anymore.
Forgive me, darling.

For you tried tricking me into loving you.
Forgive me, darling, splashing of Florida's water to
Catch me.
You are a slacker; your silence had me wondering, examining.
Why buy the cow when you can get the milk for free?

Staying alerted, have to fight off your voodoo mind.

—

35

WHY DID YOU TRY TO CHANGE ME?

Why did you try to change me? Is it because you
think you can control me if you change me?
Do you feel better with dynamic change on me and then dump me?

You're looking for a woman to take home to meet your sister
and mother at your sister's house. I find it strange; two years,
and I never visited your home. What are you trying to hide? Is
this a joke, or are we playing mind games with each other?

Why did you try to change me?

Do you think I am a mindless, subservient person
who will put your needs above mine?
Your sister monopolizes; if you give her a chance,
she will control and take your energy.

You think you can scare me, or psychologically belittle me to
control me gradually. You're looking for a spineless soul of a
woman who you can charm all the way to use as a sacrificial
lamb, so your family can use and abuse their energy.
Why did you try to change me?

You psychologically and mentally tried to beat me down,
wanting me to change to suit your old-fashioned ideology and
religious beliefs so that I can please you; is it because you know
you cannot get me? Are you using food for your sacrifices?

Alternative means of trying to trap me?
You are starting off with the charm principle and then move into
the kill zone, so your sister and mother can order me around.
Can she pressure me into loving you? I am a free and
independent woman. I don't need emotional
Comfort, demand my respect, and cannot
be ordered around by anyone.

Why did you try to change me?

The only reason why someone would try to change
another person is to use and abuse them. I have to watch
and be keen when dealing with you; look at you
Carefully, listen at all times, keep my guards up when dealing with
you. You have a strange way of thinking that does not coincide
with mine. You are hoping and wishing I would love you.
Don't trust you.

Why did you try to change me?

You stay up late at night until the morning
to worship night gods, seeking love.
However, I can't find but want much more than love. I think you
wish you could put me into trouble with my mind and soul.

Why did you try to change me?

Even if you receive love, the love you looking for,
You would not know what to do with it and
How to respect love; you are a selfish, cold
Individual, who calculates the moves of
Anyone you come into contact with, especially

Someone who is a challenge for you, Then you say,
"I love you," knowing well that's a lie.

Why did you try to change me?

Always pushing and pushing, consistently trying and
trying. I think you are a con man, deep down inside,
just waiting for the right opportunity to strike,
Looking at other women and grunting in my presence when I told you,
in the beginning, it would be difficult for this relationship to work.

Why did you try to change me?

You don't believe in marriage; only believe in consuming women's
energy and leave them emotionally and financially high and dry
when your lust for them is over, and you run out of mind games.
You disappear.
Well, this woman is not like the others and will not subject
my integrity, to your craving and advancement.

You pretend to love, but only use the body and destroy the mind.
It's not your will be done, but my will was done.
I won't allow you to change me.

—

36

WHERE IS YOUR MOTHER?

here is your mother? Is she off making more babies?
Who is going to love you and take care of you?
Where your mother? Is she shacked up with her new boyfriend
or hanging around in her mind, needing unconditional
Love,
Would she care for you unconditionally and
understand you as she loves her boyfriend?
Where is your mother?
Is life getting her down? Is she back with her baby's father?
Where is your mother? How many baby fathers does she have?
Can you find them? Did they get deported to
the lands? Are they still around?
Where is your mother? Alternatively, are they off
making more babies with other more women?
Did your mother finish school? Did she take classes in
childhood development before she became pregnant?

•

Do the babies' fathers have a car to drive her and the kids around,
or did she use the daycare at school while she tries to learn?
Where is your mother?
How about those strollers? Can't fit all of those strollers into
the bus—what a shame. Why did not the babies' fathers buy
a car for your child's mother, or take one out on credit?
Or purchase a car for yourself to drive your child mother around.
Did she pick up her check? Why is she so angry and unkempt?
Can she find a babysitter so she can finish partying
and look for love in all the wrong places?

Evette Forde

> *Where is your mother?*
>
> *Grandma has to take up the slack.*
> *Grandpa has to take up the slack.*
>
> *Maybe Auntie and Uncle could pick up the slack.*
> *Too early for children; when will she learn?*
> *Frustrated with these responsibilities,*
> *Where is your mother?*
> *I could lock kids in a closet, and on the other*
> *hand, maybe beat them to death.*
>
> *Where did the money from the check go?*
> *I have to do my nails and hair to look good.*
> *So I can replenish the earth.*
> *Where is your mother?*
> *Out last night, roaming the streets, hanging out with*
> *strange men; the babies are at home alone.*
> *Gone to karaoke*
> —

37

THE DOCTOR IS IN

Oh, I am under the weather. The doctor is in,
What are they going to run a test on today?
What are they going to find? They have to find something.
What will it be today? Blood pressure, diabetes, colon?
Rheumatism, Asthma, bronchitis, the doctor is in. Under
the weather today; the doctor is in. Call my mother.

Where is my father? Is the doctor in, Could it be my liver? Oh
yes. It could be the spices and the liquor, probably the stress.
Apparently all those curry and salt. Call the preacher.
The doctor is in, Under the weather today; the doctor is in, well, come
in. Take my pulse and check my blood pressure. What about a CAT
scan? Could it be my heart, maybe lower intestine, and colonoscopy?

My anxiety level is starting to rise with fear and
concern; call the preacher. The doctor is in,
What did the x-rays show? Can you read it correctly?
Is it my cardiac nerves? Could it be my bone marrow?
Do I need hip surgery, heart surgery?
Are my symptoms diagnosed as hypochondria?
Call the preacher; the doctor is in,

Colonoscopy, blow me up to physician and blow me up.
Find something inside; blow me up like a frog.
Blow me up inside; let the gas fill up my intestine.
Probe inside my intestine; is there a polyp inside?

Evette Forde

> *Don't forget to colorize the spot before you exit.*
> *Call the preacher; the doctor is in,*
>
> *What's up, doc? I am bleeding a lot inside?*
> *The blood is pouring out of my body like rain.*
>
> *Getting fainter and weaker by the hour,*
> *Bouncing off the wall, about to fall, reappearing in the company*
> *of the doctor once more and oh yes! Set her up with an IV; must*
> *consent to a blood refill. Call the preacher; the doctor is in,*

—

38

MUSICAL LONELINESS

In my mind, I hear a melody, sweet melody.
Open my mouth, humming and singing in my head.
The nights are long, and the days are lonely.
However, still, there is a melodious loneliness in my heart.
Come, come with me, and come with me to eternity.
Listen to the sound of loneliness, a musical loneliness.

Sit by my side; come along for the ride; look at all the
faces, the lonely faces, filled with despair. Do something,
bringing hope to their minds and hearts;
Carrying a total of harmony to them creates joy. Stay up
all night pondering and pondering. Where is my life? To
the end of the universe, touch the sky in my mind.

Listen to the sound of loneliness, a musical loneliness.
Oh, put the television on and take away my
thoughts. Put my thoughts in a distinctive
Zone; take my mind to a different consciousness.
Mind, body, and soul, traveling minds, traveling bravely through
the wilderness, I go touching the faces of all the trees, earth,
nighttime understands in my mind, looking, seeing there is light.

Listen to the sound of loneliness, a musical loneliness,
rivers and streams, waterfalls sliding, glaciers and
Mountains, walls, the brown earth beneath lined with the marks of
life. I am listening to going before Mother Wind and her sounds, her

sound, moaning and groaning, fearlessly howling in anger, warning of the outer limits and things to come. Light at the end of the tunnel; Come and see.

Listen to the sound of loneliness, musical loneliness, traveling, traveling in my mind; It sees the depth of fire, consuming and burning in rage and confinement, wanting ultimately to take hold of everything in sight. Touch the faces of fire, light the bonfire, sit around, and see the sparks as they fly into the night.

Lingering, shadows dancing, swaying in the midnight, glowing, beckoning you, singing, listen to the sound of loneliness, a musical loneliness, the fresh night air carrying my mind away. Taking me, carrying me too far places, kissing my face, touching to Mother Earth, Feeling the sparks of fire,

Cooling my face with water, darkness consumes. Nights silently bellowing into the dawn of morning, the four elements of life, speaking of life, breathing Life into me, Listen to the sound of loneliness, a musical loneliness,

—

39

SATURDAY NIGHTS

Saturday night is here; time to have some fun without fear and let down your hair. Do some cleaning, food shopping, preparing for the night. Friends are coming over; have to be on my best behavior. I could not wait; work all week, hustled and bustled; this night is here.

Get down.

What time is it? Is the liquor store open? What time does it close? If we hurry, we can get a pint or two, or maybe we can get some whiskey and rum.

I love whiskey, stretch the rum, make some punch. Where is the music? Play the music and do the dancing. Let's plug in the amplifier; let's do some salsa. I need to get hammered tonight and disappear into the night.

I called up my herb guy, had him bring some of his best stuff over. Mother wants to come over; I would have to tell her later or tomorrow,

The neighbor is a good man, but he cannot stand me. The music is too loud; maybe they will call the police. Perhaps we should invite him over to keep him from complaining.

Call up some dancing girls; Cook some exotic, different foods; there is a fight breaking out. Hide behind my couch.

Bottles are breaking; girls are flying out the door.

My adrenaline is rising; better call my mother.
The police just pulled up in front my house; noise,
Complaint, drunk and disorderly,
There is no one to make my bail; in the
tank again; it's Saturday night.

—

40

WHITE LIGHTNING

I had to go to the top of the mountain. The grass is greener; the air is fresher. It is peaceful and quiet; has to make my brew. I am going into the bushes to brew up a batch of white lightning; I have to cover my tracks if the police catch me they will convict me of running moonshine.
The cops will get me for this, but I reckon I love making this brew, keeps it coming, and keeps it coming. White lightning, if you please.

In the hills of West Virginia, making me some white Lightning; like the smell and taste, Very high proof, 200 proof; it's pure grain alcohol. Little does he know the cops will get him for brewing this crap? The cops will get you for this, but I reckon I love making this brew; keeps it coming, and keeps it coming too.

White lightning, if you please.
Stirring, cooking, and cooling, measuring and testing to finding a place by night; had to carry my corn mash. Shotgun in my hands; shoot myself a rabbit to make a stew. Little does he know the cops will get him for brewing this crap yet! He doesn't seem to mind. The cops will get you for this, but I reckon I love making this brew; keeps it coming, keeps it coming too. White lightning, if you please.

Gentle streams flowing by, stopped to look and take a smell of the young leaves, have to search for the perfect place, the flawless place to set up my illegal distillery. Little does he know the cops will

get him for brewing this crap? Cops will get you for brewing this
crap. I love the action in these dense greens, leafy green forest.

However, I reckon I love making this brew; keeps it coming;
keeps it coming. White lightning, if you please.
Young men, Hicks' Appalachian mud and mist of West Virginia;
Grandpa and Grandma taught us the formula for making this brew.
Little did they know the cops will get them for brewing this
illegal brew? Cops will get me for this, but I reckon I love
making this brew. Keeps it coming, and keeps it coming.
Mood shine white lightening; It's good for the body,
mind, and soul; white lightning, if you please.

—

41

YOU KNOCK ME OUT

You seem to think am I dreaming.
Is this really you? You knock me out!
I am thinking about you, being with you.
You knock me out!

My mind is made up!
You knock me out! My mother says no.
I want to shout out loud!
You knock me out!

Baby, all you do to me!
You knock me out! Hurling and hollowing,
You knock me out! Jumping and screaming,
You knock me out!

My life is yours. You knock me out!
In my dreams, you knock me out!
You're the best thing that happened to me.
You knock me out!

In the midnight hours, you knock me out!
Way down in the valley; you knock me out!
Sitting by the seashore, you knock me out!

Knock me out! Baby, you knock me out!
Knock me out! Baby, you knock me out!
Lord, you knock me out!

—

42

MY LOVE FOR YOU IS REAL

My love for you is real, touch me.
Hold me; smother me with your love.
This love I have for you is embedded in the love of self, grounded in it.
The depth of my soul aches with my adoration.
My love for you is real.

Sharing and caring, whatever comes our way.
Together forever, in this blissful moment,
Soul to soul, dearly and take care of each other,
my love for you is unimaginable.

The gods are in tune with this love, sending contentment
and blessings, lots of benefits, my way, as I walk with
you, holding hands in this Garden of Eden.
My love for you is real.

Nothing can come between us; the sky is the limit.
You come with me; please take my hands; let's walk this
road of life together in harmony; come on, Mama.
My love for you is real.

43

GOING UP NORTH

I am going up North for a drive out,
Going up North, to see the lakes,
Getting away from the City of Toronto;
I have to find the fresh air.

I am going up North, northwardly northward, heading
up North, and going up northward, to cool off my
head. Gridlock and confusion on the city
Streets, condos going up in the air, no-good parking,

Going up northward, have to find a cottage.
Going up north, or possibly a cabin,
Box, or something; the smells of the city are exasperating
at times, near aggravating, perhaps.
I could fit in somewhere,

Going up North, the lake is calling.
Going up North, have to do some swimming.
Maybe I should rent an RV, find a small piece of land.
I have to find some information about zoning,

Accommodation, amenities, I going up North, to sit and
see the sun. Yes, Going up North, to light a bonfire, looking
out as far as the eye can see, to see the dazzling water
shimmering bright as it shines on the surface of the water.

Traveling, going up north, or maybe I will just walk.
Going up North, carrying an old tent, a
can of beans and some rawhide

Sounds of the night are calling; have to find my old
Coleman lantern. Oh, boy I am living in the past, so confused,
Rather hide in the bushes and fight off the bears
than the traffic and people in Toronto.

Going up North; have to find a safe place to get far from
the tyranny of having to deal with the rapid way things
are politically changing, and the way the governments
through the media are trying to tug at my heartstrings to
take away my freedom of speech and freedom of choice.

Going up North
—

44

LISTEN TO THE MUSIC

Music sweet, listen to the beat.
The music is sweet, and I am moving to the beat.
Souls moving, sounds to my ears, racing,
I am on fire, listening to the music.

The sounds of music take me in another place, far away from
this dreadful place. Carry me away in your music, tantalize
me, mesmerize me, delight me, and hold me in your music.

Strings and pianos, flutes and harps, percussions, it amplifies
drums, organs, symphonies, music, and calm.

My soul lost in your bossism, cherubim harps, hearts,
mind, body, and soul; lost within the walls of your
symphonies; great is your wisdom, vision,
Splendid talent bestowed on men.

For centuries, forever knowing in depth the connection
between ears, minds, and hearts, wanting,
Longing, accepting music, embracing a longing; cleanses
souls, brings peace, joy, and harmony to the human spirit;
soothing, eliminating unwanted noise and confusion.
Listen to the music; your only connection to infinity!

—

45

I WANT TO PLAY IN THE CARIBBEAN

*Bright as the sunshine, as illuminated as can be, beaming
from ear to ear, I need to play in the Caribbean. Sun, lots of
beautiful girls to see, wants to make all of them my family. Ride
on horseback; love to go backpacking through the wilderness.
Wake up in the morning to see and feel the sun; go to the
marketplace, buy something to make a cookout.*

*Say hi! Smile a little, as you go on your way,
for tomorrow I may never know.*

*Taking a drive, heading east in the direction of the
sea; want to reach in time to see the fishermen as they
bring their first catch of fish out of the sea. The
Early-morning air smells refreshed and invigorating.*

*The pupil of my eyes looks as far as it can see. The
fishermen are coming fresh salted from the sea, with
a bounty and a variety of fishes from the sea.*

*Say hi! Smile a little as you go on your way,
For tomorrow, you may never know.*

*Hand me a bucket, filled with fresh fish. Oh, what time.
Friendly people all around me, just waiting,
looking forward to having fun in the sun;*

Let's dance and sing together; clap your hands in thanksgiving.

Say hi! Smile a little as you go on your way,
for tomorrow you may never know.

Tall coconut palm tree is swaying in the air, as they wave
gracefully as I sit under the palm tree, shading from the
heat of the sun, careful, cautious. Someone shouted, "A
coconut may come down and hit you in your head."

Say hi! Smile a little as you go, for tomorrow, you may never know.

Find a run and coconut water; they say it will make me feel as strong
as a lion, and "it's good for your daughter." Children are running
and playing, remnants of a leatherback turtle left on the beach.

Oh! Look at those small baby turtles stretching forth as
though hypnotized by some outer forces of the galaxy, as
the universe calls them into the sea. See them as they reach
the water's edge, returning them home to the sea.

As I wander around in the sand, searching,
my curiosity is killing my mind.

Pinch me! Am I still in the land of the living?
Say hi! Smile a little as you go your way, for
tomorrow you may never know.

The face of the sun is going down; what a
Beautiful sight as it lingers over the horizon, touching
the water's edges; carries me away to the edge of eternity,
for there is where I want to be. Carry me far as

The eyes can see, to the edge of eternity, for
there is where I want to stay.

Say hi! Smile a little as you go on your way,
for tomorrow you may never know.
Say hi! Smile a little as you go on your way,
for tomorrow you may never know,

Say hi! Smile a little, as you go on your way,
for tomorrow you may never know.

Say hi! Smile a little as you go as on your way,
for tomorrow you may never know.

—

MY BODY AREN'T OVERSIZED

My body is not oversized; I am just fluffy.
My body is not oversized; I am just fluffy.
Do not look down at me because I am fluffy.
Superficial people, life, living in an external world,
Maybe I find comfort in food.

My body is not oversized; I am just fluffy.
My body is not oversized; I am just fluffy.
Because of my fluffiness, you are feeling good about
yourself, got something to talk about me.
To laugh about; is it because of my fluffiness?

My body is not oversized; I am just fluffy.
My body is not oversized; I am just fluffy.
Do dress sizes bother you? Maybe I could lose a size
or two; think I am nine months pregnant?
When am I delivering the baby, I will call you?

My body is not oversized; I am just fluffy.
My body is not oversized; I am just fluffy.
Skinny and proud, fat and egotistical can't see the
differences; in you, I see a lot of confusion.
I will be damned if do, will be doomed if I don't.

My body is not oversized; I am just fluffy.
My body is not oversized; I am just fluffy.
Bake me a pie if you are my friend, I can eat it.

Without superstitions of food, you have to be careful.
Watch what you are saying; it could be you in my shoes.

My body is not oversized; I am just fluffy.
My body is not oversized; I am just fluffy.
You think being skinny means you're healthy.
It could be the start of anorexia. If you love
me, help me; don't criticize me.

Be by my side and help me through this.
My body is not oversized; I am just fluffy.
My body is not oversized; I am just fluffy.
My body is not oversized; I am just fluffy.

—

47

YOU WANT ME FOR CHEAP

Life is a blessing, money and time. Who you
think you are, you want me for cheap?
Your mother did not warn you about me. You want me for cheap.

Your father did not say anything to you
about me. You want me for cheap.
Look around and see; when you don't have anything,

You look at me. You want me for cheap.
I am not the one for you. I do not compromise
myself; you want me for cheap.
The best thing in life, you want me for cheap.

Lifelong learning, moaning, and groaning, you want me for cheap;
tired of settling for less, giving chances to losers. I am not your girl.
Mother spent lots of money for my education. You want me for cheap;
can't eat at McDonald's and think it's super. You want me for cheap.

I want a boat, a house, and a cottage. You want me for cheap. You
don't even have any ambition; you want me for cheap; want to afford
cigars. You want me for cheap. I am not your baby's mother; you
want me for cheap. I have to yell and holler! You want me for cheap.

I have to tell my mother; you want me for cheap.
Call up the preacher; you want me for cheap.
I have to visit the witch doctor. You want me for
cheap; lower expectations for yourself,
You want me for cheap.

—

48

I AM NOT YOUR GIRL

You wanted me to be your girl.
You expect me to try to love you.
With all of your bad habits, even the devil seeks
to have a girlfriend. I am not your girl.

I am not your girl. I am not your girl; my love
you cannot hold. I am not your girl.
Drama and confusion possess your soul.
Wanting my life to unfold,

This life you cannot get to hold, trying every trick in the
book; my love you cannot hold. I am not your girl.
I am not your girl. I am not you girl; my love you cannot hold.
I am not your girl.

Wanting to come my way and trying to do anything
to stay, compromising your soul for something;
I am not your girl. You cannot hold!
Bobbing and weaving, I am not your girl, crying and shaking,

I am not your girl. I am not your girl. I am not your girl; my love
you cannot hold. I am not your girl, and I am not your girl.
Father told me I am not your girl; Mother told me I am not
your girl, and the neighbor told me I am not your girl.

*The pastor told me I am not your girl; why buy the
cow when you can get the milk for free? I am not your
girl. Lying and deceiving, I am not your girl.
Why buy the milk when you can get it for free?
I am not stupid like the other girls.*

*I am not your girl. I am not your girl; my love you
cannot hold, and I am not, not your girl.*

—

49

COLORLESS VOODOO MAN

Papa Legba, I am the son of Satan.
Chant, your chant, beat your drums.
Subpoena ad testificandum Papa, Papa Legba summoned,
I want to have money, summons Papa Legba.
I want to trap women, making sure she doesn't get away.

Days are too good; the nights are unsympathetic,
close your eyes and wait for him.
Chant, your chant, beat your drums.
Colorless voodoo man, pale voodoo man, annoying voodoo man,
Bland voodoo man, transparent voodoo man, pale voodoo man,

Papa Neiza, so out of my mind.
Chant, your chant, beat your drums.
Summons Papa, Papa Neiza, summoned;
I want to have love and money, summons Papa Legba.
I want to trap women, making sure she doesn't get away.

Days are too good; the nights better; close your eyes and wait for him.
Chant, your chant, beat your drums.
Colorless voodoo man, colorless voodoo man, colorless voodoo man,
Colorless voodoo man, colorless voodoo man, colorless voodoo man,
Chant, your chant, beat your drums.
Summons Papa, Papa Neiza, summoned,
Prepare the offering table, bring food and liquor, and kill the chicken.

Dance the dance of sacrifice beat them drums faster and louder,
dance, dance, dance to the dances of sacrifice, wanting a lover,
asking for favors, for a husband, wife, battle at the altar.

Your sister and mother are causing confusion in
your mind, afraid of your kind, must find a
Black woman to distort and destroy, getting back at the
chocolate man has to find someone weak to destroy.

Chant, your chant, beat your drums.
Summons, Papa, Papa Neiza, summoned.
Colorless voodoo man, colorless voodoo man, colorless voodoo man

Colorless voodoo man, colorless voodoo man, colorless voodoo man,
Very bored with your life of privilege, Oh yeah, I suffered too.
Chant, your chant, beat your drums.
Summons Papa, Papa Neiza, summoned,
Those drums are beating louder and louder.
I am afraid, Mother; the night is dark and scary.
Fear has taken hold of me; what strange kind of
fantasy, adrenaline pumping through my veins.

Chant, your chant, beat your drums.
Summons Papa, Papa Neiza, beckoned.
Colorless voodoo man, bland voodoo man, colorless voodoo man,
Colorless voodoo man, pale voodoo man, the light-colored voodoo man

Chant, your chant, beat your drums.
Summons, Papa, Papa Neiza, summoned.
Black, white, yellow-red Africans come out in a trance,
to play, indulging, as they give their souls to Legba and
Neiza, take my mind, oh Neiza, for love and money.

While I am mesmerized, afflicted in your powers,
Chant your chant, beat your drums,
Summons, Papa, Papa Neiza, summoned.
Jesus Christ is on his way!

—

50

ALL YOU CAN EAT

I went to an all-you-can-eat buffet; what a sight to
see. Everyone was hungry, and looking at me.
I felt I was in a shark tank, had to make my way out of the tank
without getting run over, so I ate my way out of the restaurant.

People were moving were across the aisle in great pain of hunger,
looking to dive into significant portions of crab legs; here they go
to the crab's legs with butter, clams, and squid, even an octopus.

I went to an all-you-can-eat buffet; what a sight to see.
Plates and spoons, kids running around, look out,
be careful, a fight can start any minute.

I have to go and fill up on another platter, Oh, what a
lot of people chattering, swallowing, and eating;
Maybe they came out to consume all you can guzzle,
and then they will not suffer from hunger again.

I went to an all-you-can-eat buffet; what a sight to see.
Mothers and fathers gathered around. I see a table seating
twelve; might as well look out before they devour me. When the
food containers were empty and were not refilled, in time, loud
noises came from the people sitting across from my table,

Wonder if they got the right dinner or want more to eat.
The chefs are not preparing the food quickly enough; can't
cook fast enough to refill the empty food canisters.

I went to an all-you-can-eat buffet; what a sight to see.
The tablecloths could use washing and a brushing.

Do you have the all-you-can-eat coupons? Buy one
The meal, and get the other free with the purchase of a drink. Maybe
I could sneak some food home for my hamster or to hide away for
later. I went to an all-you-can-eat buffet; what a sight to see.
My friend is eating his money's worth of coupons; unbutton my
pants; call the doctor, and pass me the butter and a lot of shrimp.

I went to an all-you-can-eat buffet; what a sight to see.
Grammy slipped and fell while carrying a plate of food back to
her table; wonder if they have health and accident insurance.

Uncomfortable, have to hang in there for my friends' sake.
What a very good time I had, all I could eat forever.

—

51

I WANT A MAIL-ORDER BRIDE

My wife done left me. I am all alone, looking for some
    new adventure, and I want a mail-order bride.
I have to fight with the lawyers and ex-wife, going postal in my mind;
I have no fear, have to fight to keep my money and material goods.
    I have to travel to China, Russia, and Romania, wandering
        around the world, to find a mail-order bride.

Oh boy! What a joy; I am a man wanting to control something
    or someone, a human; I want a mail-order bride. Look at
    the money; some possess plenty. Others have a few dollars.
        My American ex-wife will be mad at me when I bring
            back May Ling from the Orient. O, wait a minute.

My granddaughter is May Ling's age. I can take her away
from her hell-on-earth life and into a life of bliss and plenty.
    May Ling, let me take you home. My family would not
        understand. She is sixteen; O I am four times her age.

She could learn to speak English and help look after me; she would
love and appreciate me and take good care of me. Life would be much
better for her and me. I like the power and attention this brings me.

O, wait a minute. My granddaughter is May Ling's age.
    This move might not go down well when I tell my family.
    Let me take you home with me. I can take you away from
    your hell-on-earth life and into a life of bliss and plenty.

*I want a mail-order bride. The Chinese girls look like young
boys and are very ready to please; maybe I should take my
chances and see what I find. O, what will my family think of
me? I have to give up my family. My son is only three, and my
granddaughter is the age of my mail-order bride, my wife.*

*An American woman is hard and coldhearted, bossy, all she wants
is my money. And my obedience; they all think I am crazy, as
crazy as I can be; I want a mail-order bride, one I can control
and dominate. I will also have to take care of her family.*

*Even take care of her family; she must be around fourteen or
fifteen. I like to make use of a situation like this, you see. I
want a mail-order bride. Her father gives her away to me; her
mother also likes me; will send her to school if it's to be.
I want a mail-order bride but wait. I am
almost seventy-eight years old.*

—

52

HAPPY BIRTHDAY, ST. PATRICK'S DAY

For My Daughter

You're considerate, loving, caring, and kind.
Your determination has brought you this far.
You're like a butterfly who wants to fly in the sky.
Your light shines like stars in the night skies;
Green is the color for this day.

I know—I know the Irish luck is on its way to you. Commissioning
Saint Patrick to deliver to you personally, a four-leaf clover filled
with all the success and joy life has to offer. Take a drink if you
may, help others if you can, but always put yourself first.

The light of the universe will guide you. Your personality
and charm are sufficient to sustain you.
My love for you is unconditional, Everlasting, Forever and always. If
I had I to give birth again, I definitely would birth another like you.

Your life has given me so much hope and strength.
My cup is filled and running over with joy
And happiness, proud, as proud as I can be,
Happy Birthday, Princess. —

53

EVERYTHING BITES

Everything has teeth, everything bites, and we are all
predators in life, camouflage, pretending, deceiving.
Life itself is a deception; how did this happen? Is this
real life? A possie of the miniature creature's unseen,
capable of biting, something is going on.

What is this all about, biting and biting, feeling the pain? Looking
down a looking glass; isolated existence, whose idea was this?
Everything has teeth, everything bites, and we are all predators in life.

Camouflage, pretending, deceiving, psychologically
creeping up on you, there are physical and mental
teeth; turn your back on them, then they bite.
Life itself is a deception; how did this happen?
Big creatures seem capable of biting;

Something is going on. What is this all about, biting
and biting, feeling the pain? Looking down a looking
glass, strange existence; whose idea was this?

Everything has teeth, everything bites, and we are all
predators in life. Camouflage, pretending, deceiving;
Life itself is a deception. How did this happen? Women
and men are capable of biting; something is going on.

What is this all about, biting and biting, feeling the pain? Looking
down a looking glass, strange existence; whose idea was this?

Everything has teeth, everything bites, and we are all predators in life.

Camouflage, pretending, deceiving;
Life itself is a deception. How did this happen? Teeth
are everywhere. Something is happening; what is this
all about, biting and biting, feeling the pain?

Looking down a looking glass, strange existence; whose idea
was this? Everything has teeth, everything bites, and we are
all predators in life, camouflage, pretending, deceiving.

Life itself is a deception; how did this happen? Men and
creatures would entice you, laugh in your face, while they lay
mental traps to trick you and destroy you, setting bait, while
slowly observing surroundings see if you take the bait.
Then they devour you physically and mentally, losing
your mind; after that, they consciously bite you.

Predators of the mind, body, and soul, creatures, and men, are
capable of eating your body and soul if you let them. Everything has
teeth, everything bites, and in some ways, we have predatory instincts.
We all are predators in life, camouflage, pretending, deceiving,
and eating each other like a virus. Whose idea was this?

Were we all created from a virus?
Or were we created to be a virus?
Sorry, I did not sign up for this.

—

54

THE FLAG

*Black people, why are you allowing yourselves to be distracted from
the real issues confronting your lives and communities? Like actual
making money, building up your communities, gaining financial
and economic strength, marrying your women and building healthy
families, taking care of your children, and curving your attitude.*

*These are some of the issues; it is not whether or not
the Confederate flag is taken down and all the other
unimportant matters that are thrown in your faces.
Hoopla; the issues are the paper and proper education
for your children; love of yourselves; building your
communities; making sure your daughters are married.*

*To their baby's fathers; turning your anger into positive
collective, productive, uplifting consciousness; organizing
yourselves; loving and respecting yourselves; stop killing
yourselves and putting down your women.
A brand-new awakening, My people, the issues are
making money and your economy, taking care of your
families and acquiring respect on the world stage.
The name of the game is economics and prosperity; healthy living;
living harmoniously; love for your beings; building your communities.
Making sure your daughters are married to their
baby's fathers; turning your anger into positive,
Collective, productive, uplifting conscious; organize;
love and respect yourselves; the new awakening.*

My people the issues are making money and spending it
in your communities, organizing your communities.
Why be distracted from the real problems? Lack of good-
paying jobs for your children, the issue is not taking
down the flag; the issues are the paper; proper education;
love of yourselves; building your communities;

Making sure your daughters are married to their baby's fathers;
turning your anger into positive, collective, productive, uplifting
conscious; organize; love and respect yourselves; the new awakening.
For too long we have to be playing second fiddle to the world.
Every hour of the day, you're being distracted away from
the real issues facing your communities, like making sure
you are not reverting yourself back to slave labor.

What's playing out on the world's stages, and how is it affecting you?

While other nations are filling their pockets with your money, for too
long we have played second fiddle to the world. Modern-day problems
facing you and your families—the issues are not taking down the flag.

And racism; the issues are the paper ($), education, love
of yourselves, jobs, building comminutes, and making sure
your daughters and sons are doing the right things.

Why be distracted from the real issues? You are having too
many babies' out of wedlock and fathers and self-abuse. The
issues are not taking down the flag; the issues are the jobs,
papers (money), proper education, love yourselves, building
your communities, making sure your daughters,

Are married to their baby's fathers, and turning your anger into
rational decisions. Collective, productive, uplifting conscious,

organize, love, and respect you. The rest will follow. The new
awakening, the way you treat one another is horrendous.

Stop the stomping of the feet in the aisles of the churches,
and stop singing "Amazing Grace." O, People of color,
why are you allowing yourselves to be distracted away
from the real issues that pertain to your life?

Still taking your lives for granted. The issues are not taking down
the Confederate flag; the issues are your economic condition. The
paper, proper education, love of yourselves, building your

Communities, making sure your daughters are
married to their baby's fathers, turning your anger into
positive collective, productive, uplifting consciousness.
Organize; love yourselves. The new awakenings!
You have to worry about your state of the union in your communities.

—

55

GAYDOM

Silent lovers of themselves, not understanding the depth of themselves,
these are the highest forms of self-hatred, jealousy, and lacking
discipline and wisdom. They compromise with their identity and give
their mind, soul, and body over to the spirit of lust for themselves.

And are blinded by ignorance, so wanting to be
loved and accepted by the fallen angels.
Some are disguised as your brother, while others make
plans to bring confusion to your mind, instilling fear.
Distorting you from the truth about yourselves, and the richness of
you, continually exploiting your creativeness; you are the chosen ones.

Can't you see?

Stand up—you are the gods of this universe. Because when all else and
fallen angels become bored and weary, and everything fails, you keep
on creating music and dance. You owe it to yourselves to be virtuous.
You say black men have no morals, so you associate
them with gaydom and being weak.
Men of color are not feeble and are not receptive to gaydom. They
are creative, reliable, and do not discriminate, with feelings that
go dark. If you frustrate and confuse any race of people, they
too would become angry and bitter toward your aggression.

The sexual revolution of gaydom was exposed to destroy the
relationship and bring discord among men and women.

Evette Forde

And weaken the relation between male and female,
while destroying manhood and its intelligence.
The issue of being gay is not a civil rights issue but one of morality.

Being a black man and gaydom has nothing to do with civil rights.
It has to do with morality. Rise, and see that past civil rights struggles
were fought by dedicated men of color with conviction who died trying
to set your mind and body free from economic and social prejudices.

The march on Selma was for the world to see black men and women
standing up to the authorities for their right to exist and treated fairly.
Not for fighting for the right to be gay. Why is everything negative?
Like whatever is linked to or tied to people of color and the black man?

Even the entire mainstream television programming is
designed to be discriminating against people of color.
We are portrayed in a very negative light, or as if
we don't even exist in your scheme of things.

Somewhere between the gathering of minds or in someone's
twisted mind, they decided to link blackness with being
gay, weak, compromising, angry, violent, and ashamed
and disappointed. Where is the real leadership in the
black community to fight against this notion?

Some of them are aware of the previous struggles and the purpose of
the conflict and the dark man's ordeals. Fighting for respect, equality,
payment for cotton-field labor and the truth should be on the minds
of these leaders. Killing and confusing the minds of the black youths,
Confusing their sexuality;

The issue of being gay is not a civil rights issue.
It's one of morality.

The civil right movements in the 1950s and 1960s and
always were fought for people of color to attain and gain
their God-given rights to be an individual and privileges
denied them by the administering authorities.
The movement did not fight for people to receive the rights to be gay.

It is time to set the record straight, clarifying and
separating these two issues. Gay leaders and organizers
should have fought the church for their right to be gay,
and use a different platform to fight for and promote.

Their agenda and not intertwined their issues with the black issues.
The dark-skinned people have been through too much. They
have enough problems with their own economic and personal
identities to wrestle with society over the issues of gaydom.

—

56

SUMMERTIME FUN

Wow! What a winter. Have to shake off winter's grip and these winter blues, slowly stretching my soul toward spring. How lovely, magically, and majestically, the earth releases varieties of hormones.

Necessary to wake up the plants and flowers, making them come to life, slowly promptly, regenerating into the sphere—wow! Summer time, it's here. It is time to take out my gears, make a spin around, wanting to suck up and bask in the summer sun.

Take in, absorb, glorify all the summer fun; the earth slowly turning on its axis, rotating, bringing The sun closer once more to my existence,

There are fun activities everywhere, two—and three- day concerts in the boondocks, sitting in the Parks, barbecues all over, swimming, camping,

Dundas Square excitement, Pan American games, Adventures to the lakes, sunshine Caribbean Carnival, (Caribana) by the lake shore, white-water rafting. Let's go to the X Toronto, food and fun, Art in the Park. Tall ships are coming into the harbor. How much of this excitement can I take?

In this summer, my blood is just pumping with excitement. I have to see and do as much as I can. Where is my Hibachi? I must go to Canadian Tire to purchase a barbecue set.

*Going to the park to roast some meat; maybe I'll
take a drive to Rogue Valley River to see the river
surging, gliding, whining after a thunderstorm.*

*The campers are there with their RVs and trailers
camping, Gay Pride parade; those guys know how to
throw a party. Salsa music and dancing in the park,*

*The Distillery District, drive cross-country up to Lindsay or
Berry, Oshawa, Ontario for barbecue festivals or possible
go to Scarborough's Roy Thompson's Park instead.*

*There is a barbecue festival taking place over there too.
Eat some barbecue; pulled pork, corn on the cob. Drink
lemonade and listen to some country music.*

*The sun shining bright and hot taking away
All of my winter blues, warm and inviting,
Appreciating, holding me tight. The Gay Pride parade
is extraordinary; Caribana is on its way.*

*I have to visit Louis Saldenah's Mas-K Club to purchase a costume
for Caribana. Must go down to the lake shore and shake my tail
feather to the beat of sweet calypso music—fun in the sun.*

*The girls are coming to play and have some fun
in the sun, shaking off their winter blues.
Celebrating life, moving to the music, everyone's enjoying the beat.
Drink a rum and Coca-Cola and some coconut water for dehydration.*

*Move your waist down to the ground; lots of fun in
the sun. So many Mas bands to choose from—Harold
Saldanha's, Mas-K Club, celebrated yearly portrayals.*

They present secular creations, thirteen times band of
the year winner; what joy and happiness he brings to the
summer. Ontario, Canada—yours to discover!

The competition is steep. Girls and boys, young
and old have to represent their band.
Leaders' costume creation, dance and dance the
Costumes, dance the costumes in front of the
judges; the judges are waiting.

For you to appear on the stage, dance for your supper,
Dance for your life, the world is watching.
You are celebrating life and love; no time for discrimination and
the blues; the sun always shines brightly on Caribana weekend.

Love you, women, and behave like yourselves. Mr. John Tory
the beautiful mayor of the City of Toronto and the premier are
on board. Get on board with the program, everyone! Bring
yourselves from around the world; come and see; come and
feel the spirit of the people of Toronto. Celebrating life!

—

57

GO TO HELL

If you thought I would fall for your deceptions, go to hell. You are not the person I want to give my positive energy. For a long time, you were taking me for granted; all of you were looking at my so-called distress situations and using me for your idiosyncratic edification. The time has come for you to face your personal world, using your courage and strength to sustain you.

Go to hell. I was once bitten, so I am twice shy. Through it all, I had faith and hope in myself and God. The struggles I had to face in life were bravely faced. I met my particular Waterloos using love, courage, and strength and saw the light at the end of each of my tunnels.

Every time I find the strength to rebound from one of my life's challenge, you show up with your problems and try to make your problems greater than mine. Your self-induced drama; you bring them for me to take my mind off my upward mobility.

Just to distract me, so I take my eye off my prize. I had to abandon my projects simply to find myself in the jaws of limbo. Go to hell; you will have to do your dirty bidding. The time has come for me to rise to my full potential, leaving you behind.

Go to hell; you will have to deal with the darkness that lives in your mind and heart. There will be no one left to help and bring comfort to you. Hey! You always tried to kill the messenger; this messenger would not hang around you to be killed.

Haters go to hell; I must be about my calling, not
your personal dreams, and aspirations.
Good luck with your bitter thought toward my family and
me. I will live long enough to see my dreams come true.

Go to hell with the inherence and the self-hating, and the
hating. Your world filled with confusion and negative thoughts.
I am not ignorant and confused; I hold no bitterness toward
you. Good luck and go to hell. You will need it. Go to hell.
—

58

MATERIALISM

*All your life you chased after materialism. For a piece of
silver, you sold your soul to the devil just for the hip of owning
more of all this materialism. Don't sit on my chairs; don't
play my stereo. I don't trust you around my material things.
You love material things and wealth over your families.*

*You hate yourself and love others.
Your tangible things are worth more than your family and your soul.*

*Steadfastly complain about simple things with no substance.
Your soul belongs to materialism, mainly seeking praises and
wanting to be loved by others, while subconsciously shying from
wanting to love yourself, always pushing your children away.*

*At no time were you receptive to their love for you. Never
really learned to love yourself and give yourself the praises,
lying to you by not loving and being proud of yourself.*

*Leasing others, loving others, taking your strength and energy and
giving it to others for nothing, ignoring the love your children
have for you, always putting others above God and your family.*

*Well well, you will have to answer to yourself for these things.
Oh, you say to yourself, "Why don't my children want me? Why
do they not love me?" Maybe it's because they see you not loving
yourself and putting material things above them and God.*

*God knows men were not put on earth to worship material
things. He created you to worship him first and then the
material things. You were blinded by material things and could
not see the love and adoration your children had for you.*

*It hurts the soul to know the true love of a mother, knowing that
deep down inside, their mother did not love herself or them. The
maker of humankind, help my mom to know; guide her soul
to a place where it can welcome, receive, and accept love.*

*Unconditional loves the kind that lasts forever and will never
fade away; it is a sin to love your God over materialism is a sin.
Material things were placed on earth for you to enjoy and to
bring comfort. They were not put on earth for you to worship.
Love yourself first, and praise yourself. Then you will
have the wisdom and understanding to love others,
enjoy material things, and enjoy your life.*

—

59

CRYSTAL CITY

Crystal City is a place where highly orderly structural
Entities' minds exist where brilliant minds maintain
Universal order,
Where minds, speak to souls, reaching hearts, listening,
obeying each other, they are forever keeping us together
in the universe while dwelling in a different sphere.
As, they reach out their minds to the unknown,
stretching forth their minds and souls to us,
Collectively supplying us with pure discipline, knowledge,
wisdom, fortitude, virtue, giving and receiving energy.
One unit with a common thought governed by the Godhead of the
universe, The head concealed, grand and excellent, extending invisible
fiber-optic thoughts, communicating with the ones. Who are willing
to receive, terrestrial minds residing in a place in the universe.

Wherein infinity of order is perpetuated in a completely sterile,
chaos-free zone, organize, orderly lily-white robes, without a
face or identity, heartless, minds and eyes combined are darkly
and richly embedded into their faceless structures, looking out
at you with their eyes implanted at the back of the brain.

The cerebellum is structured, forward vision, insights
unknown, penetrating, overseeing the universe.

Their minds are calculative, master chess players of the world
overseeing us all. Manipulating life in the universe, presenting
themselves from an everlasting higher order, one,

They are timely and accurately, constantly, visually, uniquely arranging atoms, ions, and molecules into crystalline liquid, solid. With their minds and gowns made of unadulterated, lily-white pure textile sharp.

The milieu in Crystal City is white and cold.

The kind of coldness you cannot feel. Let there be light, broader than the minds of some humans, magnifying, these lights forming electromagnetic carrier's waves that are modulated to carry information through the universe.

These waves are transmitting to the spirit of the ones who believe and are discipline and receptive, the one who is not afraid to receive information of truth.

This light takes information from the depth of Crystal City and transmits information to the minds and souls of those who believe and knows that Crystal City exists.

—

60

CELEBRATE MY LIFE.

Celebrate my life through the tears and pain.
Celebrate my life through the joy and laughter.
Celebrate my life through the hopes and disappointments.

The time I spent with my family and friends was wonderful.
Michael, the archangel is beside me vigorously protecting
and fighting for the sanctification of my soul.
Heavenly Father of Universe in his glory
waits to welcome me into his gates.

Celebrate my life through the pain and tears.
Celebrate my life through the joy and laughter.
Celebrate my life through the hopes and disappointments.

All in all, I gave life my best.
Find ways to love and respect each other.
Never be too hasty to respond to matters.
Always remember to keep the peace.
Celebrate my life through the tears and pain.
Celebrate my life through the joy and laughter.
Celebrate my life through the hopes and disappointments.

Here, at the end of my life's journey,
I did not enter the world to stay.
I came to be a part.
To give love, joy, to enjoy and leave,
So don't cry, or worry it is well with my soul.

Celebrate my life through the tears and pain.
Celebrate my life through the joy and laughter.
Celebrate my life through the hopes and disappointments.

Look after and care for each other. Fight the good fight.
The joy comes from knowing to live again. You must first die.
Live, live each day as though it is your last.
Find the strength to love and give.
May the God of life blesses and guides you,
through your sorrows and bewilderment.
Memory of an Angel
September 5ᵗʰ, 2016

—

WORDS OF WISDOM

♥ Praise the LORD, the All Mighty God, whose love dwells in all living things,

♥ It is laborious to smile. Be polite to someone, or take the time to help someone; as difficult as this may be, you must. However, be careful; it can backfire. Implement at your risk.

♥ Ignorance of a person's mind is worse than abusing and killing the human body.

♥ For those who don't believe there is one God, and he is capable, I hope one day all will realize that he is the one and only God. He is the way to joy and everlasting life.

BENEDICTION

"Now may our God and Father himself, and our LORD Jesus, direct our way unto you: and the LORD make you to increase and abound in love one toward another, and toward all men, even as we also *do* toward you; to the end he may establish your hearts unblamable in holiness before our God and Father, at the coming of our LORD Jesus with all his saints." (*1 Thessalonians 3:11-13 (ASV)*

GLOSSARY

Amplification—Increase, strengthening

Calculative—controlling a situation for your advantage, causing someone not to trust you

Camouflage—Hide, conceal, cover up

Caribana —a festival of Caribbean culture held each summer in the city of Toronto, Ontario, Canada

Colonoscopy—A test that allows your doctor to look at the inner lining of your large intestine

Confederate—Unite, amalgamate, join together

Corazón Sagrado de Jesús; Amor tan grande que es difícil de entender Sacred Heart of Jesus; — love so great it's hard to fathom

Dehydration—Lack of moisture

Electromagnetic—A magnetic field that is produced by a current of electricity

El Shaddai—Might, strength, power God

Exacerbating—to make something worse

Florida water—Nineteenth-century formula used in rituals

Gaydom—the gay population; a condition that causes one to seek constant attention

Goons'—bullies or thugs, especially ones hired to terrorize or do away with opposition

Hipness—the characteristic of being hip; coolness; trendiness

Idiosyncratic—All your own, characteristic, personal

Ignorance—Lack of knowledge, unawareness

Implement—to put into operation or to do something

Incandescence— the quality or state of being incandescent; especially; emission by a hot body of radiation that makes visible

Incandescent— emitting light as a result of being heated

Incarnation—Living form, life, manifestation

Indigenous—Homegrown

Jesu mites ET humilis corde—Sacred Heart of Jesus; love so great it's hard to fathom

Laborious—Painstaking, difficult

Le coeur sacré de Jésus—Sacred Heart of Jesus

Legalize—Permit, make legal, make lawful

Louis Saldenah, Mas-K Club— Scotia Bank Caribbean Carnival

Manipulating—Control, direct, influence, maneuvering

Manipulation—Exploitation

White lightning—very high proof moonshine, liquor, alcohol

Materialism—Greediness, hoarding

Mojo—Magic, charm, talisman, or spell

Papa Legba—the gatekeeper to the spirit world

Papa Neiza—a term used in the West Indies to refer to folk Magic, sorcery, Obeah man

Pathway—Passageway

Pestilence—Deadly disease

Receptacle—A container or vessel, holder

Resurrection—Rebirth

Sacred Heart of Jesus; — love so great it's hard to fathom (Sagrado Corazón de Xesús; - Amor tan grande que é difícil de entender)

Sacred Heart of Jesus; — love so great it's hard to fathom (Sacred Heart Íosa; - Grá mór mar sin tá sé deacair a fathom)

Selah—to lift up the LORD

Symphonies—an elaborate musical composition for full orchestra

Tangible—Concrete, solid

Tantalizing—Temptation, persuade

Terrestrial—Global, earthly, knowing, worldly wise

The Rafle du Vel'd'Hive: dHiv Police—Roundup when the Jews of Paris were rounded up by French police

The X Toronto—the Canadian National Exhibition Unadulterated— Pure, neat, unmodified, complete vain, victoriously—successfully

Yeshua of Nazareth—Jesus of Nazareth or Jesus Christ

Printed in the United States
By Bookmasters